JIM MANTHORPE is a wildlife cameraman and writer, the author of the first edition of this book. He has written and updated dozens of Trailblazer guidebooks over the years, from Ladakh to Canada. Based in the Scottish Highlands, he has a particular love for wild places and wildlife and has filmed eagles, otters and orcas for various BBC programmes including *Springwatch*. He's also the author of *Scottish Highlands Hillwalking*, *Great Glen Way*, *Tour du Mont Blanc*, *Pembrokeshire Coast Path* and *Iceland Hiking*, all from Trailblazer.

HENRY STEDMAN (right) researched and wrote this 8th edition. He's been writing guidebooks for more than 25 years and is the author or co-author of over a dozen Trailblazer titles including *Kilimanjaro*, *Inca Trail*, *Coast to Coast Path*, *Hadrian's Wall Path*, *London LOOP* and all three books in the *South-West Coast Path* series. On most walks he's accompanied by Daisy: two parts trouble to one part Parson's Jack Russell. When not travelling, Henry lives in Battle, East Sussex, editing and arranging climbs on Africa's highest mountain through his company, Kilimanjaro Experts.

Authors

South Downs Way

First edition: 2004, this eighth edition 2024

Publisher Trailblazer Publications
The Old Manse, Tower Rd, Hindhead, Surrey, GU26 6SU, UK ▱ trailblazer-guides.com

British Library Cataloguing in Publication Data
A catalogue record for this book is available from the British Library

ISBN 978-1-912716-47-0

© **Trailblazer** 2004, 2007, 2009, 2012, 2015, 2018, 2022, 2024: Text and maps

Series Editor: Anna Jacomb-Hood **Editor and layout**: Nicky Slade
Cartography: Nick Hill **Proofreading and index**: Jane Thomas and Bryn Thomas
Photographs (flora): all © Bryn Thomas except p67: red admiral © Jane Thomas;
p68: bee orchid © Tim Muddle
All other photographs: © Henry Stedman unless otherwise indicated

The maps in this guide were prepared from out-of-Crown-
copyright Ordnance Survey maps amended and updated by Trailblazer.

Acknowledgements

Thanks to Zoe, Henry & Daisy for visiting me on my last night on the trail and camping
with me at the YHA – great fun. And to Joel Newton for the updates, and for joining me on
the last leg across the Seven Sisters – a glorious day and a lovely way to end the trip. To
the other walkers we met during this update walk, thanks for your suggestions. I'm also
grateful to all those readers who wrote in with updates and recommendations, particularly
William Allberry, Stuart Blackburne, Ian Cairns, Anne Conchie, David Cocovini, Susan
Corbett, Bea Delannoy and Olivier, Rodney Duggua, Keith Good, Rachel and Karl-Peter
Hammer, Tricia Hayne, Andrew Hilton, Jennie Hiscock, Susie Lapwood, Richard Marshall,
Jasmin McMillan, Heather and Steve Oxley, Nick Price, Trudi & Andy Rintoul, Catherine
Sharp, Danny Shone, Malcolm Simister, Andrew Stanley, Sue Tucker, and Sue Wood.
  Back at Trailblazer HQ, many thanks to Nicky Slade and Nick Hill for their stellar work
on editing and mapping, and Jane and Bryn Thomas for proofreading and the index.

A request

The author and publisher have tried to ensure that this guide is as accurate and up to date
as possible. Nevertheless, things change. If you notice any changes or omissions that should
be included in the next edition of this book, please write to Trailblazer (address above) or
email us at ▱ info@trailblazer-guides.com. A free copy of the next edition will be sent to
persons making a significant contribution.

Warning: coastal walking and long-distance walking can be dangerous

Please read the notes on when to go (pp13-16) and outdoor safety (pp54-6). Every effort
has been made by the author and publisher to ensure that the information contained herein
is as accurate and up to date as possible. However, they are unable to accept responsibility
for any inconvenience, loss or injury sustained by anyone as a result of the advice and information given in this guide.

Updated information will be available on: ▱ **trailblazer-guides.com**

Photos – Front cover: On the cliffs above Beachy Head Lighthouse. **This page**: Walking
west towards Belle Tout. **Previous page**: Marching up to Chanctonbury Ring. **Overleaf**:
Local landmarks, the two windmills above Clayton are known as Jack and Jill. This is Jill.

Printed in Malaysia; print production by D'Print (☎ +65-6581 3832), Singapore

South Downs
WAY

64 maps & guides to 49 towns and villages
with large-scale walking maps (1:20,000)

PLANNING – PLACES TO STAY – PLACES TO EAT

Winchester–Eastbourne & Eastbourne–Winchester

JIM MANTHORPE &
HENRY STEDMAN

TRAILBLAZER PUBLICATIONS

INTRODUCTION

About the South Downs Way

PART 1: PLANNING YOUR WALK

Practical information for the walker

Budgeting 27

Itineraries

What to take

Getting to and from the South Downs Way

PART 2: MINIMUM IMPACT WALKING & OUTDOOR SAFETY

Minimum impact walking

Outdoor safety and health

PART 3: THE ENVIRONMENT & NATURE

Conservation of the South Downs

Flora and fauna

Contents

PART 4: ROUTE GUIDE AND MAPS

Contents

About this book

This guidebook contains all the information you need to undertake all or parts of the South Downs Way. The hard work has been done for you so you can plan your trip without having to consult numerous websites and other books and maps. When you're packed and ready to go, there's comprehensive public transport information to get you to and from the trail and detailed maps (1:20,000) to help you find your way along it. It includes:

● Reviews of campsites, hostels, B&Bs, guesthouses, pubs and hotels
● Walking companies if you want an organised tour or your luggage carried
● Itineraries for all levels of walkers
● Answers to all your questions: when is the best time to walk, how hard is it, what to pack and the approximate cost of the trip
● Walking times and how to use GPS tracklogs as a back-up to navigation
● Cafés, pubs, tea-shops, restaurants, and shops/supermarkets along the route
● Rail, bus and taxi information for the towns and villages on or near the Way
● Street maps of the main towns and villages
● Historical, cultural and geographical background information

Note that this edition of the guide is liable to more change than usual. Some of the B&Bs, hotels, pubs, restaurants and tourist attractions may not survive the hardships caused by rising fuel prices, inflation and staff shortages. Do forgive us where your experience on the ground contradicts what is written in the book; please email us – info@trailblazer-guides.com so we can add your information to the updates page on the website.

❏ MINIMUM IMPACT FOR MAXIMUM INSIGHT

Nature's peace will flow into you as the sunshine flows into trees. The winds will blow their freshness into you and storms their energy, while cares will drop off like autumn leaves. **John Muir** (one of the world's first and most influential environmentalists, born in 1838)

Why is walking in wild and solitary places so satisfying? Partly it is the sheer physical pleasure: sometimes pitting one's strength against the elements and the lie of the land. The beauty and wonder of the natural world and the fresh air restore our sense of proportion and the stresses and strains of everyday life slip away. Whatever the character of the countryside, walking in it benefits us mentally and physically, inducing a sense of well-being, an enrichment of life and an enhanced awareness of what lies around us. All this the countryside gives us and the least we can do is to safeguard it by supporting rural economies, local businesses, and low-impact methods of farming and land-management, and by using environmentally sensitive forms of transport – walking being pre-eminent.

INTRODUCTION

The 100-mile (160km) line of chalk hills known as the South Downs stretches from the historic city of Winchester, in Hampshire, across Sussex to the Pevensey Levels by Eastbourne. For centuries travellers and traders have used the spine of the Downs as a route from one village to the next.

Today that route is still used by walkers, outdoor enthusiasts and others who simply need to escape from

> **For centuries travellers and traders have used the spine of the Downs as a route from one village to the next.**

congested towns and cities. London, Brighton, Southampton and other urban areas are all within an hour or two of the South Downs, making these beautiful windswept hills an important recreational area for the millions who live in the region.

A traverse from one end to the other following the South Downs Way national trail is a great way of experiencing this beautiful landscape with its mixture of rolling hills, steep hanging woodland and windswept fields of corn. Add to this the incredible number of pretty Sussex and Hampshire villages with their friendly old pubs, thatched cottages and gardens bursting with blooms of roses, foxgloves and hollyhocks in summer, and one begins to understand the appeal of the Downs as a walking destination.

Above: A typically quaint thatched cottage in the village of Amberley.

INTRODUCTION

The official start (or end) of the South Downs Way is now the City Mill in Winchester, marked by a wooden sign outside it. Until 2017, the trail began from Winchester Cathedral (**above**) – in our opinion a much more appropriate starting point. It's well worth visiting.

The South Downs Way begins in the cathedral city of Winchester from where it heads across rolling hills and the Meon Valley with its lazy, reed-fringed chalk-bed river and charming villages. At Butser Hill the Way reaches the highest point of the Downs with views as far as the Isle of Wight and, in the other direction, the North Downs. Continuing along the top of the ridge the Way passes through ancient stands of mixed woodland, past the Roman villa at Bignor and on towards the sandstone cottages of Amberley. Close by is the fascinating town of Arundel with its grand cathedral and even grander castle rising above the trees on the banks of the River Arun. Then it is on to Chanctonbury Ring with its fine views across the Weald of Sussex. The next stretch climbs past the deep valley of Devil's Dyke and over Ditchling Beacon to Lewes with its crooked old timber-framed buildings and the famous Harvey's Brewery. Finally, the path reaches the narrow little lanes of Alfriston with more historic pubs than one has any right to expect in such a small village. The walk's grand finale includes the meandering Cuckmere River and the roller-coaster Seven Sisters chalk cliffs – before reaching the final great viewpoint of Beachy Head, overlooking the seaside town of Eastbourne.

The eastern end of the Way is also marked with a wooden sign (**left**), on the outskirts of Eastbourne. Most walkers will want to continue into this seaside town with its impressive Victorian pier (**below**).

Above, left: A statue of King Alfred the Great (849-99) stands in his capital, Winchester. **Centre**: Hanging on the wall in the Great Hall in Winchester is the table top said to be from King Arthur's Round Table. As it dates only from the 13th century it's too young to be genuine but still impressive at about 800 years old. **Right**: Arundel Castle rises above Arundel town which is five minutes by train from Houghton Bridge.

Walking the Way can easily be fitted into a week's holiday but you should allow more time to be able to explore the many places of interest such as Arundel, Lewes and Winchester itself ... not to mention the lure of all those enchanting village pubs that are bound to make the trip longer than intended!

History

There has been a long-distance route running along the top of the South Downs for far longer than walking has been considered a leisure activity. The well-drained chalk hilltops high above the densely forested boggy clay below were perfect for human habitation and were certainly in use as far back as the Stone Age.

From this time onwards a complex series of trackways and paths developed across the land and it is believed that by the Bronze Age there was an established trade route along the South Downs. All along the crest of the Downs escarpment there is evidence of Iron Age hill-forts and *tumuli* (ancient burial grounds), many of them very well preserved, particularly the Old Winchester hill-fort site in Hampshire.

In more recent times the land was cleared and enclosed, and the flat hilltops were put under the plough. Although this process erased many of the lesser tracks the most sig-

Lewes Castle was built shortly after the Battle of Hastings in 1066.

nificant remained: the one which ran east–west along the edge of the escarpment.

It was not until 1972, amid rapidly growing public interest in walking, that the then Countryside Commission designated the 80 miles from Eastbourne to the Sussex-Hampshire border the first long-distance bridleway in the UK. Later, the final section through Hampshire was added bringing the length of the South Downs Way to 100 miles and giving it a spectacular start in the historic city of Winchester. Today the route is growing in popularity with walkers, cyclists and horse-riders alike, who tend to mingle with ease.

Easy walking below an impressive row of copper beeches to the east of Buriton.

How difficult is the path?

The South Downs Way is one of the most accessible and easiest of Britain's long-distance paths. Those on foot will find the route usually follows wide, well-drained tracks in keeping with its designation as a long-distance bridleway, catering for cyclists and horse-riders as well as walkers. If anything walkers may, on occasion, crave a few more lightly trodden paths since the route always sticks to the well-beaten track.

This 100-mile walk can be conveniently divided into sections starting and stopping at any of the numerous little villages that sit at the foot of the escarpment or in a fold in the hills. One thing to note, though, is that because the Way generally follows the high ground along the top of the South Downs, to reach the villages offering accommodation, pubs and shops you usually have to descend steeply off the Downs and climb back onto them to continue, which can make pub lunches less attractive! When calculating the day's timings you need to bear in mind this extra walking time involved.

How long do you need?

Walkers will find that **the whole route can be tackled over the course of a week** but it is well worth taking a couple of extra days to enjoy the beautiful downland villages that are

Above: A peaceful place to rest your legs: St Peter's Church, Southease.

Right: Walking west towards Cocking. The chalk trail runs over the downs far ahead.

Above: For a change from a B&B you could stay in a cosy shepherd's hut (**left**). You'll certainly see a lot of sheep, including some striking breeds such as the Badger Face (**right**).

passed along the Way. It is also worth taking time to explore the former capital of Saxon England, Winchester, a historic town with a beautiful cathedral. At the other end of the walk Eastbourne is, to be polite, perhaps a little less interesting but is not entirely without charm, and will keep those who like to sit on a windy seafront happy for hours.

See pp32-4 for suggested itineraries covering different walking speeds

Below: St Pancras Church, Kingston-near-Lewes.

Above: On the Way, west of Truleigh Hill. **Below**: Through the woods near Winchester.

When to go

The south-east of England has probably the best climate in a country maligned for its fickle weather. It doesn't suffer from too much rain and enjoys more hours of sunshine than other parts of the United Kingdom; indeed, Eastbourne proudly boasts of being the UK's sunniest place! The route can be followed at any time of year but the chances of enjoying good weather do depend on the season.

SEASONS
Spring
A typical spring is one of sunshine and showers. From March to May a day walking on the Downs may involve getting drenched in a short sudden shower only to be dried off by warm sunshine a few minutes later. However, the weather can vary enormously from year to year, sometimes with weeks of pleasantly warm sunny weather and in other years days of grey drizzle. In general this is a great time to be on the Downs. Walker numbers are low and the snowdrops, bluebells and primroses decorate the bare woodland floors.

Summer
It can get surprisingly hot and sunny from June to September but again the weather can

❏ MAIN FESTIVALS & EVENTS

May/June

● **Charleston Festival** (🖥 charleston.org.uk) Held at Charleston (see p162) in the last week or two of May. Arts and literature abound.

● **Goodwood Race Course** (🖥 goodwood.com) Horse-racing takes place here **between May and October**; booking accommodation in the area can be tricky when meetings are being held, so check the website for schedules.

● **Goodwood Festival of Speed** (🖥 goodwood.com) Held over three days in late June on the Goodwood Estate a few miles south of Cocking; see box p106.

● **Eastbourne International** (🖥 lta.org.uk) Women's tennis championship, a very popular pre-Wimbledon warm-up held in Eastbourne each June.

July/August

● **Qatar Goodwood Festival** (🖥 goodwood.com) Known in horse-racing circles as 'Glorious Goodwood', this is one of the highlights of the flat-racing season and is held over five days at the end of July or start of August.

● **Winchester Hat Fair** (🖥 hatfair.co.uk) Originally a buskers' festival, now a celebration of street arts and community; all events are free but contributions are welcome – just put your money in the hat. First weekend of July.

● See 🖥 visitwinchester.co.uk/whats-on/festivals for details of the other festivals in Winchester, including the **Grange Opera Festival** (early July) and **Boomtown** (4 days in early Aug), the UK's biggest independent music and theatrical festival.

● **Airbourne: Eastbourne International Airshow** (🖥 eastbourneairshow.com) Held in Eastbourne mid to late August.

● **Arundel Festival** (🖥 arundelfestival.co.uk) takes place over the last 10 days of August – folk, rock and classical music, comedy and Shakespeare plays.

September

● **Goodwood Revival** (🖥 goodwood.com) Historic motor race meeting that attracts classic car enthusiasts and lovers of all things vintage; held at Goodwood over three days in mid September.

November

● **Lewes Bonfire Night Celebrations** (🖥 lewesbonfirecelebrations.com) Largest bonfire-night celebration in the country, held on 5 November unless it's a Sunday.

Above: With several pubs and an excellent village shop, Alfriston makes a great place for a stop. **Right**: Looking west over Birling Gap and the cliffs known as the Seven Sisters.

vary from one year to the next. Always be prepared for wet weather but also be confident of enjoying some balmy summer days, too. Occasionally it can be a touch too hot for walking. This can be a problem as there is not much water on the Downs so fill up your water bottles whenever you can. Visitor numbers are high at this time of year, as you might expect, so it can be a little difficult to enjoy a solitary day on the Way. The hills are colourful in summer with wild flowers in bloom in the meadows, red poppies among the corn and

> **The big advantage of summer walking is that it remains light until well after nine in the evening so there is never any rush to finish a day's walk.**

fields of bright yellow oil-seed rape. Hay-fever sufferers may not agree that this is such a good thing. However, everyone seems to be in a good mood and the pubs are brimming with all sorts of folk, from fellow walkers to country gents. The big advantage of summer walking is that it remains light until well after nine in the evening so there is never any rush to finish a day's walk.

Autumn

Autumn is probably the season when you can reliably expect to be rained on. The weather from September to November tends to be characterised by low-pressure systems rolling in from the Atlantic one after another, bringing with them prolonged spells of rain, mist and strong winds. On the positive side those who enjoy a bit of peace and quiet will find very few fellow walkers out and about at this time of year. Furthermore, it is not all rain and wind. Sometimes the weather can surprise you with a day of frost and cold sunshine that can make a day on the Way a real treat. It's important to remember that some businesses reduce their opening hours at this time of year or even close all together.

Winter

Southern England doesn't experience as many cold snowy winters as it once did. From December to February these days it's usually relatively mild with wet weather and occasional spells of colder, dry weather. Any snow that does fall is usually during January and February. It is more likely the further east you go since it is the south-east corner that gets caught by the snow showers that roll in from the North Sea, when the wind is from the north or east. Many walkers will appreciate winter walking for the wilder weather it offers and the days of solitary sauntering along the high windswept crest of the Downs. The best days are the cold, frosty ones when the air is clear and the views stretch for miles. Bear in mind that in winter some businesses, particularly in the more remote villages, are closed. It is always wise, for example, to call a pub before turning up expecting dinner.

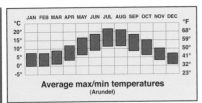

Average max/min temperatures
(Arundel)

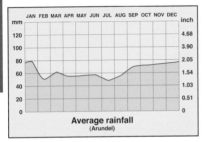

Average rainfall
(Arundel)

TEMPERATURE

Generally, temperatures are comfortable year-round. In winter, warmer clothes will be needed as the temperature drops towards and, on occasion, just below freezing. Summer is usually pleasantly warm with temperatures around 16°C to 23°C but temperatures as high as the 30s Celsius do occur on at least a few days during July or August which can make walking on exposed sections of the Way uncomfortable.

RAINFALL

The weather in England is affected mostly by the weather systems that come from the south-west. These are usually low-pressure systems that contain a lot of rain. Rain can and does fall in any month of the year but dry weather is usually more likely in the early summer.

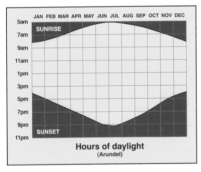

Hours of daylight
(Arundel)

DAYLIGHT HOURS

If walking in autumn, winter and early spring, you must take account of how far you can walk in the available light. Also bear in mind that, depending on the weather, you may get a further 30-45 minutes of usable light before sunrise and after sunset.

PLANNING YOUR WALK

Practical information for the walker

ROUTE FINDING

There is very little opportunity to get lost along the Way. It would be an easy route to follow even without the waymark posts, which are usually marked with the National Trail 'acorn' symbol. An acorn on a **yellow** chevron indicates that this route is a footpath, so exclusively for pedestrians. A **blue** background indicates that the trail is a bridle-way and can therefore also be used by horses and cyclists. A **purple** background quaintly adds a pony and trap. A **red** or **white** background warns that the route can also be used by motorbikes. Bear in mind that other footpaths may be indicated on the waymark posts so **follow the acorn**. Nevertheless, it is hard to go astray and there are usually other walkers around who you can ask for directions.

GPS on your smart phone

These days individuals who don't routinely clutch a **smart phone** every waking hour are regarded as eccentric. But not all devoted users appreciate that a modern mobile can receive a **GPS** signal from space as well as estimate your position often as accurately using **mobile data** signals from hilltop masts. These signals are two differ-ent things: GPS comes free from American, Russian or European satellites and is everywhere all the time but works best outdoors. Much stronger 4- or 5G mobile signals beam off towers up to 40 miles away and are what you pay the phone company for.

Accessing an online map with mobile data (internet via your phone signal, not wi-fi), your position can be pinpointed with great accuracy. But with no signal your phone will use GPS to display your position as a dot on the screen. Except that, *unless you import a map into your phone's internal storage* (which may require an app and even a small financial outlay), without a signal the kilobit-sized 'tiles' which make up a **zoomable online map** cannot be down-loaded. The internet browser's cache may retain a few tiles until the signal resumes or until you walk off that tile's coverage. Much will depend on your service provider.

The best way to use your mobile as an accurate navigation aid is to **download a mapping app plus maps covering the route** (see box p41). That will work with GPS where there is no phone signal. The online map which shows the South Downs Way most accurately and consistently is the well-known OS 1:25k Explorer series. Predigital era hikers won't need persuading of OS maps' readability and reliability. On these maps, National Trails are marked as three green dashes then a green diamond, plus a 'South Downs Way' every once in a while. Ideally, your on-screen location dot is pulsing right on that track. Currently, the **OS Maps app** (🖥 shop.ordnancesurvey.co.uk/apps) costs just £6.99 for a month – less than a single OS paper map. By the year it's much cheaper.

Although there are free online maps and mapping apps, they don't have the same reliability and might have adverts, or full functionality disabled until you cough up some money. On some of these apps the South Downs Way is shown but not always identified alongside other adjacent paths and tracks, and so downloading a tracklog and our waypoints (see below) should clarify the route.

When considering whether or not to use satellite navigation on your phone, one thing to note is that it may **drain battery power faster than usual**. Having the phone on standby and minimal other apps working will maximise your battery life, but obviously carrying a back-up power bank makes sense.

Tracklogs

A **tracklog** is a continuous winding line marking the walk from end to end, displayed on your screen; all you have to do is keep on that line. If you lose it on the screen you can zoom out until it reappears and walk towards it. A tracklog can be traced with a mouse off a digital map, or recorded live using a GPS enabled device. When recorded live, tracklogs are actually hundreds of waypoints separated by intervals of either time or more usefully distance (say, around 10 metres). Some smartphones or mapping apps can't display a tracklog with over 500 points so they get truncated into fewer straight lines, resulting in some loss in precision.

National Trails have a free tracklog at 🖥 nationaltrail.co.uk/en_GB/trails – look for 'GPX downloads'.

Waypoints and what3words

Besides those navigation options, this book offers an additional one. The maps in the book all feature at least one numbered **waypoint**, marked directly onto the map. Where a tracklog is a continuous line, waypoints are single points like cairns. These waypoints correlate to the list on pp183-4 which gives the grid reference and description. For these waypoints we've now also listed the three-word geocode used by **what3words** (🖥 what3words.com, p56 and pp188-92) which could be useful in an emergency.

You can either manually key the nearest presumed waypoint from the list at the back of this book into your phone/GPS (a process prone to user errors), or just download the list for free at 🖥 trailblazer-guides.com/gps-waypoints.

In summary

Stepping back a bit, we're on the South Downs Way, not the Tibetan plateau, so you'll rarely need to refer to your phone for navigation. Waymarking is mostly crystal clear; often so is the track beneath your feet, and this book's hand-drawn maps show what lies ahead. It's worth repeating that the vast majority of people who walk the South Downs Way do so perfectly successfully without GPS.

South Downs Way app
A Trailblazer South Downs Way app is now available. For more information see the Trailblazer website: 🖳 trailblazer-guides.com.

ACCOMMODATION

The South Downs lie in a populous area so there are plenty of villages and towns within easy reach of the Way, most of which offer accommodation for the walker. However, the Way generally follows the high ground along the top of the South Downs escarpment while the villages lie at the foot of the hills. This tends to leave the walker with a small detour to reach a bed at the end of each day. Bear this in mind when calculating times and distances from the maps in Part 4. As a general rule it is a good idea to allow an extra hour each day for the walk to and from your accommodation.

Camping
There is virtually no opportunity for wild camping on the South Downs so campers must rely on organised campsites. Fortunately, there are enough to make it feasible to camp your way along almost the entire trail, with a couple of exceptions. Those who do camp will certainly appreciate the experience: the pampered comforts of a B&B are outweighed by the chance to sleep under the stars and be woken by the sun, should it happen to be showing.

Refer to the itinerary charts for campers on p33 to help organise a schedule, and pay particular attention to the list below for all camping options that are right on the trail, rather than in more distant downland villages, which are a pain to get to and from with a heavy rucksack. Campsites generally charge between £10 and £30 per tent and one camper. Some of the more organised sites have showers and washing facilities while others are merely a place to pitch a tent in the grass. You can also camp at some YHA hostels.

Campsites right on the trail include: **Holden Farm Camping** (p84; Map 4); **Meon Springs** (pp91; Map 8); **The Sustainability Centre** (p93; Map 9); **Littleton Farm Camping** (p114; Map 16); **Bignor Farms Camping** (p115; Map 17a); **Washington Park Campsite** (p130; Map 21); **White House Caravan &**

PLANNING YOUR WALK

❑ **TIPS FOR BOOKING ACCOMMODATION**
Always **book your accommodation well in advance** because of the high demand for beds in summer and during events such as those held at Goodwood (see box p106). For the chain hotels this strategy generally yields the most competitive rates.

If you are booking with an independent accommodation provider you will usually get the best price by **booking direct with them** rather than via one of the online agencies. In recent years it has become increasingly common for B&Bs and even glamping sites to impose a **minimum booking of two nights**, especially during summer weekends. However, it is always worth contacting them directly to ask about single nights as they may have gaps between other bookings, or be more willing to accept single-night guests at short notice. Alternatively, you could stay two or more nights in one location and use public transport to get to/from your accommodation at the end/start of each day.

❑ YHA: YOUTH HOSTELS ASSOCIATION

Despite the name, anyone of any age can join the YHA. This can be done at any hostel or by contacting the **Youth Hostels Association of England and Wales** (YHA; ☎ 01629-592700, 🖳 www.yha.org.uk). A year's membership costs £15 if paid by direct debit, £20 by credit card/bank transfer.

YHA hostels are easy to book, either online or by phone, and you can stay even if you aren't a member though members are entitled to a 10% discount (this is valid for a member booking for up to 16 people at the same time and is applicable to the rate and meals) so it is worth joining if you expect to stay in a YHA hostel several times in a year. Note that photo ID must be shown at check-in. They also have showers, communal space, a drying room, a fully equipped kitchen and a café-restaurant offering meals. Bedding is provided but not towels, though they can be rented.

Campsite (p134; Map 22); **YHA Truleigh Hill** (p139; Map 23); **Housedean Farm** (p156; Map 29); and **Alfriston Camping Park** (p168; Map 35).

If you really want to camp in greater isolation where there is no recognised site you may find it worthwhile asking a landowner for permission to do so.

Hostels and budget accommodation

The South Downs Way is poorly served by hostels. There's a great one at Truleigh Hill (YHA Truleigh Hill, p139), and at Southease (YHA South Downs, p158). You don't need to be a member to stay at these (see box above re YHA membership). There is also the **independent** South Downs Eco Lodge (p93), which is part of the Sustainability Centre near East Meon.

Other budget lodgings include: a **bunkhouse** (Houghton Bridge), **yurts** and/or **shepherd's huts** (at the Sustainability Centre, Manor Farm near Cocking, Pyecombe, at Housedean Farm Campsite near Lewes and at Rose Cottage in Alciston) and **log cabins/land pods** and **bell tents** (at YHA South Downs, YHA Truleigh Hill, and also at Housedean Farm). These generally include bedding (though not always, so check in advance), saving you from having to carry your own sleeping bag.

Bed and breakfast

Some B&Bs can be quite luxurious and come at a price, but generally speaking, all the Downs walker really wants is a warm bed and a hot bath. For this reason most of the B&Bs listed in this guide are recommended because of their usefulness to the walker and convenience to the Way, not for how many stars the tourist board has awarded them.

Bed and breakfast owners are often proud to boast that all rooms are **en suite**. This enthusiasm for private facilities has led proprietors to squeeze a cramped shower and loo cubicle into the last spare corner of the bedroom. Not having an en suite room is sometimes preferable as you may get sole use of a bathroom across the corridor and a hot bath is just what you need after a day's walking – and you will also probably save a few pounds each night.

It can be hard to find establishments with **single** rooms. **Twin** rooms and **double** rooms are often confused but a twin room usually comprises two single beds which can either be pushed together for a couple or kept separate. A double room has one double bed. **Triple/quad** rooms are for three/four people and usually consist of a double bed and one or two single beds or bunk beds, but occasionally three/four single beds.

B&Bs do of course provide **breakfast**. Some also provide a packed lunch or an evening meal but you will need to request this in advance and there will be an extra charge. Most B&Bs, however, are close enough to a pub or restaurant and if not the owner may give you a lift to one.

B&Bs in this guide vary, from £30 per person (pp) **for two sharing** in the most basic accommodation to £60-75pp (or more) for the most luxurious places with en suite facilities; most charge £40-50pp. Many places do not have a single room so for single occupancy of a double room they may still charge the full room rate. If you are on a budget you could ask for a room-only rate (ie no breakfast) which will usually be about £5-10 less.

Guesthouses, hotels, pubs and inns
Guesthouses are usually more sophisticated than B&Bs, offering evening meals and a lounge for guests; rates are around £40-70 per person (pp) for two sharing. **Pubs and inns** offer bed and breakfast of a medium to high standard and have the added advantage, of course, of having a bar downstairs and also generally offer food, so it's not far to stagger back to bed. However, the noise from tipsy punters below your room might prove a nuisance if you want an early night. Prices usually range from £45pp to £60pp per night for two sharing. Generally, **hotels** tend to be more expensive, ranging from £40pp to £100pp (or more) for two sharing. However, branches of chain hotels such as Travelodge (Winchester; see p75) and Premier Inn (Eastbourne; p186) can provide better value if booked in advance.

Airbnb
The rise and rise of Airbnb (🖥 airbnb.co.uk) has seen private homes and apartments opened up to overnight travellers on an informal basis. While accommodation is primarily based in cities, the concept has spread to tourist hotspots in more rural areas, but do check thoroughly what you are getting and the precise location. While the first couple of options listed may be in the area you're after, others may be far too far afield for walkers. Be aware that these places are not registered B&Bs, so standards may vary, yet prices may not necessarily be any lower. This guide does not specifically mention Airbnb accommodation owing to its highly variable and often temporary nature.

FOOD AND DRINK
Breakfast and lunch
If staying in a B&B, guesthouse or hotel you'll usually be served a full cooked breakfast which may be more than you are used to. However, some places offer a lighter continental breakfast which you may prefer first thing in the morning and some also are happy to provide vegetarian/vegan breakfasts with prior warning. If requested in advance, and for an additional cost (or instead of break-

PLANNING YOUR WALK

fast, if you are planning an early start), many places can also provide you with a packed lunch. Alternatively, breakfast and packed lunches can be bought along the Way from one of the great cafés and bakeries, or made yourself from supermarket or village store ingredients. Remember that certain stretches of the walk are devoid of places to eat so check the information in Part 4 to ensure you don't go hungry.

Evening meals

The **pubs** that grace the pretty flint villages of the Downs rank as some of the most authentic country inns in England. Many of them date from the 14th or 15th centuries and have fascinating histories.

Food can vary from cheap traditional pub grub to high-quality cuisine served in a pub restaurant. For the serious 'connoisseur' drinker the best thing about the downland pub is the range of real ales on offer (see box opposite).

While evening meals in the villages are often limited to whatever the local pub is serving, some of the larger towns such as Winchester, Eastbourne, Lewes and Petersfield are home to some top quality **restaurants**.

Those on a budget, or walkers who stumble into town late in the evening, will find a number of late-night **takeaway** joints offering everything from kebabs and pizzas to Indian and Chinese and, of course, traditional fish & chips.

Self-catering supplies

If you are camping, fuel for the stove and other equipment is an important consideration. Supplies can be found at any of the outdoor shops in Winchester and Eastbourne, whilst en route there are outdoor shops in Petersfield and Lewes as well as hardware stores, which stock camping-stove fuel. Some of the bigger campsites also sell camping-stove fuel, while some provide fire pits and sell bundles of kindling. Check Part 4 for more detailed information about each.

Drinking water

Depending on the weather you may need to drink as much as 3-4 litres of water a day. If you're feeling lethargic it may well be that you haven't drunk enough, even if you're not feeling particularly thirsty.

Although drinking directly from streams and rivers can be tempting, it is not a good idea. Streams that cross the path tend to have flowed across farmland where you can be pretty sure any number of farm animals have relieved themselves. Combined with the probable presence of farm pesticides and other delights, it is best to avoid drinking from these streams. Fortunately, there are quite a few **drinking-water taps** along the Way; we've marked them on our route maps. They are also marked on the South Downs Way trail map on the National Trails website (🖳 nationaltrail.co.uk/south-downs-way – click on 'Trail information & Map'). Also remember that, unless otherwise specified, all tap water in the UK, even that from the taps in public toilets, is safe to drink.

Where drinking-water taps are thin on the ground, remember that you can always ask staff in shops, cafés or pubs to fill your bottle or pouch from the tap.

❏ REAL ALE
There's a plethora of local breweries for the real-ale connoisseur to get excited about. Probably the most famous Sussex brewery, and certainly the oldest, is **Harvey's** (🖳 harveys.org.uk) of Lewes (p152) which dates from 1790. Beers to look out for include their Sussex Best and Armada Ales, while in September they release their seasonal Southdown Harvest Ale which they proudly describe as the 'taste of the South Downs'. It's also worth seeking out ales from **Long Man Brewery** (🖳 longmanbrewery.com), in Litlington. Then there's **Riverside Brewery** (🖳 riversidebreweryltd.co .uk) in Upper Beeding who do a Beeding Best Bitter (4.2%), with a hint of liquorice, and a hoppy Steyning Steamer (4.0%). You can try **Flower Pots IPA** (🖳 www.theflowerpots.co.uk) right where it's brewed, at the Flower Pots Inn in Cheriton.

In England, licensed premises (ie places that serve alcohol) are required by law to provide customers with free tap water, but kind staff will sometimes be happy to help fill up your bottle even if you're not buying anything from them.

MONEY

Since the COVID pandemic, cash is less acceptable than it once was and many establishments, even small and seasonal businesses, now prefer you to pay by card. Nevertheless, it is worth having some **cash** for those that may not, such as some B&Bs and campsites.

While Eastbourne and Winchester at each end of the Way have banks and **ATMs** (cashpoints/cash machines), the villages in between do not. If you find yourself without a penny on the Way it is only a short detour to some of the larger towns; banks and/or ATMs can be found in Petersfield, Midhurst, Arundel, Storrington, Steyning and Lewes.

Shops that do take cards, such as supermarkets, will sometimes advance cash against a debit card (a transaction known as '**cashback**') as long as you buy something for at least £5 at the same time. Pubs sometimes do the same.

Getting cash from a post office

Several banks in Britain have an agreement with the post office allowing customers with a debit card and PIN to make cash withdrawals at post office counters throughout the country. For a full list of banks that are part of this scheme contact the Post Office (🖳 www.postoffice.co.uk/branch-finder). This is a useful service particularly if no ATM is available.

OTHER SERVICES

Many villages and all the towns have at least one **food shop** or **supermarket** and a **post office**. Post offices can be useful for sending unnecessary equipment home which may be weighing you down.

In Part 4 mention is given to services that may be of use to the walker such as **banks**, **ATMs**, **outdoor equipment shops**, **pharmacies/chemists**, **tourist information centres** and **public toilets**.

WALKING COMPANIES AND BAGGAGE TRANSFER

Several companies provide 'self-guided holidays' which include detailed advice and notes on itineraries, maps, accommodation booking, daily baggage transfer and transport at the start and end of your walk. If the thought of carrying a heavy rucksack doesn't appeal there is a company which will transfer your luggage to your next B&B.

PLANNING YOUR WALK

❑ INFORMATION FOR FOREIGN VISITORS

● **Currency** The British pound (£) comes in notes of £50, £20, £10 and £5, and coins of £2 and £1. The pound is divided into 100 pence (usually referred to as 'p', pronounced 'pee') which come in silver coins of 50p, 20p, 10p and 5p, and copper coins of 2p and 1p.

● **Money** Up-to-date **rates of exchange** can be found on 🖳 xe.com/currencyconverter, at some post offices, or at any bank or travel agent.

● **Business hours** If we assume that the whole COVID pandemic is behind us by the time you read this, you'll find most **shops and supermarkets** are open Monday to Saturday 7/8am-8pm (sometimes up to 15 hours a day) and on Sunday from about 9am to 5 or 6pm, though main branches of supermarkets generally open on Sunday 10am-4pm or 11am-5pm. Occasionally, especially in rural areas, you'll come across a local shop that closes at lunchtime on one day during the week, usually a Wednesday or Thursday; this is a throwback to the days when all towns and villages had an 'early closing day'.

Main **post offices** are open at least from Monday to Friday 9am-5pm and Saturday 9am-12.30pm; branches in villages stores are often now open the same hours as the store. **Banks** typically open at 9.30am Monday to Friday and close at 3.30pm or 4pm though in some places they may open only two or three days a week and/or in the morning only; **ATMs** (**cash machines**) though are open all the time as long as they are outside; any inside a shop or pub will only be accessible when that place is open. Note that ATMs that charge (see p22), such as Link machines, may not accept foreign-issued cards.

Pub hours are less predictable; although many open daily 11am-11pm; often in rural areas opening hours are Monday to Saturday 11am-3pm & 5 or 6-11pm, Sunday 11am/noon-3pm & 6 or 7-10.30pm. Last entry to most **museums and galleries** is half an hour, or an hour, before the official closing time.

● **National (bank) holidays** Most businesses are shut on 1 January, Good Friday (March/April), Easter Monday (March/April), first and last Monday in May, last Monday in August, 25 December and 26 December.

● **School holidays** State-school holidays in England are generally as follows: a one-week break late October, two weeks over Christmas and the New Year, a week mid February, two weeks around Easter, one week at the end of May/early June (to coincide with the bank holiday at the end of May) and five to six weeks from late July to early September. Private-school holidays fall at the same time, but tend to be slightly longer.

● **Travel/medical insurance** Although Britain's National Health Service (NHS) is free at the point of use, that is only the case for residents. All visitors to Britain should be properly insured, including comprehensive health coverage. Though Britain has left the EU, the **European Health Insurance Card (EHIC)** does still

Baggage transfer
● **South Downs Bag Transfers** (☎ 01962-867728, 🖳 southdownsbagtrans fers.co.uk, Winchester) Maximum weight per bag 20kg. Currently available April to end Sep only.

For an agreed charge some **B&B owners** may be prepared to take your luggage on to your next accommodation; it's always worth enquiring. Some **taxi companies** are also prepared to transfer luggage on an ad hoc basis.

entitle EU nationals (on production of the EHIC, so ensure you bring it with you) to necessary medical treatment under the NHS while on a temporary visit here. To make sure this is still the case when you visit, however, contact your national social security institution. Also note that the EHIC is not a substitute for proper medical cover on your travel insurance for unforeseen bills and for getting you home should that be necessary. Also consider cover for loss and theft of personal belongings, especially if you are camping or staying in bunkhouses, as there may be times when you'll have to leave your luggage unattended.

● **Weights and measures** In Britain, milk can be sold in pints (1 pint = 568ml), as can beer in pubs, though most other **liquids** including petrol (gasoline) and diesel is sold in litres. Distances on road and path signs is given in miles (1 mile = 1.6km) rather than kilometres, and yards (1yd = 0.9m) rather than metres.

The population remains divided between those who still use inches (1 inch = 2.5cm), feet (1ft = 0.3m) and yards for **distances** and those who are happy with millimetres, centimetres and metres; you'll often be told that 'it's only a hundred yards or so' to somewhere, rather than a hundred metres or so.

Most food is sold in metric weights (g and kg) but the imperial weights of pounds (lb: 1lb = 453g) and ounces (oz: 1oz = 28g) are frequently displayed too. The **weather** – a frequent topic of conversation – is also an issue: while most forecasts predict temperatures in Celsius (C), some older people continue to think in terms of Fahrenheit (F; see the temperature chart on p16 for conversions).

● **Smoking & vaping** The ban on smoking in public places relates not only to pubs and restaurants, but also to B&Bs, hostels and hotels. These latter have the right to designate one or more bedrooms where the occupants can smoke, but the ban is in force in all enclosed areas open to the public – even in a private home such as a B&B. Should you be foolhardy enough to light up in a no-smoking area, which includes pretty well any indoor public place, you could be fined £50, but it's the owners of the premises who suffer most if they fail to stop you, with a potential fine of £2500.

Although the ban does not apply to vaping, premises can and do impose their own restrictions on the use of e-cigarettes indoors.

● **Time** During the winter, the whole of Britain is on Greenwich Mean Time (GMT). The clocks move one hour forward on the last Sunday in March, remaining on British Summer Time (BST) until the last Sunday in October.

● **Telephone** The international country access code for Britain is ☎ 44 followed by the area code minus the first 0, and then the number you require. Within Britain, to call a landline number with the same code as the landline phone you are calling from, the code can be omitted: dial the number only. If you're using a mobile phone that is registered overseas, consider buying a local SIM card to keep costs down.

● **Emergency services** For police, ambulance, fire or coastguard dial ☎ 999 or ☎ 112.

Self-guided holidays
Note: unless specified all companies listed both offer the walk and can tailor-make a holiday in either direction.
● **Absolute Escapes** (☎ 0131-610 1210, 🖳 absoluteescapes.com, Edinburgh) Itineraries of 6-9 days.
● **British & Irish Walks** (☎ 01242-254353, 🖳 britishandirishwalks.com, Gloucestershire) Itineraries along the whole and parts of the Way.
● **Celtic Trails Walking Holidays** (☎ 01291-689774, 🖳 celtictrailswalkinghol idays.co.uk, Monmouthshire) The whole Way (west to east only) in 8-11 days' walking/9-12 nights and short breaks of 2 days' walking/ 3 nights.
● **Contours Walking Holidays** (☎ 01629-821900, 🖳 contours.co.uk, Derby-shire) Has a variety of packages from 2-day tasters to the whole walk.
● **Embark Walking Holidays** (☎ 01873 379100, 🖳 embarkwalkingholidays .com, Wales) Offer the full walk over 7 to 11 nights, or in smaller sections and short breaks over 3-6 nights. Can provide walks with dogs.
● **Footpath Holidays** (☎ 01985-840049, 🖳 footpath-holidays.com, Wiltshire) Has been organising walking holidays for 40 years. A 9-night full walk, or parts of the Way using Alfriston as a base and also offer inn-to-inn.
● **Footprints of Sussex** (🖳 footprintsofsussex.co.uk, West Sussex) Has been organising SDW walks for 30 years, based in Sussex and within South Downs NP. Offers the Original, Full or as sections. Also organises an annual, supported rather than guided, walk each June (🖳 southdownsway.com).

❏ MOUNTAIN BIKING THE SOUTH DOWNS WAY
The South Downs Way is perfect for mountain bikers. As Britain's first long-distance bridleway it was specifically geared to horse-riders, cyclists and walkers. The entire route can be followed on two wheels on wide tracks which are, on the whole, well drained, with only a few very steep sections either side of the major river valleys. There are some sections where walkers and cyclists must follow different routes; these are marked with blue chevrons indicating byways and yellow chevrons for footpaths.

Tips for cycling the Way
● **Camp rather than staying in B&Bs** Cycling gives you the perfect opportunity to experience the joys of camping without having to carry any of your gear on your back. Strap a tent, sleeping bag and roll mat onto your bike, and off you go! See pp19-20 for a list of campsites that are on the Way itself, rather than in the surrounding countryside far below.
● **Stick to the Way** Most of the downland villages are some distance below the Way itself, and whilst it's a joy to freewheel down to them for a pub lunch, it can be tough pulling your bike back up onto the trail afterwards. Plan accordingly; it's far better to stay on the Way, if at all possible.
● **Be prepared for punctures** It hardly needs saying but don't forget your puncture repair kit (and know how to use it!) as well as your pump. Though famed for its chalk, much of the South Downs Way also contains super-sharp fragments of flint, which can cause havoc for even the sturdiest mountain-bike tyres.
● **Pack wet-weather gear** Chances are it will rain at some stage, and when it does the Way gets muddy; sometimes very muddy. Come prepared with wet-weather gear, including waterproof panniers, mudguards and a rag to wipe down any dirty gear.

● **Freedom Walking Holidays** (☎ 07733-885390, 💻 freedomwalkingholidays
.co.uk, Oxfordshire) A 7- to 8-day full-walk itinerary.

● **Let's Go Walking** (☎ 01837-880075, 💻 www.letsgowalking.com, Devon)
The whole path in 9 days' walking/10 nights.

● **Macs Adventure** (☎ 0141 530 8886, 💻 macsadventure.com, Glasgow) The
full Way (west to east only) in 6-8 days and a short break in 5 days.

● **Mickledore** (☎ 01768-772335, 💻 mickledore.co.uk, Cumbria) Have itineraries offering the whole route in 6-9 days, or each half of the Way, and a short
break 2-day circular walk.

● **Responsible Travel** (☎ 01273-823700, 💻 responsibletravel.com, East
Sussex) The whole Way in 9 nights/10 days and 10 nights/11 days.

● **S-Cape Travel UK** (☎ 01768 807617, 💻 www.s-capetravel.eu, Cumbria) 10
days – 9 nights itinerary in either direction; tailor-made walks west to east only.

● **South Downs Discovery** (☎ 01925 914182, 💻 southdownsdiscovery.com)
South Downs Way specialists offering itineraries for 2-10 days.

● **Walk the Trail** (☎ 01326 567252, 💻 www.walkthetrail.co.uk; Cornwall)
Offer the whole path as well as in sections.

Guided holidays

● **Her on a Hill** (☎ 07444 794 300 💻 heronahill.com, South Yorkshire) Offers
guided group walking holidays for women along parts of the South Downs Way.
Itinerary varies from year to year.

● **Secret Hills Walking Holidays** (☎ 01694-723600, 💻 secrethillswalking
.co.uk; Shropshire) Specialise in sole guided walking breaks. Offer itinerary
with 4½ days' walking/4 nights.

TAKING DOGS ALONG THE WAY   [see also pp192-3]

Dogs are allowed on the South Downs but should be kept on a lead whenever
there are sheep around. Considering the Downs is a prime sheep-farming area
this is most of the time and it is worth remembering that farmers are perfectly
within their rights to shoot any dog they believe to be worrying their sheep.

DISABLED ACCESS

In the summer of 2016 the South Downs Way became the first fully inclusive
National Trail when it was completed in its entirety by a wheelchair user using
a state-of-the-art pony cart, specially developed by PonyAxeS (💻 ponyaxes
.com/south-downs-way). Unfortunately, for those without access to such car-
riages, some parts of the South Downs Way are still quite inaccessible to disabled people, despite many of the councils taking steps to improve access to the
Sussex and Hampshire countryside.

Nevertheless, there are stretches of the Way that can be followed quite easily, particularly where roads provide direct access to the top of the hills such as
at **Ditchling Beacon** (see p147). Here there are gates designed for wheelchair
users and there are also plenty of benches at intervals along the path to the west
of Ditchling Beacon. **Devil's Dyke** (see p141) is another good spot where

access is relatively easy and the path not too rough. **Seven Sisters Country Park** (see box p174) has good facilities for the disabled both in the park and at the visitor centre and access to the beach at Cuckmere Haven is quite straightforward. Further west the easiest stretches of the Way can be found to the west of **Bignor Hill** (see p115), where there's a car park near the top, and on **Harting Down** (pp102-3) which has a relatively long stretch of gentle, level pathways. **Queen Elizabeth Country Park** (p94) has wide, level tracks and easy access.

For more information see 🖥 accessiblecountryside.org.uk/southeast.

Budgeting

ACCOMMODATION

Camping

Campsites generally charge £10-15 per person (pp) so if camping and cooking all your own food expect to need £20-30pp per day. However, it is always best to allow for more than you think necessary, to cover those occasional luxuries such as a hot meal in a cosy pub after a day walking in the pouring rain. Bearing this in mind it is worth counting on at least £25pp per day.

Hostels and budget accommodation

There are very few hostels and only one bunkhouse on the Way, so you won't be able to use this type of accommodation exclusively. However, combined with camping, other budget places such as cabins, land pods, shepherd's huts and bell tents, or one or two nights in B&Bs, it can still be fairly cost-effective.

The YHA charges for beds in its **hostels** following the modern online model with lowest prices during quieter periods and rates increasing with popularity of location and date. Beds in dormitories cost around £15-22pp, while rooms (£29-60 for up to two sharing) are surprisingly good for such a budget price. All rates are 10% less for YHA members. Hostels usually have a self-catering kitchen, allowing you to keep food costs down. However, if you want to eat in their restaurant/café, expect to pay around £7 for breakfast, around the same for a packed lunch and £12 for an evening meal. To cover the cost of a night in a private room in a hostel and the occasional bar meal and drink, count on at least £40pp per day. For a dorm bed, £30pp may be more accurate. If you eat out most nights this figure is likely to be £45/55pp per day (dorm/private room) or more.

The only true **bunkhouse** on the Way, called South Downs Bunkhouse (Houghton Bridge; see p117), will set you back from £32.50pp per night and also has a self-catering kitchen.

Log cabins and **land pods** are often no-frills options from around £20-30pp for two sharing, while **shepherd's huts** vary hugely depending on what is offered by way of facilities and luxury, but could be more in the range of £40-60pp. For a group of three or four, a **bell tent** or **yurt** could be an economical option as they start from around £75 a night. These don't usually have self catering facilities so you will need to add the cost of meals out to your daily budget.

B&B-style accommodation

Rates for bed and breakfast in a **B&B**, **pub** or **guesthouse** are usually £40-80pp (**hotels** are likely to be more) for two sharing a room. Breakfast is, of course, almost always included in the rate but you will need to buy your lunch and evening meal so you will probably need around £60-100pp per day.

MEALS OUT AND EXTRAS

The cost of eating out obviously depends on what you choose and where, but if you buy a **cooked breakfast** in a café (around £9), a **sandwich** in a pub at lunchtime (£8-12) and a **main meal** in the evening (£14-20) you will need to add at least £40pp per day to your accommodation costs.

If you like a pint or two of beer in the evening, remember that one costing less than £5 is a rare thing in the south of England.

Don't forget all those little things that push up your daily bill – laundry, souvenirs, hot drinks, beer, ice-cream, buses, more beer and travel to and from the Way. All these will probably add up to between £50 and £100 for the trip.

Itineraries

Part 4 of this book (the Route Guide) has been written so that it can be used by hikers walking the South Downs Way in either an eastward or westward direction, following a colour coding: **E ➜** and **W ⬅**. For more details see p71. This guidebook is divided into daily stages but these are not rigid. Instead, it's structured to make it easy for you to plan your own itinerary. The South Downs Way can be tackled in any number of ways, the most challenging of which is to do it all in one go; this requires about one week. Others may prefer to walk it over a series of short breaks, coming back year after year to do a bit more.

To help plan your walk the **colour maps** at the end of the book have **gradient profiles** and there is also a **planning map** (see opposite inside back cover). The **table of town and village facilities** (pp30-1) gives a rundown on the essential information you will need regarding accommodation possibilities and services. See pp19-20 for details of campsites that are closest to the trail. Alternatively, you could follow one of the **suggested itineraries** below. There is also a list of recommended **day and weekend walks** (see p35) which cover the best of the path, most of which are well served by public transport. The **public transport map** is on p48.

Once you have an idea of your approach turn to **Part 4** for detailed information on accommodation, places to eat, and other services in each place on the route. Also in Part 4 are route descriptions to accompany the trail maps.

WHICH DIRECTION?

There are many criteria that will determine in which direction to tackle the Way. It always seems a good idea to finish a walk with something that is worth

(cont'd on p36)

PLANNING YOUR WALK

VILLAGE AND TOWN FACILITIES
Winchester to Eastbourne – Walking East E→

PLACE* & DISTANCE* APPROX MILES / KM	BANK/ ATM	POST OFFICE	INFO	EATING PLACE	FOOD SHOP	CAMP-SITE	HOSTEL BARN	B&B HOTEL
Winchester 0	✔	✔	TIC	✔✔✔	✔	✔(2¼)		✔✔✔
Chilcomb 2 / 3.2						✔(2)		✔
Cheriton 4½ / 7.2 (+1.5)		✔		✔		✔		✔
Exton & Meonstoke 5½ / 8.8		✔		✔✔	✔			✔
East Meon 5 / 8 (+1)		✔		✔✔	✔	✔		✔✔
Around Butser Hill 2 / 3.2				✔✔		✔	H	✔✔
Buriton 5½ / 8.8 (+0.5)				✔✔				✔
Petersfield (+2)	✔	✔	TIC	✔✔✔	✔	✔(1¼)		✔✔✔
South Harting 3½ / 5.6 (+0.5)		✔		✔✔	✔			✔✔
Cocking 7 / 11.2 (+0.5)		✔		✔	✔	✔		✔✔
Heyshott 2 / 3.2 (+0.5)				✔				
Graffham 1½ / 2.4 (+1)		mobile		✔	✔	✔		✔
Upwaltham 2 / 3.2				✔		✔		
Sutton & Bignor 2 / 3.2 (+1)				✔		✔		✔✔
Bury 2½ / 4 (+1)		mobile		✔				
Houghton Bridge & Amberley 1 / 1.6	✔			✔✔	✔		B	✔✔
Arundel (+5)	✔	✔		✔✔	✔			✔✔
Storrington 3 / 4.8 (+1.5)	✔	✔		✔✔	✔			
Washington 3 / 4.8 (+0.5)				✔		✔		✔
Steyning, Bram &UB 4 / 6.4 (+1)	✔	✔		✔✔	✔	✔	YHA (2½)	✔✔
Fulking 6½ / 10.4 (+0.5)				✔				
Poynings 2 / 3.2 (+0.5)				✔✔				✔
Pyecombe 2 / 3.2				✔	✔	✔		✔✔
Clayton 1 / 1.6 (+0.5)				✔				✔
Ditchling 1½ / 2.4 (+1.5)		✔		✔✔	✔	✔(½)		✔✔
Plumpton 2 / 3.2 (+0.5)				✔				
Lewes 1 / 1.6 (+3)	✔	✔	TIC	✔✔✔	✔			✔✔✔
Housedean Farm 2¾ / 4.5						✔		
Kingston-nr-Lewes 2¼ / 3.5 (+1)				✔				
Rodmell & Southease 4 / 6.4				✔			YHA	✔
West Firle 3½ / 5.6 (+1)		✔		✔	✔			✔
Alciston & Berwick 2½ / 4 (+1)		✔		✔✔				✔✔
Alfriston 2 / 3.2				✔✔✔	✔	✔		✔✔✔
Litlington 1 / 1.6				✔✔				
Exceat/Westdean 1½ / 2.4				✔				✔
Birling Gap 4 / 6.4				✔				✔
Beachy Head 2¾ / 4.5				✔✔				
Alternative (inland) route from Alfriston:								
Milton Street 1 / 1.6 (+0.5)								✔
Jevington 2½ / 4				✔				✔
***End SDW** (inland)* 4½ / 7.2	✔	✔		✔	✔			✔✔
End of SDW (Meads) 1¼ / 2		✔		✔✔	✔			✔✔
Eastbourne (pier) 1½ / 2.4	✔	✔	TIC	✔✔✔	✔		YHA	✔✔✔

NOTES

*PLACE Places in bold are on the path; those not in bold are a short walk off the route
*DISTANCE = from the place above. Distances given are between places directly on the route
Bracketed distance eg (+1) shows additional distance in miles off the route

PLANNING YOUR WALK

VILLAGE AND TOWN FACILITIES
W← Eastbourne to Winchester – Walking West

PLACE* & DISTANCE* APPROX MILES / KM	BANK/ ATM	POST OFFICE	INFO	EATING PLACE	FOOD SHOP	CAMP SITE	HOSTEL BARN	B&B HOTEL
Eastbourne (pier) 0	✔	✔	TIC	✔✔✔	✔		YHA	✔✔✔
Start of SDW (Meads) 1½ / 2.4		✔		✔✔	✔			✔
Alternative (inland) route to Alfriston:								
Jevington 4½ / 7.2				✔				✔
Milton Street 2½ / 4 (+0.5)								✔
Alfriston (inland route) 1 / 1.6	mobile			✔✔✔	✔	✔		✔✔✔
Beachy Head 1¼ / 2				✔✔				
Birling Gap 2¾ / 4.5				✔				✔
Exceat/Westdean 4 / 6.4				✔				✔
Litlington 1½ / 2.4				✔✔				
Alfriston 1 / 1.6				✔✔✔	✔	✔		✔✔✔
Alciston & Berwick 2 / 3.2 (+1)		✔		✔✔				✔✔
West Firle 2½ / 4 (+1)		✔		✔	✔			✔
Rodmell & Southease 3½ / 5.6				✔			YHA	✔
Kingston-nr-Lewes 4 / 6.4 (+1)				✔				
Housedean Farm 2¼ / 3.5						✔		
Lewes 2¾ / 4.5 (+3)	✔	✔	TIC	✔✔✔	✔			✔✔✔
Plumpton 1 / 1.6 (+0.5)				✔				
Ditchling 2 / 3.2 (+1.5)		✔		✔✔✔	✔	✔ (½)		✔✔
Clayton 1½ / 2.4 (+0.5)				✔				✔
Pyecombe 1 / 1.6				✔	✔	✔		✔✔
Poynings 2 / 3.2 (+0.5)				✔✔				✔
Fulking 2 / 3.2 (+0.5)				✔				
Steyning, Bram &UB 6½ / 10.4 (+1)	✔	✔		✔✔✔		✔	YHA (2½)	✔✔✔
Washington 4 / 6.4 (+0.5)				✔		✔		✔
Storrington 3 / 4.8 (+1.5)	✔	✔		✔✔✔	✔			
Arundel (+5)	✔	✔		✔✔✔	✔			✔✔✔
Houghton Bridge & Amberley 3 / 4.8	✔			✔✔✔			B	✔✔✔
Bury 1 / 1.6 (+1)		mobile		✔				
Sutton & Bignor 2½ / 4 (+1)				✔		✔		✔✔
Upwaltham 2 / 3.2				✔		✔		
Graffham 2 / 3.2 (+1)		mobile		✔	✔	✔		✔
Heyshott 1½ / 2.4 (+0.5)				✔				
Cocking 2 / 3.2 (+0.5)		✔		✔	✔	✔		✔✔
South Harting 7 / 11.2 (+0.5)		✔		✔	✔			✔✔
Petersfield (+2)	✔	✔	TIC	✔✔✔	✔	✔ (1¼)		✔✔✔
Buriton 3½ / 5.6 (+0.5)				✔✔				✔
Around Butser Hill 5½ / 8.8				✔✔		✔	H	✔✔
East Meon 2 / 3.2 (+1)		✔		✔✔	✔	✔		✔✔
Exton & Meonstoke 5 / 8		✔		✔✔✔	✔			✔
Cheriton 5½ / 8.8 (+1.5)		✔		✔		✔		✔
Chilcomb 4½ / 7.2						✔ (2)		✔
Winchester 2 / 3.2	✔	✔	TIC	✔✔✔	✔	✔ (2¼)		✔✔✔

B&B/HOTEL	✔ = one place ✔✔ = two ✔✔✔ = three or more
BUNK/HOSTEL	YHA = YHA hostel H = independent hostel B = bunkhouse
CAMPSITE	Bracketed distance eg (½) shows distance from South Downs Way
EATING PLACE	✔ = one place ✔✔ = two ✔✔✔ = three or more
INFO	TIC = Tourist information centre

PLANNING YOUR WALK

STAYING IN B&B-STYLE ACCOMMODATION – West to East

	Relaxed pace			Medium pace			Fast pace		
	Place	Approx distance		Place	Approx distance		Place	Approx distance	
Night		miles	km		miles	km		miles	km
0	Winchester			Winchester			Winchester		
1	Cheriton	8	12.8	Cheriton	8	12.8	Meonstoke	12	19.3
2	Meonstoke	7	11.2	East Meon	13	20.9	South Harting	16½	26.5
3	East Meon	6	9.6	South Harting	12½	20.1	Amberley	20	32.2
4	Buriton	8½	13.6	Graffham	10½	16.9	Pyecombe	20½	33
5	Cocking	11	17.7	Amberley	9	14.4	Rodmell	15	24.1
6	Amberley	13½	21.7	Steyning	13	20.9	Alfriston	9	14.4
7	Steyning	13	20.9	Lewes*	16	25.7	Eastbourne	12½	20.1
8	Pyecombe	9½	15.2	Alfriston	17	27.3			
9	Lewes*	5½	8.4	Eastbourne	12½	20.1			
10	Rodmell	9	14.4						
11	Alfriston	8	12.8						
12	Eastbourne	12½	20.1				* See Notes below		

STAYING IN B&B-STYLE ACCOMMODATION – East to West

	Relaxed pace			Medium pace			Fast pace		
	Place	Approx distance		Place	Approx distance		Place	Approx distance	
Night		miles	km		miles	km		miles	km
0	Eastbourne			Eastbourne			Eastbourne		
1	Alfriston	12½	20.1	Alfriston	12½	20.1	Alfriston	12½	20.1
2	Rodmell	8	12.8	Lewes*	17	27.3	Rodmell	9	14.4
3	Lewes*	9	14.4	Steyning	16	25.7	Pyecombe	15	24.1
4	Pyecombe	5½	8.4	Amberley	13	20.9	Amberley	20½	33
5	Steyning	9½	15.2	Graffham	9	14.4	South Harting	20	32.2
6	Amberley	13	20.9	South Harting	10½	16.9	Meonstoke	16½	26.5
7	Cocking	13½	21.7	East Meon	12½	20.1	Winchester	12	19.3
8	Buriton	11	17.7	Cheriton	13	20.9			
9	East Meon	8½	13.6	Winchester	8	12.8			
10	Meonstoke	6	9.6						
11	Cheriton	7	11.2						
12	Winchester	8	12.8				* See Notes below		

B&B – Notes
*Lewes is three miles off the trail but frequent public transport is available from Housedean Farm (see p156), very near the path, or it's a three-mile walk from trail to town.

(The three miles to Lewes have not been included in the above mile counts.)

CAMPING – West to East

	Relaxed pace			Medium pace			Fast pace		
Night	Place	Approx distance miles	km	Place	Approx distance miles	km	Place	Approx distance miles	km
0	Winchester*			Winchester*			Winchester*		
1	Holden Farm	7	11.2	Holden Farm	7	11.2	Meon Springs	17	27.3
2	Meon Springs	10	16.1	Butser Hill	13	20.9	Manor Farm†	18	28.9
3	Butser Hill	6	9.6	Manor Farm†	16	25.7	Amberley*	12	19.3
4	Manor Farm†	13	20.9	Amberley*	12	19.3	Pyecombe	20	32.2
5	Graffham	3½	5.7	Truleigh Hill	14	22.5	Alfriston	22	35.4
6	Amberley*	8½	13.6	Ditchling	9	14.4	Eastbourne*	12½	20.1
7	Washington	7	11.2	Southease#	11	17.7			
8	Truleigh Hill	8	12.8	Alfriston	8	12.8			
9	Pyecombe	6	9.6	Eastbourne*	12½	20.1			
10	Housedean Fm	8	12.8						
11	Southease#	7	11.2						
12	Alfriston	8	12.8						
13	Eastbourne*	12½	20.1						

† Manor Farm is on the Way (just south of Cocking)
\# No camping but pods and fixed bell tents at YHA
* See Notes below

CAMPING – East to West

	Relaxed pace			Medium pace			Fast pace		
Night	Place	Approx distance miles	km	Place	Approx distance miles	km	Place	Approx distance miles	km
0	Eastbourne*			Eastbourne*			Eastbourne*		
1	Alfriston	12½	20.1	Alfriston	12½	20.1	Alfriston	12½	20.1
2	Southease#	8	12.8	Southease#	8	12.8	Pyecombe	22	35.4
3	Housedean Fm	7	11.2	Ditchling	11	17.7	Amberley*	20	32.2
4	Pyecombe	8	12.8	Truleigh Hill	9	14.4	Manor Farm†	12	19.3
5	Truleigh Hill	6	9.6	Amberley*	14	22.5	Meon Springs	18	28.9
6	Washington	8	12.8	Manor Farm†	12	19.3	Winchester*	17	27.3
7	Amberley*	7	11.2	Butser Hill	16	25.7			
8	Graffham	8½	13.6	Holden Farm	13	20.9			
9	Manor Farm†	3½	5.7	Winchester*	7	11.2			
10	Butser Hill	13	20.9						
11	Meon Springs	6	9.6						
12	Holden Farm	10	16.1						
13	Winchester*	7	11.2						

† Manor Farm is on the Way (just south of Cocking)
\# No camping but pods and fixed bell tents at YHA
* See Notes below

Camping – Notes In some cases it is necessary to walk up to a mile for the campsite but see pp19-20 for a list of campsites directly on the trail.

* No campsites at places marked with an asterisk. For **Winchester** consider Morn Hill Caravan Club Campsite: it is two miles north-east of Chilcomb and 1½ miles north of the Cheesefoot Head car park (both Map 2), or 2¼ miles from Winchester but accessible by bus from Winchester bus station. For **Eastbourne** stay in the YHA, or catch the last train home. For **Amberley** there's the bunkhouse at nearby Houghton Bridge.

PLANNING YOUR WALK

STAYING IN HOSTELS/BUDGET ACCOMMODATION – West to East

Night	Relaxed pace Place	Approx distance miles	km	Medium pace Place	Approx distance miles	km	Fast pace Place	Approx distance miles	km
0	Winchester*			Winchester*			Winchester*		
1	Cheriton*	8	12.9	Exton*	12	19.3	East Meon	18	28.9
2	East Meon	13	20.9	Butser Hill	7	11.3	Cocking	18	28.9
3	Buriton*	9	14.5	Cocking	16	25.8	Houghton Br	11	17.7
4	Cocking	11	17.7	Houghton Br	11	17.7	Truleigh Hill	15½	25
5	Houghton Br	11	17.7	Truleigh Hill	15½	25	Southease	21	34
6	Washington*	7	11.3	Ditchling*	10½	16.9	Eastbourne	20½	33
7	Truleigh Hill	8½	13.7	Southease	12	19.3			
8	Ditchling*	10½	16.9	Alciston	7	11.3			
9	Southease	12	19.3	Eastbourne	13½	21.7			
10	Alciston	7	11.3						
11	Eastbourne	13½	21.7						

Budget accommodation includes hostels, bunkhouses, log cabins, bell tents and shepherd's huts. Check carefully whether bedding is provided.

*No hostels/budget accommodation; alternative accommodation available

STAYING IN HOSTELS/BUDGET ACCOMMODATION – East to West

Night	Relaxed pace Place	Approx distance miles	km	Medium pace Place	Approx distance miles	km	Fast pace Place	Approx distance miles	km
0	Eastbourne			Eastbourne			Eastbourne		
1	Alciston	13½	21.7	Alciston	13½	21.7	Southease	20½	33
2	Southease	7	11.3	Southease	7	11.3	Truleigh Hill	21	33.8
3	Ditchling*	12	19.3	Ditchling*	12	19.3	Houghton Br	15½	25
4	Truleigh Hill	10½	16.9	Truleigh Hill	10½	16.9	Cocking	11	17.7
5	Washington*	8½	13.7	Houghton Br	15½	25	East Meon	18	28.9
6	Houghton Br	7	11.3	Cocking	11	17.7	Winchester*	18	28.9
7	Cocking	11	17.7	Butser Hill	16	25.8			
8	Buriton*	11	18.5	Exton*	7	11.3			
9	East Meon	9	14.4	Winchester*	12	19.3			
10	Cheriton*	13	20.9						
11	Winchester*	8	12.8						

Budget accommodation includes hostels, bunkhouses, log cabins, bell tents and shepherd's huts. Check carefully whether bedding is provided.

*No hostels/budget accommodation; alternative accommodation available

❏ THE BEST DAY AND WEEKEND WALKS

Day walks

Exton to Buriton   **12 miles/19.3km (see pp88-97)**

The best of the East Hampshire downland, passing over Old Winchester Hill and its magnificent hill-fort remains and Butser Hill, the highest hill on the Downs, with far-reaching views over the Meon Valley and Queen Elizabeth Country Park.

There are no bus services at Exton but there are to East Meon so if you need to use public transport it is easiest to start there.

Amberley to Steyning   **13 miles/20.9km (see pp126-34)**

Starting in one of the prettiest villages on the Way and ending in one of the most beautiful towns, this walk provides extensive views from the spine of the Downs, taking in the famous local landmark of Chanctonbury Ring.

Devil's Dyke to Ditchling Beacon   **5 miles/8km (see pp141-9)**

Possibly the most spectacular dry valley on the Downs, Devil's Dyke is the magnificent starting point of this short section that continues by climbing over the isolated Newtimber Hill before ending at the beauty spot of Ditchling Beacon. There are seasonal bus services (Sat, Sun & public holidays only) to both Devil's Dyke and Ditchling Beacon.

Kingston-near-Lewes to Southease   **5 miles/8km (see pp159-61)**

One of the quieter stretches of the Downs with fine views of Mount Caburn on the other side of the Ouse Valley and some literary history into the bargain at Rodmell, once the home of Virginia Woolf.

Exceat to Eastbourne via Cuckmere Haven   **9 miles/14.4km (see pp170-8)**

Arguably the finest day of walking anywhere between Winchester and Eastbourne, following the rollercoaster tops of the Seven Sisters chalk cliffs to the high point of Beachy Head high above Eastbourne.

Alfriston to Eastbourne via Jevington   **10 miles/16km (see pp180-3)**

This inland route is not as spectacular as the coastal route to Eastbourne but equally enjoyable, encompassing the beautiful Cuckmere Valley, the ramshackle timber-framed houses of Alfriston and the curious Long Man of Wilmington chalk figure.

Weekend walks

Buriton to Amberley   **23½ miles/38km (see pp97-120)**

Stopping off in either Cocking or Midhurst for the night, this section takes in the fine wooded sections close to Buriton and the airy Harting Down on the first day, followed by Bignor Hill with its Roman road, Stane Street, on the second day.

Amberley to Pyecombe   **20½ miles/33km (see pp120-46)**

Extensive views and the curious, enchanted Chanctonbury Ring are the highlights of the first day with a wide choice of places to stay in historic Steyning, or Bramber with its castle. The second day follows the open top of the Downs all the way to the impressive valley of Devil's Dyke.

Circular walk (Eastbourne, Alfriston, Cuckmere Haven)   **19 miles/30.5km**

The Exceat to Eastbourne and Alfriston to Eastbourne walks (see p170 & p180) can be combined to make a wonderful circular walk and can be started and finished anywhere on the circuit. You'll pass through the beautiful villages of Jevington, Alfriston, Litlington and Westdean as well as walking the entire coastal section from Cuckmere Haven to Eastbourne.

PLANNING YOUR WALK

(cont'd from p29) walking towards. With this in mind, although Winchester is a more attractive town to finish in than Eastbourne, the scenery improves towards the eastern end of the South Downs Way and what finer place to con- clude the walk than by the sea and on top of the white cliffs of the Seven Sisters and Beachy Head? Another factor is the prevailing wind which normally comes from the south-west. Having the wind at your back is a great help so this would also suggest starting at Winchester and finishing at Eastbourne.

Although the maps in Part 4 are arranged in a west to east direction, times and route descriptions are given for walking in both directions so they can be easily followed in reverse order.

SUGGESTED ITINERARIES

The itineraries are based on different accommodation types – B&B-style accommodation (p32), campsites (p33) and hostels/budget accommodation (p34) – with each divided into three categories of walking speed. They really are only suggestions and all of them can be easily adapted by using the more detailed information on accommodation found in Part 4; the distance chart on pp194-5 will also help you plan your itinerary.

Don't forget to add your travelling time from/to your accommodation both before and after the walk.

See box p35 for suggestions of a number of day and weekend walks cover- ing the best of the South Downs Way; these are accessible using public transport (see pp46-8) unless specified.

What to take

Deciding how much to take with you can be difficult. Experienced walkers know that you really should take only the bare essentials but at the same time you need to ensure you have all the equipment necessary to make the trip safe and comfortable.

KEEP YOUR LUGGAGE LIGHT

Carrying a heavy rucksack really can ruin your enjoyment of a good walk and can also slow you down a great deal, turning an easy 7-mile day into an inter- minable slog. Be ruthless when you pack and leave behind all those little home comforts that you tell yourself don't weigh that much really. Always pack the essentials, of course, but try to leave behind anything that you think might 'come in handy' but probably won't. This advice is even more pertinent to campers who have the added weight of camping equipment to carry. And remember, in the south of England you are never far from a shop where you can buy it if necessary.

HOW TO CARRY IT

The size of the **rucksack** you need depends on your sleeping and eating plans. If you are camping and cooking for yourself you will probably need a 65- to 75-litre rucksack which can hold the tent, sleeping bag, cooking equipment and food.

The hostels provide bedding (though not towels) and have cooking facilities, so if staying in these a 40- to 60-litre rucksack should be sufficient. The budget accommodation options such as log cabins and bell tents usually provide bedding but may not have cooking facilities so check and plan accordingly.

If you have gone for the B&B option you will probably find a 30- to 40-litre daypack is more than enough to carry your lunch, waterproofs, spare clothes and guidebook. If you've booked a self-guided holiday, or are using a baggage-transfer service (see p25), you could even just take a suitcase plus a small **day pack** for the essentials for the day.

Whatever size your rucksack is, ensure it has a stiffened back and can be adjusted to fit you comfortably; this will make carrying the weight much easier. Rucksacks are decorated with seemingly pointless straps but if you adjust them correctly it can make a big difference to your personal comfort while walking. Make sure the hip belt and chest belt (if there is one) are fastened tightly as this helps distribute the weight; most of it should be carried on your hips.

When packing the rucksack make sure you have all the things you are likely to need during the day – this guidebook (of course!), a map, a water bottle, waterproofs, packed lunch – near the top or in the side pockets. Try always to put things in the same place and memorise where they are so you can find them easily when you need them. There is nothing more annoying than pulling everything out of your pack to find that lost banana when you're starving or your waterproofs when it's just started raining.

Even though most rucksacks come with their own rain cover, it is still a good idea to keep everything inside it in **canoe bags**, **waterproof rucksack liners** or strong plastic bags (or bin-liners). If you don't it's bound to get wet.

FOOTWEAR

Boots versus trainers Your footwear is arguably the most important item of gear that can affect the enjoyment of your hike. In summer you can get by with a light pair of running trainers or trail shoes, especially if you're carrying only a small pack, although this is an invitation for wet, cold feet if there is any rain and they don't offer support for your ankles. On the plus side, lightweight running trainers dry off after a rainstorm much more quickly than big heavy hiking boots. Some of the terrain can be quite rough and wet, though, so many people prefer a pair of good walking boots. If going down this route, remember they must fit well and be properly broken in: it is no good discovering that your boots are slowly murdering your feet two days into a one-week walk.

Socks The traditional wearing of a thin liner sock under a thicker wool sock is no longer necessary if you choose a high-quality sock specially designed for walking. A high proportion of natural fibres makes them much more comfortable. Three pairs are ample, although you may need more if it rains a lot.

Extra footwear Some walkers like to have a second pair of shoes to wear when not on the trail. Trainers, sport sandals, or flip flops are all suitable as long as they are light. Flip flops are certainly useful for campsite shower blocks.

CLOTHES

Experienced walkers will know the importance of wearing the right clothes. Always expect the worst weather even if the forecast is good. Modern technology in outdoor attire can seem baffling but it basically comes down to the old multi-layer system: a base layer to transport sweat away from your skin; a mid-layer to keep you warm; and an outer layer or 'shell' to protect you from the rain.

Underwear and base layer As with socks, two or three changes of your normal **underwear** is fine. Cotton absorbs sweat, trapping it next to the skin which will chill you rapidly when you stop exercising. A thin lightweight **thermal top** made from a synthetic material is better as it draws moisture away, keeping you dry. It will be cool on its own in hot weather and warm when worn under other clothes in cooler conditions.

Mid layers In the summer a woollen jumper or mid-weight polyester **fleece** will suffice. For the rest of the year you will need an extra layer to keep you warm. Both wool and fleece, unlike cotton, have the ability to stay reasonably warm when wet.

Outer layer A decent **waterproof jacket** is essential year-round and will be much more comfortable (but also more expensive) if it's also 'breathable' to prevent the build up of condensation on the inside. This layer can also be worn to keep the wind off.

Leg wear Whatever you wear on your legs it should be light, quick-drying and not restricting. Many British walkers find **polyester tracksuit bottoms** comfortable. Poly-cotton or microfibre trousers are excellent. Denim jeans should never be worn; if they get wet they become heavy, cold and cling to your legs. A pair of **shorts** is nice to have on sunny days; many hikers wear '**zip-off**' **trousers**, so you can convert them into shorts if preferred, making these the most versatile and suitable option for the South Downs. Thermal **long-johns** or thick tights are cosy if you're camping but are probably unnecessary even in winter.

Waterproof trousers are necessary most of the year. In summer a pair of windproof and quick-drying trousers is useful in showery weather.

Gaiters are not really necessary but may come in useful in wet weather, when the vegetation around your legs is dripping wet.

Other clothes A **warm hat** and **gloves** should always be kept in your rucksack; you never know when you might need them. In summer you should also carry a **sun hat** with you, preferably one which covers the back of your neck. For cooling off on beaches, or in local swimming pools, take a **swimsuit**.

TOILETRIES

Take only the minimum: unless staying in B&Bs, you'll need a small bar of **soap** or small bottle of **shower gel**, either of which can also be used instead of shaving cream and for washing clothes; a tiny tube of **toothpaste** and a **toothbrush**; and one roll of **loo paper** in a plastic bag. If you are planning to defecate outdoors you will also need **bags** to pack out the loo paper and a lightweight **trowel** for burying the evidence (see p51 for further tips).

You'll also need a **towel** (if camping or staying in a hostel though at the latter they can usually be rented), **razor**, **deodorant**, **tampons/sanitary towels** and a high-factor **sunscreen** and **lip balm**.

FIRST-AID KIT

Medical facilities in Britain are excellent so you need only take a small kit to cover common problems and emergencies. A basic kit will contain a pack of **aspirin** or **paracetamol** for treating mild to moderate pain and fever; **plasters/ Band Aids** for minor cuts; **blister patches** such as 'moleskin', 'Compeed' or 'Second skin'; a **bandage** for holding dressings, splints or limbs in place and for supporting a sprained ankle; an **elastic knee support** for a weak knee; a small selection of different-sized **sterile dressings** for wounds; **porous adhesive tape**; **antiseptic wipes**; **antiseptic cream**; **safety pins**; **tweezers** and a small pair of **scissors**. Pack the kit in a waterproof container.

GENERAL ITEMS

Essential
The following should be in everyone's rucksack: a **water bottle/pouch** (holding at least one litre); a **torch** (flashlight), if you don't have one on your phone, in case you end up walking after dark; **emergency food** which your body can quickly convert into energy; a **penknife**; a **watch** with an alarm; and a **bag** for packing out any rubbish you accumulate. A **whistle** is also worth taking. It can fit in a pocket and although you are very unlikely to need it you may be grateful of it in the unlikely event of an emergency (see p56).

Of course, a **smartphone** can do the job of some of the above (torch, watch, alarm), as well as being a **GPS**, **map**, **camera**, **compass** – oh, and a phone too. Phone reception on the South Downs is generally good. Most people will regard their phone as an essential bit of kit, but obviously if it isn't charged up it becomes just 200g or so of dead (but precious) weight. So a **power/battery pack** is also essential, to reduce the chances of it running out of power while you're walking, together with the appropriate **chargers** for both, and **leads** to connect battery pack and phone.

Useful

The quality of the camera on a smartphone these days is impressive, though most serious photographers would still prefer to use an **SLR**. That said, it can be liberating to travel without one once in a while; a **notebook** can be a more accurate way of recording your impressions (but remember to take some **pens**). Other items include a **book** to pass the time on train journeys; a pair of **sunglasses**; **binoculars** for observing wildlife; **walking poles** to take the strain off your knees and a **vacuum flask** for carrying hot drinks. Although the path is easy to follow a 'Silva' type **compass** could be a good idea.

CAMPING GEAR

Campers need a decent **tent** (or bivvy bag if you enjoy travelling light) that's able to withstand wet and windy weather; a two- to three-season **sleeping bag**; a **sleeping mat**; a **stove** and **fuel** (there is special mention in Part 4 of which shops stock fuel); a **mug**; a **spoon**; a wire/plastic **scrubber** for washing up; and a pan or **cooking pot**. One pot is fine for two people; some pots come with a lid that can be used as a plate or frying pan. You can also buy camping pot sets that pack away neatly into one pot.

MONEY

Since the pandemic, accepting payment by **debit/credit card** has become much more widespread, even for small and seasonal businesses. But there's still a place for **cash**, so bring about £200 and replenish from supermarket **ATMs** in towns. You can also get cash at **village post offices** with a debit card. For further details see 🖥 postoffice.co.uk (Products & Services; then Branch & banking services).

MAPS

The **hand-drawn maps** in this book cover the trail at a scale of 1:20,000 – plenty of detail and information to keep you on the right track; the **colour maps** at the back of the book are at a smaller scale covering the surrounding area.

To explore even further afield you might be interested in Ordnance Survey maps (OS; 🖥 ordnancesurvey.co.uk). The best maps for walkers are the 1:25,000 OS Explorer Maps (orange cover). The website sells the whole set of relevant maps for the South Downs Way as a bundle for a discounted £72.74 (or £95.14 if weatherproof), a set that includes OL3 (Meon Valley), OL8 (Chichester), OL10 (Arundel & Pulborough), OL11 (Brighton & Hove), OL25 (Eastbourne & Beachy Head) and OL32 (Winchester) and OL 33 (Haslemere & Petersfield). All OS maps listed here are £12.99 for standard paper (£16.99 for weatherproof). OS also offers **digital maps** (see box opposite), which come free with the paper map or you can download them separately for a fee.

The *AZ Adventure Series South Downs Way map* (🖥 collins.co.uk/pages/a-z-maps-atlases; £8.95) includes the relevant section of the OS maps at a scale of 1:25,000 and also has an index.

❏ DIGITAL MAPPING   see also pp17-18

There are numerous software packages now available that provide Ordnance Survey (OS) maps for a smartphone, tablet, PC, or GPS unit. Maps are downloaded into an app from where you can view, print and create routes on them.

For a subscription of £6.99 for one month or £34.99 for a year (on their current offer) **Ordnance Survey** (🖳 ordnance survey.co.uk) allows you to download and use their UK maps (1:25,000 scale) on a mobile or tablet without a data connection for a specific period. Their app works well.

Memory Map (🖳 memory-map.co.uk) currently sell OS Explorer 1:25,000 and Landranger 1:50,000 mapping covering the whole of Britain with prices from £22.50/13.50 (1:25k/1:50k) for a one year subscription. **Anquet** (🖳 anquet.com) has the full range of OS 1:25,000 maps covering all of the UK from £28 per year annual subscription.

Maps.me is free and you can download any of its digital mapping to use offline. You can install the Trailblazer waypoints for this walk on its mapping but you'll need to convert the .gpx format file to .kml format before loading it into maps.me. Use an online website such as 🖳 gpx2kml.com to do this then email the kml file to your phone and open it in maps.me.

Harvey (🖳 store.avenza.com/collections/harvey-maps) currently use the US Avenza maps app for their *South Downs Way* map (1:40,000, $14.99).

It is important to ensure any digital mapping software on your smartphone uses pre-downloaded maps, stored on your device, and doesn't need to download them on-the-fly, as this may be expensive and will be impossible without a signal. Remember that battery life will be significantly reduced, compared to normal usage, when you are using the built-in GPS and running the screen for long periods.

PLANNING YOUR WALK

There's also a single-sheet Harvey's *South Downs Way Map* (Harvey Maps, £14.95, 🖳 harveymaps.co.uk) at a scale of 1:40,000.

A Trailblazer **South Downs Way app** is available; for more information see the Trailblazer website 🖳 trailblazer-guides.com.

RECOMMENDED READING

Many bookshops and most of the tourist information centres along the South Downs Way stock many of the following books.

An interesting read recounting **one person's experience** of his walk is *The South Downs Way* (Mainstream, 2002) by Martin King. Other books worth considering are: *Alone on the South Downs Way: one woman's solo journey from Winchester to Eastbourne* by Holly Worton (Tribal, 2016); *The South Downs Way* by Belinda Knox (Frances Lincoln, 2008), a photographic based guide, or *Whan That Aprille: For the Curious: An Exploration of the South Downs Way in Hampshire*, Heather Lacey (Redback Publishing; 2016).

For **bird identification** there are plenty of books to choose from including the *Collins Bird Guide* by Lars Svensson et al (2010) and the more portable RSPB's *Pocket Guide to British Birds* by Simon Harrap (Bloomsbury Wildlife, 2018), in which birds are identified by their plumage and song.

❑ SOURCES OF FURTHER INFORMATION

Tourist information

● **Tourist/Visitor Information Centres** (TICs) are based in towns throughout Britain; they provide all manner of locally specific information and a few offer accommodation booking. However, some are staffed by volunteers who can help with information but not book accommodation; they also generally have limited opening hours. The following TICs lie on or near the Way: **Winchester** (see p75); **Petersfield** (see p98); **Lewes** (see p152); **Eastbourne** (see p184).

In addition there are some **visitor centres** such as the ones at Queen Elizabeth Country Park (see p94) and Seven Sisters Country Park (see box p174). Visitor centres generally only have information about the actual attraction.

● **Friends of the South Downs** (South Downs Society) See p61.

Organisations for walkers

● **Backpackers' Club** (🖳 backpackersclub.co.uk) Aimed at people who are interested in lightweight camping through walking and other activities. Membership costs £20/30 per year for an individual/family and includes a quarterly magazine and a comprehensive advisory & information service; they also organise weekend trips.

● **The Long Distance Walkers' Association** (🖳 ldwa.org.uk) Membership includes a journal (Strider) three times per year with details of challenge events and local group walks as well as articles on the subject. Membership costs £18/25.50 a year for individuals/families (£15/22.50 if paying by direct debit).

● **Ramblers** (🖳 ramblers.org.uk) A charity that looks after the interests of walkers throughout Britain and promotes walking for health. Annual membership costs from £41, and includes their quarterly Walk magazine as well as access to their app and their library of walking routes plus walks arranged by the various regional groups.

One of the best field guides to **flora** is *Wild Flowers of Britain and Ireland* by Marjorie Blamey et al (Bloomsbury Natural History, 2013). Now sadly out of print, but used copies may be available online; the best guidebook specifically aimed at the **wildlife of the region** is the hardcover *Downland Wildlife – A Naturalist's Year in the North & South Downs* by John S Burton, illustrated by John Davis (George Philip, 1992).

There are also numerous **fieldguide apps** for both iPhone and Android, for identifying flowers, butterflies and birds by their song as well as by their appearance. One to consider for birds is Merlin Bird ID 🖳 merlin.allabout birds.org.

Getting to and from the South Downs Way

It could not be easier to reach the South Downs from London as there are numerous road and rail links not just to Winchester and Eastbourne, at either end of the walk, but to many other points along the Way. Most parts of the South Downs Way are no more than 1½-2 hours from the capital. Access from other parts of Britain often involves going via London but there are rail services to Winchester and Southampton via Reading. The rail line running across the south coast goes from Dover to Ashford International, then to Hastings and along the coast to Eastbourne and Brighton; from Brighton there are services to Portsmouth and Southampton.

See below for routes from continental Europe to the south coast of England.

❏ GETTING TO BRITAIN

● **By air** The nearest international airport to Winchester is Southampton Airport (🖥 www.southamptonairport.com) on the south coast. The alternative would be to fly to London's Gatwick (🖥 gatwickairport.com) or Heathrow airports (🖥 heathrow.com), both of which serve destinations worldwide. Further away but with a direct rail connection to Brighton is Luton Airport (🖥 www.london-luton.co.uk); Gatwick also has a direct train connection to Eastbourne (via Lewes), see box p44.

Another option is London City Airport (🖥 londoncityairport.com); the Docklands Light Railway is connected to the airport terminal; from there take a train to Canning Town and transfer to the Jubilee line (underground) for Waterloo Station.

● **From Europe by train** Eurostar (🖥 eurostar.com) operates a high-speed passenger service via the Channel Tunnel between Paris/Brussels and London. The Eurostar terminal in London is at St Pancras International station.

For information about the various rail services to Britain from the continent contact your national rail service provider, or visit 🖥 railteam.eu.

● **From Europe by coach** Flixbus (🖥 flixbus.co.uk) have a huge network of long-distance coach services connecting over 500 cities in 25 European countries to London. This is also a more environmentally sustainable way to travel, although obviously it takes longer than flying and may not work out much cheaper.

Megabus (🖥 uk.megabus.com) is part of the Stagecoach group and it operates low-cost coach services from a number of destinations in Europe to London and other cities including Winchester.

● **From Europe by car** Eurotunnel ('Le Shuttle'; 🖥 www.eurotunnel.com) operates a shuttle **train** service for vehicles via the Channel Tunnel between Calais and Folkestone, taking an hour between the motorway in France and the motorway in England. There are many **ferry** routes between France (Caen, Calais, Cherbourg, Dieppe, Dunkerque, Le Havre and St Malo) and the south coast ports of England such as Dover, Newhaven, Poole and Portsmouth. There are also services from Spain (Bilbao and Santander) to Portsmouth. Look at 🖥 directferries.com for a full list of companies and services.

❏ **USEFUL RAIL SERVICES**   **[see map p48]**

Note: not all stops are listed here, nor are all shown on the map. Check the relevant operator's website for full details.

Southern (🖳 southernrailway.com, Southern On Track app)
(**Note**: services from London Victoria usually also stop at Clapham Junction, East Croydon and Gatwick Airport)
● London Victoria to Horsham via Three Bridges & Crawley, Mon-Sat 2/hr, Sun 1/hr
At Horsham the trains divide:
    to Bognor Regis via Christ's Hospital (1/hr), Billingshurst, Pulborough, **Amberley** & Arundel, Mon-Sat 2/hr, Sun 1/hr
    to Portsmouth & Southsea via Barnham, Chichester & Havant, daily 1/hr
    to Southampton Central via Barnham, Chichester & Havant, daily 1/hr
● London Victoria to **Eastbourne** via Haywards Heath, **Plumpton**, **Lewes**, Glynde, **Berwick**, Polegate, **Eastbourne**, daily 1-2/hr
● Hastings to Brighton via **Eastbourne**, **Berwick**, **Glynde**, **Lewes** & Falmer, daily 1-2/hr
● Brighton to Seaford via Moulsecoomb, Falmer, **Lewes**, **Southease** & Newhaven Town, daily 1-2/hr

South Western Railway (🖳 southwesternrailway.com, SWR app)
● London Waterloo to Weymouth via Woking, **Winchester**, Southampton Airport, Southampton & Bournemouth, daily 1-2/hr
● London Waterloo to Portsmouth Harbour via Guildford, Haslemere & **Petersfield**, daily 2/hr
● London Waterloo to Southampton Airport & Southampton Central via Woking & **Winchester**, daily 2/hr

Cross Country Trains (🖳 crosscountrytrains.co.uk, CrossCountry app)
● Manchester to Bournemouth via Birmingham, **Winchester** & Southampton, Mon-Sat 1/hr

NATIONAL TRANSPORT

By rail

The two main rail operators for services to locations along the South Downs are Southern (from London Victoria to the south coast) and SouthWest Trains (from London Waterloo stopping at Winchester and Petersfield). Other providers are: Thameslink (from Bedford to Brighton via Luton Airport and St Pancras International) and Cross Country (from Manchester/Birmingham to Bournemouth and calling at Winchester). See the box above and map on p48 for contact and service details.

Timetables, ticket and fare information can be found on the rail operators' websites, apps or through **National Rail Enquiries** (☎ 03457-484950, 🖳 nationalrail.co.uk, app available); you can purchase tickets through the relevant rail operator's website. Note, it is much cheaper if you book tickets in advance and especially if you can travel on trains at a specific time.

You could also save money on longer journeys with sections run by different operators by buying split tickets. **Trainline** (🖳 thetrainline.com) now offers this, known as SplitSave, as an option where applicable. See their website for an explanation of how it works.

It is also often possible to book train tickets that include (discounted) bus travel to your ultimate destination; enquire when you book your train ticket or look at Plus Bus's website (🖳 plusbus.info).

By car
The south of England is overrun with dual carriageways and bypasses so there is no shortage of major roads to follow down to the Downs. On holiday weekends, however, be prepared for long tailbacks as everyone heads for the coast. There are main roads from London passing through Winchester, Petersfield, Cocking, Amberley, Arundel, Washington, Pyecombe, Lewes, Brighton and Eastbourne.

By air
Although there are local airports, such as Brighton City Airport at Shoreham, the easiest way to fly to the South-East from other corners of the UK is to get a flight to Gatwick or Southampton; see box p43. Bear in mind the environmental cost of flying.

By coach
Coach travel is generally cheaper but takes longer than the train. **National Express** (🖳 nationalexpress.com, National Express Coach app) is the principal coach (long-distance bus) operator in Britain and currently runs two services that stop in Winchester (but none to Eastbourne):
● **032** London Victoria coach station to/from Southampton via **Winchester**, daily 8/day
● **203** Heathrow Airport to/from Portsmouth via **Winchester**, Southampton & Fareham, daily 9/day.

A second operator, **Megabus** (🖳 uk.megabus.com), operates a cheap coach between **Winchester** and Glasgow via Manchester and Oxford three or four times a week.

LOCAL TRANSPORT
Hampshire, West Sussex and East Sussex have good local transport networks which make getting to and from the Way and planning linear day and weekend walks fairly easy.

The public transport map on p48 summarises all the useful routes; see the box on pp46-7 overleaf for details (though not all stops are listed). Where school bus services may be of use to walkers they are mentioned in the relevant place in the route guide. The tourist information centres along the Downs can provide, free of charge, a comprehensive local transport timetable for their particular region.

Most bus companies permit up to two **dogs** on a bus but it is also up to the discretion of the driver and dogs must be on a lead, well behaved and sitting under the seat or on their owner's lap; definitely not actually on a seat.

☐ LOCAL BUS SERVICES

[see map p48]

No	Operator	Route and frequency details
		Note: not all stops are listed for all routes.
1	bluestar	Southampton to **Winchester**, Mon-Sat 3/hr, Sun 2/hr
1	Stagecoach	**Midhurst** to Worthing via Petworth, Pulborough, **Storrington, Washington** & Findon, Mon-Sat 1/hr, Sun 6/day
2	B&H	Rottingdean to **Steyning** via Brighton, Shoreham, **Upper Beeding** & **Bramber**, daily 1/hr (3/hr R'dean to Shoreham)
3/3A	Stagecoach	Foot of Beachy Head to **Eastbourne** via Meads, Mon-Sat 4/hr, Sun 1/hr
12/12A/12X	B&H	(Coaster) Brighton to **Eastbourne** via Rottingdean, Newhaven, Seaford, **Exceat** (Seven Sisters Park Centre) & East Dean, Mon-Sat 3/hr, Sun 4/hr)
13X	B&H	Brighton to **Eastbourne** via Rottingdean, Newhaven, Seaford, **Exceat** (Seven Sisters Park Centre), **Birling Gap & Beachy Head**, Sun & public holidays only, 3/day
23	Metrobus	Crawley to Worthing via Horsham, Ashington & **Washington**, Mon-Sat approx 1/hr, Sun & public hols 5-6/day
29/29A	B&H	Brighton to Tunbridge Wells/Heathfield via Falmer, **Housedean Farm (A27)**, **Lewes** & Uckfield, Mon-Sat 3/hr, Sun 2/hr
37	Stagecoach	Havant to **Petersfield** via Waterlooville, Clanfield, **Queen Elizabeth Country Park** (request stop), Mon-Fri 1/hr, Sat 8/day
38	Stagecoach	Alton to **Petersfield**, Mon-Fri 4/day
47	CCB	Cuckmere Valley Ramblerbus: **Berwick** Station circular route via **Alfriston**, Seaford, **Seven Sisters Country Park, Litlington & Lullington**, late Mar to late Oct Sat, Sun & public hols 1/hr.
54	Stagecoach	**Petersfield** to Chichester via **South Harting & Uppark**, Mon-Sat 5/day
60	Stagecoach	Chichester to **Midhurst** via **Cocking**, Mon-Sat 2/hr, Sun 1/hr
64	Stagecoach	Alton to **Winchester** via Alresford & Morn Hill campsite, daily 2/hr
67	Stagecoach	**Winchester** to **Petersfield** via Alresford, **Cheriton**, Bramdean, West Meon & **East Meon**, Mon-Fri 4-6/day, Sat 3/day plus 1/day Winchester to/from West Meon only
70	Stagecoach	**Midhurst** to Guildford via Haslemere station, Mon-Sat 1/hr
74/74A/74B	Compass	Horsham to **Storrington**, Mon-Fri 1/day (continues to Amberley station & Houghton on school days), Tue & Thur 4/day
77	B&H	Brighton to **Devil's Dyke**, mid June to mid Sep daily 1-2/hr; mid Sep to mid June Sat, Sun & public hols only, 8/day
79	B&H	Brighton (station) to **Ditchling Beacon**, late Apr to mid Sep Sat, Sun & public holidays 1/hr
85	Compass	Chichester to **Arundel**, Mon-Fri 3/day
85A	Compass	Chichester to **Arundel** via Barnham, Mon-Fri 2/day
91	Stagecoach	**Midhurst** to **Petersfield** via **South Harting**, Mon-Sat 1/day
92/93	Stagecoach	**Midhurst** to **Petersfield**, Mon-Sat 6/day

94	AMK	**Petersfield** to **Buriton**. Mon-Fri 3/day
99	Compass	Chichester to Petworth via Upwaltham (no other stops unless prebooked ☎ 01243-858854; bookable stops include Goodwood, Graffham Down, Graffham, Sutton & Bignor), Mon-Sat 6/day except public holidays
100	Compass	Burgess Hill to Horsham via Henfield, **Upper Beeding, Bramber, Steyning, Washington, Storrington & Pulborough**, Mon-Sat approx 1/hr
123	Compass	Newhaven to **Lewes** via **Southease. Rodmell & Kingston-near-Lewes**, Mon-Fri 8/day, Sat 6/day, Sun 3/day
125	Compass	Lewes to **Eastbourne** via **Glynde, Charleston, Berwick, Alfriston & Wilmington**. Mon-Fri 2/day plus 1/day terminating at Alfriston
126	CCB	**Berwick** to Seaford via **Alfriston**, Mon-Sat 1-2/day
166	Compass	**Lewes** to Hayward Heath via **Plumpton** & Wivelsfield, Mon-Fri 5/day, Sat 4/day
270	Metrobus	East Grinstead to Brighton via Burgess Hill, Hassocks & **Pyecombe**, Mon-Sat approx 1/hr, Sun & public hols 3/day
271/272	Metrobus	Crawley to Brighton via Burgess Hill, Hassocks & **Pyecombe**. Mon-Fri 2/hr, Sat & Sun 4/day
273	Metrobus	Crawley to Brighton via Hickstead, Hassocks & **Pyecombe**. Mon-Fri 7/day, Sat 6/day

Additional limited frequency services (not shown on the map):

CCB (operated by volunteers): **25 Lewes to Eastbourne** via **Glynde, Charleston, Berwick, Alfriston & Wilmington**. Sat 3/day plus 1/day Alfriston to Eastbourne (see also Compass Travel No 125 above) ● **26** Seaford to **Eastbourne** via **Alfriston, Berwick** (Drusillas), **Wilmington**, Polegate & Willington, Sun & public hols 4/day plus 1/day **Alfriston to Eastbourne** (see also Compass Travel service 119/125 above) ● **40** Seaford to **Berwick** via **Exceat, Westdean**, Charleston, **Litlington, Lullington, Wilmington & Alciston**. Tue & Fri 1/day ● **42** Hailsham to **Berwick** circular route via Alciston & Alfriston Wed 1/day ● **43 Eastbourne to Berwick** via Hailsham and Polegate, Mon 1/day ● **44 Berwick to Eastbourne** via Alciston & Wilmington, Tue & Thur 2-3/day .

Compass: 69 Alfold to Worthing via **Pulborough, Bury, Houghton & Arundel**, Tue & Fri 1/day ● **71 Storrington** to Chichester via Pulborough, **Bury & Houghton**, Wed 1/day

Operator contact details
AMK (☎ 01428 751675, ⌨ amk.co.uk) ● **bluestar** (☎ 01202-338421, ⌨ bluestarbus.co.uk) ● **Brighton & Hove Buses (B&H):** ☎ 01273-886200, ⌨ buses.co.uk; Brighton & Hove Buses app) ● **Compass Travel** (☎ 01903-690025, ⌨ compass-travel.co.uk) ● **Cuckmere Community Bus (CCB:** ☎ 01323-870920, ⌨ cuckmerebuses.org.uk) ● **Metrobus** (☎ 01293-449191, ⌨ metrobus.co.uk, Metrobus app) ● **Stagecoach** (⌨ stagecoachbus.com; Stagecoach Bus app).

PLANNING YOUR WALK

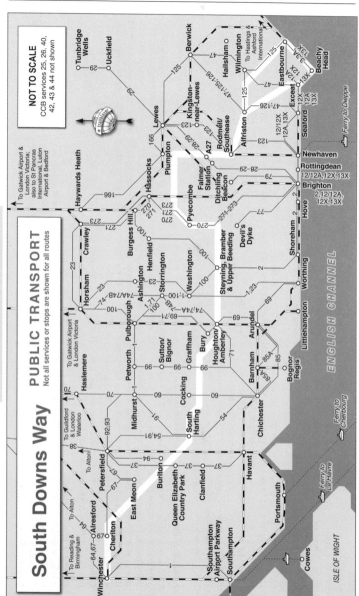

South Downs Way

PUBLIC TRANSPORT
Not all services or stops are shown for all routes

NOT TO SCALE

CCB services 25, 26, 40, 42, 43 & 44 not shown

ENGLISH CHANNEL

ISLE OF WIGHT

MINIMUM IMPACT & OUTDOOR SAFETY

Minimum impact walking

Walk as if you are kissing the Earth with your feet
Thich Nhat Hanh *Peace is every step*

The popularity of the 'Great Outdoors' as an escape route from the chaos of modern living has experienced something of a boom over the last couple of decades or so. It is therefore important to be aware of the pressures that each of us as visitors to the countryside exert upon the land. The South Downs are particularly vulnerable, situated as they are in the most populous corner of the British Isles. Thousands of people explore the network of trails that criss-cross these historic chalk hills.

Minimum impact walking is all about a common-sense approach to exploring the countryside, being mindful and respectful of the wildlife and those who live and work on the land. Those who appreciate the countryside will already be aware of the importance of safeguarding it. Simple measures such as not dropping litter, keeping dogs on leads to avoid scaring sheep and leaving gates as you find them will already be second nature to anyone who regularly visits the countryside. However, there are several other measures that are not quite so well known and are worth repeating here.

ECONOMIC IMPACT

Buy local

Rural businesses and communities in Britain have been hit hard in recent years by a seemingly endless series of crises, most recently COVID. In addition, they have to compete with the omnipresence of chain supermarkets that are now so common in towns across Britain.

Faced with such competition local businesses struggle to survive. Visitors to the countryside can help these local businesses by 'buying locally'. It's a fact of life that money spent at local level – perhaps in a market, or at the greengrocer, or in an independent pub – has a far greater impact for good on that community than the equivalent spent in a branch of a national chain store or restaurant. It's a step too far to advocate that walkers should boycott the larger supermarkets, which after all do provide local employment. But if we want to keep these local shops and post offices, we need to use them. The more money that circulates locally and is spent on local labour and materials, the greater the impact on the local economy.

Encourage local cultural traditions and skills

No two parts of the countryside look the same. Buildings, food, skills and language evolve out of the landscape and are moulded over hundreds of years to suit the locality. Discovering these cultural differences is part of the pleasure of walking in new places. Visitors' enthusiasm for local traditions and skills brings awareness and pride, nurturing a sense of place; an increasingly important role in a world where economic globalisation continues to undermine the very things that provide security and a feeling of belonging.

ENVIRONMENTAL IMPACT

By choosing a walking holiday you are already minimising your impact on the environment. Your interaction with the countryside and its inhabitants, whether they be plant, animal or human, can bring benefits to all. The following are some ideas on how you can go a few steps further in helping to minimise your impact on the natural environment while walking the South Downs Way.

Use public transport whenever possible

Both Sussex and Hampshire have a good public transport system (see pp46-8). There are plenty of options to get the walker to the Downs, making driving there unnecessary, and also various bus services linking the Way with nearby towns and villages as well as offering convenient start and finish points for day walks.

Never leave litter

Leaving litter shows a total disrespect for the natural world and others coming after you. As well as being unsightly, litter kills wildlife, pollutes the environment and can be dangerous to farm animals. Please take your rubbish with you so you can dispose of it in a bin in the next village. It would be very helpful if you could pick up litter left by other people, too.

● **Is it OK if it's biodegradable?** No. Apple cores, banana skins, orange peel and the like are an eyesore, encourage flies, ants and wasps and ruin a picnic spot for others. They also promote a higher population of scavengers such as carrion crows and magpies, an explosion of which can have a detrimental effect on rarer bird species. Those who use the excuse that orange peel is natural and biodegradable are simply fishing for an excuse to clear their conscience. Biodegradable? Yes, but surprisingly slowly. Natural? The South Downs have never been known for their orange groves.

● **The lasting impact of litter** A piece of orange peel left on the ground takes six months to decompose; silver foil 18 months; a plastic bag 10 years; clothes 15 years; and an aluminium can 85 years.

Erosion

● **Stay on the main trail** The effect of your footsteps may seem minuscule but when they are multiplied by several thousand walkers each year they become rather more significant. Avoid taking shortcuts, widening the trail or taking more than one path; your boots will be followed by many others. This is particularly pertinent on the South Downs where there is such a huge volume of visitors.

● **Consider walking out of season** Unfortunately, most people prefer to walk in the spring and summer which is exactly the time of year when the vegetation is trying to grow. Walking on the South Downs in the autumn and winter can be just as enjoyable and eases the burden on the land during the busy summer months. The quieter season also gives the walker a greater chance of a peaceful walk away from the crowds with fewer people competing for accommodation.

Respect all wildlife, plants and trees
If you come across wildlife keep your distance and don't watch for too long. Your presence can cause considerable stress, particularly if the adults are with young or in winter when the weather is harsh and food is scarce. Young animals are rarely abandoned. If you come across young birds keep away so that their mother can return. Never pick flowers – leave them for others to enjoy too – and try to avoid breaking branches off or damaging trees in any way.

The code of the outdoor loo
As more and more people discover the joys of the outdoors, issues like toilet business rapidly gain importance. How many of us have shaken our heads at the sight of toilet paper strewn beside the path or, even worse, someone's dump left in full view? Human excrement is not only offensive to our senses but, more importantly, can infect water sources.

● **Where to go** Wherever possible **use a toilet**. Public toilets are marked on the trail maps in this guide and you will also find facilities in pubs, cafés and campsites along the Way. If you do have to go outdoors choose a site at least **30 metres away from running water** and 200 metres from any high-use areas such as hostels and beaches, or from any sites of historic or archaeological interest. Carry a small trowel and dig a small hole about 15cm (6") deep in which to bury your excrement. It decomposes quicker when in contact with the top layer of soil or leaf mould. Use a stick to stir loose soil into your deposit as well, as this speeds up decomposition even more. Do not squash it under rocks as this slows down the composting process. If you have to use rocks to cover it make sure they are not in contact with your faeces.

● **Toilet paper and tampons** Toilet paper takes a long time to decompose whether buried or not. It is easily dug up by animals and may then blow into water sources or onto the path. The best method for dealing with it is to **pack it out**. Put the used paper inside a paper bag which you then place inside a biodegradable bag. Then simply empty the contents of the paper bag at the next toilet you come across and throw the bag away. You should also pack out **tampons** and **sanitary towels** in a similar way and for the same reasons.

Wild camping
There is very little opportunity for wild camping along the length of the Downs. Most of the land is private farmland and much of this is arable cropland. If the urge to camp away from an organised site is too much to resist always ask the landowner first. If the opportunity for wild camping is there, take it. Camping

in such an independent way is an altogether more fulfilling experience than camping on a designated site.

Remember that by camping off the beaten track you accept added responsibilities. By taking on board the following suggestions for minimising your impact the whole experience of wild camping will be a far more satisfying one.

● **Be discreet** Camp alone or in small groups and spend only one night in each place. Pitch your tent late in the day and leave as early the next day as you can.

● **Never light a fire** The deep burn caused by camp fires, no matter how small, seriously damages the turf and takes years to recover. Use a camp stove instead.

● **Don't use soap or detergent** There is no need to use soap; even biodegradable soaps and detergents pollute streams. Wash up without detergent; use a plastic or metal scourer, or failing that some bracken, grass or grit.

● **Leave no trace** Enjoy the skill of moving on without leaving any sign of having been there. Before heading off check your campsite and pick up any litter (even if not left by you), so leaving the place in a better state than you found it.

ACCESS

The south-eastern corner of England is the most populated area of the British Isles and is criss-crossed by some of the busiest roads in the country. Thankfully, there are also countless public footpaths and rights of way for the large local population and visitors alike. But what happens if you want to explore some of the local woodland or tramp across a meadow? Most of the land on the South Downs is agricultural land and, unless you are on a right of way, it's off limits. However, the 'Right to Roam' legislation (see opposite) opened up some previously restricted land to walkers.

Rights of way

As a designated National Trail the South Downs Way is a public right of way – this is either a footpath, a bridleway or a byway; the South Downs Way is made up of all three. Rights of way are theoretically established because the owner has dedicated them to public use. However, very few rights of way are formally dedicated in this way. If the public has been using a path without interference for 20 years or more the law assumes the owner has intended to dedicate it as a right of way. If a path has been unused for 20 years it does not cease to exist; the guiding principle is 'once a highway, always a highway'.

On a public right of way you have the right to 'pass and repass along the way' which includes stopping to rest or admire the view or to consume refreshments. You can also take with you a 'natural accompaniment' which includes a dog, but

---

❑ **LAMBING**
Most of the Way passes through private farmland, some of which is pasture for sheep. Lambing takes place from mid March to mid May when dogs should not be taken along the path. Even a dog secured on a lead is liable to disturb a pregnant ewe. If you should see a lamb or ewe that appears to be in distress contact the nearest farmer.

obviously could also be a horse, on bridleways and byways. All 'natural accompaniments' must be kept under close control.

Farmers and land managers must ensure that paths are not blocked by crops or other vegetation, or otherwise obstructed, and the route is identifiable and the surface is restored soon after cultivation. If crops are growing over the path you have every right to walk or ride through them, following the line of the right of way as closely as possible. If you find a path blocked or impassable you should report it to the appropriate highway authority as they are responsible for maintaining public rights of way. Along the Way the highway authorities are Hampshire, West Sussex and East Sussex county councils. The councils are also the surveying authority with responsibility for maintaining the official definitive map of public rights of way.

THE COUNTRYSIDE CODE

Respect everyone
● Be considerate to those living and working in the countryside
● Leave gates and property as you find them
● Do not block access to gateways or driveways when parking
● Follow local signs and keep to marked paths, even if they're muddy.

Protect the environment
● Take all your litter home
● Do not light fires
● Always keep dogs under control and in sight.
● Dog poo – bag it and bin it in any public waste bin
● Care for nature – do not cause damage or disturbance

Enjoy the outdoors
● Check your route and local conditions
● Plan your adventure – know what to expect and what you can do
● Enjoy your visit, have fun, make a memory

Right to roam

For many years groups such as the **Ramblers** (see box p42) and the **British Mountaineering Council** (🖥 thebmc.co.uk) campaigned for new and wider access legislation. This finally bore fruit in the form of the Countryside & Rights of Way Act of November 2000, colloquially known as the CRoW Act or 'Right to Roam'. It came into full effect in 2005 and gave access for 'recreation on foot' to mountain, moor, heath, down and registered common land in England and Wales. In essence it allows walkers the freedom to roam responsibly away from footpaths, without being accused of trespass, on about four million acres of open, uncultivated land. The areas of access land open to walkers are shown on OS Explorer maps. 'Right to Roam' does not mean free access to wander over farmland, woodland or private gardens, and much of the true chalk grassland of the South Downs has long since been ploughed up. Along with this, most of what remains is already annexed as national and local nature reserves where access is relatively unrestricted anyway, so the results of the CRoW Act on the South Downs Way might not be quite as liberating as expected.

For those who wish to get off the beaten track and away from the crowds there are plenty of lesser-known rights of way. Follow any of these and you are likely to spend the whole day alone, which is not an easy thing to do in this part of England. However, if you want to leave the path entirely and beat your own trail through the woods and fields always check with local landowners.

Those who do exercise their 'right to roam' should remember that this added freedom comes with the responsibility to respect the immediate environment. This is particularly pertinent on the South Downs where most of the land is worked by farmers and is the home to a variety of wildlife. Always keep this in mind and try to avoid disturbing domestic and wild animals.

Outdoor safety and health

AVOIDANCE OF HAZARDS

Walking does not come much more hazard-free than on the South Downs. However, these low southern hills should be given as much respect as their loftier counterparts. Good preparation is just as important here as it is on the northern mountains. The following common-sense advice should ensure that those out for a day trip as well as those embarking on the whole route enjoy a safe walk. Always make sure you have **suitable clothes** to keep you warm and dry, whatever the conditions, as well as a spare change of inner clothes.

Take more **food** than you expect to eat. High-energy snacks such as chocolate, fruit, biscuits and nuts are useful for those last few gruelling miles each day. Make sure you have at least a one-litre **water bottle** or **pouch** that can be refilled when the opportunity arises. You need to drink plenty of water when walking; 3-4 litres per day depending on the weather. There are a few drinking water taps placed conveniently along the path; these are marked on the maps in Part 4. If you start to feel tired, lethargic or get a headache it may be that you are not drinking enough. Thirst is not always a good indicator of when to drink; stop and have a drink every hour or two, even if you're not feeling thirsty, and note the colour of your urine – the lighter the better. If you are not needing to urinate much and your urine is dark yellow, increase your fluid intake.

You should always take a torch, whistle, simple first-aid kit (see p39) and compass, though the latter may not be necessary as the trail is clear. A whistle is also unlikely to be used due to the close proximity of people and villages. The **emergency signal** is six blasts on the whistle or six flashes with a torch.

Try to be aware of where you are throughout the day. **Check your location** on the map or phone regularly. Getting lost on the Downs is unlikely to be a major cause for concern but it can turn a pleasant day's walk into a stressful trudge back in the dark, praying that the pub chef has not gone home.

If you are walking alone you must appreciate and be prepared for the increased risk. Let someone know your route before you set off (which could be a friend or your booked accommodation for that night) and remember to let them know you've arrived safely. Carrying a mobile phone can be useful though you cannot rely on a strong signal, or your phone's battery life.

Be aware that, because much of the South Downs Way is on a chalk ridge high above the surrounding countryside, there may be a steep climb down to, and back up from the adjacent towns and villages.

To ensure you have a safe trip it is well worth following this advice:
● Keep to the path – avoid steep sections of the escarpment and old quarries
● Be aware of the increased possibility of slipping over in wet or icy weather, especially where the chalk is exposed
● Whether you choose to wear hiking boots, trainers or even hiking sandals, be sure that your footwear has good grip and is well worn-in before you start
● Be extra vigilant with children
● Take extra care when leading dogs through areas of grazing animals
● In an emergency dial ☎ 999.

FOOTCARE

Caring for your feet is vital; you're not going to get far if they are out of action. Wash and dry them properly at the end of the day, change your socks every day and if it is warm enough take your boots and socks off when you stop for lunch to allow your feet to dry out. It is important to 'break in' new boots or shoes before embarking on a long walk. Make sure they are comfortable and try to avoid getting them wet on the inside. If you feel any 'hot spots' stop immediately and apply blister plasters (eg Compeed) and leave them on until the area is pain free or the tape starts to come off. If you have left it too late and a blister has developed it's still worth putting on a blister plaster (or a regular one if you don't have any blister plasters) to protect it from abrasion. Popping it can lead to infection. If the skin is broken keep the area clean with antiseptic and cover with a non-adhesive dressing material held in place with tape.

SUNBURN, HYPERTHERMIA & HEATSTROKE

Owing to climate change, summers in the UK are becoming increasingly warm, so **sunburn** can be a risk, even on overcast days. The only surefire way to avoid it is to stay wrapped up but that's not always an option. You should always wear a hat, preferably a wide-brimmed one, and use plenty of high-factor sunscreen, reapplied regularly throughout the day. Don't forget your lips, nose, the back of your neck and under your chin to protect against rays reflected from the ground.

Hyperthermia occurs when the body generates too much heat, eg heat exhaustion and heatstroke. Symptoms of **heat exhaustion** include thirst, fatigue, giddiness, a rapid pulse, raised body temperature, low urine output and, if not treated, delirium and finally a coma. The best cure is to drink plenty of water. **Heatstroke** is another matter altogether, and even more serious. A high body temperature and an absence of sweating are early indications, followed by symptoms similar to hypothermia (see p56) such as a lack of co-ordination and convulsions. Coma and death will follow if treatment is not given instantly. Sponge the victim down, wrap them in wet towels, fan them, and get help immediately.

HYPOTHERMIA

Hypothermia, also known as exposure, occurs when the body can't generate enough heat to maintain its normal temperature, usually as a result of being wet,

MINIMUM IMPACT & OUTDOOR SAFETY

cold, unprotected from the wind, tired and hungry. The risk of hypothermia while walking on the Downs is low. However, it is worth being aware of the dangers. Hypothermia is easily avoided by wearing suitable clothing, carrying and eating enough food and drink, being aware of the weather conditions and checking the morale of your companions.

Early signs to watch for are feeling cold and tired with involuntary shivering. Find some shelter as soon as possible and warm the victim up with a hot drink and some chocolate or other high-energy food. If possible give them another warm layer of clothing and allow them to rest until feeling better.

If untreated, strange behaviour, slurring of speech and poor co-ordination will become apparent and the victim can quickly progress into unconsciousness, followed by coma and death. In the unlikely event of a severe case of hypothermia, quickly get the victim out of wind and rain, improvising a shelter if necessary. Rapid restoration of bodily warmth is essential and best achieved by bare-skin contact: someone should get into the same sleeping bag as the patient, both having stripped to their underwear with any spare clothing under or over them to build up heat. Send urgently for help.

WEATHER FORECASTS

The South Downs is one of the driest parts of what has historically been a notoriously wet island. However, the weather can still change from blazing sunshine to a stormy wet gale in the space of a day. The wind, in particular, can be surprisingly severe along the top of the Downs. Couple this with rain and a nice walk can turn into a damp battle against the elements. For detailed local weather outlooks online see 🖥 www.bbc.co.uk/weather, or 🖥 www.metoffice.gov.uk.

DEALING WITH AN ACCIDENT

● Use basic first aid to treat the injury to the best of your ability.
● Try to attract the attention of anybody else who may be in the area. The emergency signal is six blasts on a whistle, or six flashes with a torch.
● If possible leave someone with the casualty while others go to get help. If there are only two people, you have a dilemma. If you decide to get help leave all spare clothing and food with the casualty.
● Telephone ☎ 999 and ask for the ambulance service (or coastguard if relevant). They will assist in both offshore and onshore incidents. Be sure you know exactly where you are before you call. Report the exact position of the casualty (the proven 🖥 what3words app, see below, can make this easier) and their condition.

> ❏ **WHAT3WORDS**
> On the app **What3words** (🖥 what3words.com) the world is divided into three-metre squares and each has its own three-word geocode so it makes it easy to tell people where you are.
> **See pp188-92 for the what3words references for the waypoints in this book.**

THE ENVIRONMENT & NATURE

Conservation of the South Downs

Ever since the Industrial Revolution and the rapid development over the last 200 years the English countryside has been put under a great deal of strain. The South Downs were once wooded hills, home to wolves, wild boar and other species that have long since departed. The need to feed an increasing population led to much of the countryside being cleared and ploughed. The result of this is the landscape we see today, although the traditional patchwork pattern of fields and hedgerows has been replaced in some parts of the Downs by much larger fields, the hedgerows having been torn out.

The South Downs is, then, a man-made landscape; even the woodland has been coppiced and the meadows ploughed at one time or another. This is not necessarily a bad thing, however. The resulting habitat is a rare one that provides an essential niche for endangered species, most notably the butterflies for which the Downs are famous.

Although the Downs, positioned in a populous corner of England, continue to be put under pressure from road and housing projects, the increasing awareness of the value of our natural (or perhaps semi-natural) heritage has resulted in greater efforts in the conservation. There are several local and national, voluntary and government groups, who help protect the species, habitats and buildings of the Downs. They also help visitors to get the most out of their trip whilst trying to ease the pressure brought by the increase in tourist numbers.

The elevation of the South Downs to National Park status has, on the whole, provided increased environmental protection, but the work of these groups is still absolutely vital to maintaining the health and beauty of the area.

GOVERNMENT AGENCIES AND SCHEMES

Natural England

Natural England (🖥 www.gov.uk/government/organisations/natural-england) is the single government body responsible for identifying, establishing and managing National Parks, National Landscapes (formerly known as Areas of Outstanding Natural Beauty or AONBs), National Nature Reserves, Sites of Special Scientific Interest, and Special Areas of Conservation.

THE ENVIRONMENT & NATURE

□ **HOW THE SOUTH DOWNS BECAME A NATIONAL PARK**

The South Downs almost became one of the first designated national parks back in the 1950s but the proposal was rejected on the grounds that the area did not offer sufficient recreational possibilities for the public. This seems rather surprising today when you consider the number of walkers, cyclists, horse-riders and paragliders who use the hills. National Park status is not just about providing an area of fun for outdoor enthusiasts, however. It is about protecting the area from harmful development such as road building, a real problem in the South-East, and preserving the natural and cultural heritage of the area.

In 1999 the Department of the Environment, now Department for Environment, Food and Rural Affairs (DEFRA), proposed that the Countryside Agency, now part of Natural England, designate the South Downs a National Park. A Designation Order was published in late 2002 and in November 2003 a public inquiry began, to hear the views of those likely to be affected by the change. In 2006 a report was passed to the Secretary of State. After several more delays and legal wrangles, in 2009 it finally was announced that the South Downs would receive National Park status, and the newly appointed **South Downs National Park Authority** (🖥 southdowns.gov.uk) officially assumed responsibility for it on 1st April 2011.

Although at 1648 sq km it is not the largest in area (that distinction going to the Lake District National Park at 2292 sq km), being only an hour from London it encompasses several large towns including Petersfield and Lewes, and is by far the most densely populated of all the National Parks.

The highest level of landscape protection is the designation of land as a **National Park** which recognises the national importance of an area in terms of landscape, biodiversity and as a recreational resource. This designation does not signify national ownership and they are not uninhabited wildernesses, making conservation a knife-edged balance between protecting the environment and the rights and livelihoods of those living in the park. In April 2011 the South Downs became England's ninth National Park, and its most densely populated. Some 85% of the land within the South Downs National Park is agricultural, so this balancing act is particularly critical here.

The next level of protection within the National Park includes **National Nature Reserves (NNRs)** and **Sites of Special Scientific Interest (SSSIs)**. The **NNRs** along the course of the South Downs Way (SDW) include: Beacon Hill (see p86), just before the village of Exton; Old Winchester Hill (see p88), just after Exton; and Butser Hill (see p93) several miles further along the path. Though there are no NNRs near the Way in West Sussex, in East Sussex Lullington Heath (p180) lies right on the trail, and Castle Hill and Lewes Downs (ie Mount Caburn; see pp155-6) both lie very near to it too.

SSSIs range in size from little pockets protecting wild flower meadows, important nesting sites or special geological features, to vast swathes of upland, moorland and wetland. They are a particularly important designation as they have some legal standing. They are managed in partnership with the owners and occupiers of the land who must give written notice before initiating any operations likely to damage the site and who cannot proceed without consent from

Natural England. SSSIs along the SDW include: Cheesefoot Head (see p81), Butser Hill (see p93), Harting Down, Heyshott Down (see p109), Chanctonbury Hill (see p136), Beeding Hill to Newtimber Hill, and Seaford to Beachy Head.

Special Areas of Conservation (SACs) are designated by the European Union's Habitats Directive and provide an extra tier of protection to the areas that they cover. Along the SDW Butser Hill NNR and SSSI is also a SAC.

Historic England

Historic England (🖳 historicengland.org.uk) is the name for the government department responsible for looking after and promoting England's historic environment and is in charge of the listing system, giving grants and dealing with planning matters.

CAMPAIGNING AND CONSERVATION ORGANISATIONS

The **National Trust** (NT; 🖳 nationaltrust.org.uk) is a charity which, through ownership, aims to protect threatened coastline, countryside, historic houses, castles, gardens and archaeological remains for everyone to enjoy. It manages large sections of the Downs including an area of chalk grassland on the Seven Sisters between the hamlet of Crowlink and Birling Gap (see p175), Harting Down (p103), Devil's Dyke and Newtimber Hill (see pp141-3 for both). It also owns various properties on the Way, such as Monk's House (p158) in Rodmell and Alfriston Clergy House (p164), its first-ever property, bought in 1896.

English Heritage (🖳 www.english-heritage.org.uk) has been a charitable trust since April 2015. It cares for over 400 historic buildings, monuments and sites in England; Wolvesey Castle (Old Bishop's Palace) in Winchester (see p74) and Bramber Castle (p137) are just two of the properties it manages.

The **Wildfowl & Wetlands Trust** (WWT; 🖳 wwt.org.uk) is the biggest conservation organisation for wetlands in the UK; their centre at Arundel (see p122) is well-known and very popular with visitors year-round.

The **Wildlife Trusts** (🖳 wildlifetrusts.org) undertake projects to improve conditions for wildlife and promote public awareness of it as well as acquiring land for nature reserves to protect particular species and habitats. The Sussex Wildlife Trust (🖳 sussexwildlifetrust.org.uk) manages: Amberley Wildbrooks network of ponds and marshland; Ditchling Beacon; Seaford Head, south of

---

❏ NATIONAL TRAILS

The South Downs Way is one of 16 National Trails (🖳 nationaltrail.co.uk) in England and Wales. These are Britain's flagship long-distance paths which grew out of the post-war desire to protect the country's special places, a movement which also gave birth to National Parks and AONBs (now rebranded National Landscapes). The Pennine Way was the first to be created.

National Trails in England are designated and largely funded by Natural England Natural Resources Wales and are managed on the ground by a National Trail Officer. They co-ordinate the maintenance work undertaken by the local highway authority and landowners to ensure that the trail is kept to nationally agreed standards.

Alfriston; and Southerham Farm and Malling Down, both near Lewes. The Hampshire and Isle of Wight Wildlife Trust (🖥 hiwwt.org.uk) manages six near Winchester alone, including St Catherine's Hill and Deacon Hill, as well as several other small reserves a few miles off the trail.

The **Royal Society for the Protection of Birds** (RSPB; 🖥 rspb.org.uk) was the pioneer of voluntary conservation bodies and although it doesn't have any reserves directly on the South Downs Way, there is one near Pulborough, where the wet grassy meadows attract ducks, geese, swans and wading birds; and at Amberley Wildbrooks, part of the Arun Valley Special Protection Area, where wildfowl including Bewick's swan, wigeon, teal, shoveler and pintail like to winter. The reserve is a short walk from Amberley village.

Butterfly Conservation (🖥 butterfly-conservation.org) was formed to prevent the decline in the number of butterflies and moths. The two branches relevant to the SDW are Hampshire and the Isle of Wight (🖥 hantsiow-butterflies .org.uk) and Sussex (🖥 sussex-butterflies.org.uk). Beachy Head, Cissbury Ring and Malling Down are important sites for butterflies.

There are also smaller conservation groups such as **Murray Downland Trust** (🖥 murraydownlandtrust.org.uk) which manages five reserves (Heyshott Escarpment, Heyshott Down, Buriton Down, Under Beacon, and The Devil's Jumps) in West Sussex and East Hampshire. The Trust's main objective is to 'rescue and enhance neglected areas of unimproved chalk downland' but it also looks after some ancient monuments in the area such as the Bronze Age archaeological site (see p110). Access to the Trust's sites is permitted except when the area should be left undisturbed for conservation reasons. The trust relies on volunteers to help clear the land in its care and sheep are often brought in during the winter months to eat the scrub that threatens the grassland.

❑ GEOLOGY OF THE DOWNS

How the chalk Downs were formed

It helps to examine the geology of the region as a whole in order to understand how the South Downs reached their present-day form. South-East England is made up of three bands of rock and sediment, the deepest layer being sandstone, the one above clay and the top layer chalk. Over time these layers were pushed up, probably due to tectonic plate movements, with Africa nudging into Europe. Through the ensuing millennia the soft chalk was eroded through weathering, exposing first the clay and then the more resistant sandstone. The North and South Downs are all that remains of the chalk that lies over the deeper clay and sandstone layers. They are still being eroded.

One interesting feature of the Downs is the lack of streams. Chalk is highly permeable so streams flow only very briefly during periods of very heavy rainfall.

Flint

Flint is a mineral found in bands within chalk and has played a big part in the history of the Downs. When man first developed the ability to make tools the folk who lived on the Downs used flakes of flint to make arrowheads and knives. It was also found to be a very useful stone for making sparks to start fires. Today flint can be seen in local village architecture, being a very versatile building stone, often paired with red brick.

The Friends of the South Downs (⌨ friendsofthesouthdowns.org.uk), formerly the South Downs Society, campaigns specifically for the conservation and enhancement of the landscape of the South Downs. It was formed in 1926 and is supported entirely by donations and subscriptions (membership costs £30/40 individual/joint members). Their current projects include replacing stiles with kissing gates throughout the park, to enable those walkers who are unable to climb stiles to still enjoy the Downs, and introducing benches along the route of the South Downs Way. They also arrange a programme of strolls and walks, on and around the Downs, throughout the year.

Fauna and flora

The South Downs region is essentially a man-made landscape. Centuries of farming have shaped these rolling hills and left a unique habitat for a variety of common and not-so-common species. Left alone the South Downs would revert to scrub and woodland. This may not appear to be a great tragedy. However, the habitat that would be lost is a much scarcer one that provides sanctuary to a variety of endangered species which rely on the unique chalk grassland environment. The Downs are not free of trees either. The plough never reached the steep scarp slope that runs along the northern edge of the Downs. Indeed there is a healthy balance between the open grassland of the high ground and the deciduous beech woodland which can claim to be some of the oldest and most undisturbed woodland in Britain.

MAMMALS

The well-drained soil of chalk downland is ideal habitat for the **badger** (*Meles meles*), a sociable animal with a distinctive black-and-white-striped muzzle. Badgers live in family groups in large underground 'setts'. They are rarely spotted since they tend to emerge after dark to hunt for worms in the fields. Sadly, they are more commonly seen dead on the road: after hedgehogs they are the most inept at crossing roads.

Although the **fox** (*Vulpes vulpes*) prefers to come out at night it is not exclusively nocturnal; particularly in summer it may be out in broad daylight in some of the quieter corners of the hills though the best time to spot a fox is at dusk when you might see one trotting along a field or woodland edge.

Introduced from North America in the 19th century, the outstanding success of the **grey squirrel** (*Sciurus carolinensis*) in colonising Britain is very much to the detriment of other native species, particularly the red squirrel. Greys are bigger and stockier than reds and to many the reds, with their tufted ears and small beady eyes, are the more attractive of the two. Sadly there are no red squirrels on the Downs. The **roe deer** (*Capreolus capreolus*) is a small, native species of deer that tends to hide in woodland. They can sometimes be seen, alone or in pairs, on field edges or clearings in the forest but you are more likely to hear the sharp dog-like bark made when they smell you coming.

The **rabbit** (*Oryctolagus cuniculus*) is seemingly everywhere on the Downs, with the well-drained, steep grassland being ideal for their warrens. However, if the Downs were made for any one species it is probably the **brown hare** (*Lepus europaeus*) which, if you are observant, can be seen racing across the fields on the hilltops. Hares are bigger than rabbits, with longer hind legs and ears, and are far more graceful than their prolific little cousins.

Some other small species to keep an eye out for include the carnivorous **stoat** (*Mustela erminea*), its smaller cousin the **weasel** (*Mustela nivalis*), the **hedgehog** (*Erinaceus europaeus*) and several species of **voles**, **mice** and **shrews**.

At dusk **bats** can be seen hunting for moths and flying insects along hedgerows, over rivers and around street lamps. All 17 species in Britain are protected by law. The smallest, most common species is the **pipistrelle** (*Pipistrellus pipistrellus*). Although only about 4cm long it can eat up to 3000 insects in one night. You may also be lucky enough to see the slighter larger **Daubenton's bat** (*Myotis daubentonii*) hunting for mosquitoes over rivers and ponds.

REPTILES

The **adder** (*Vipera berus*) is the only poisonous snake in Britain. It is easily recognised by the distinctive zigzag markings down its back and a diamond shape on the back of its head. On summer days adders bask in sunny spots, such as on a warm rock or in the middle of a path so watch your step. Adders tend to move out of the way quickly but should you be unlucky enough to inadvertently step on one and get bitten, sit still and send someone else for help. Their venom is designed to kill small mammals, not humans. A bite is unlikely to be fatal to an adult but *is* serious enough to warrant immediate medical attention, especially in the case of children. Nevertheless, the likelihood of being bitten is minuscule. Walkers are far more likely to frighten the adder away once it senses your footsteps.

The **grass snake** (*Natrix natrix*), an adept swimmer, is a much longer, slimmer snake with a yellow collar around its neck. It's non-venomous but does emit a foul stench should you attempt to pick one up. It's much better for you and the snake to leave it in peace.

The **common lizard** (*Lacerta/Zootoca vivipara*) is a harmless creature which can often be seen basking in the sun on rocks and stone walls. About 15cm long, it is generally brown with patterns of spots or stripes. However, you are far more likely to hear them scuttling away through the undergrowth as you approach.

A curious beast, looking like a slippery eel or small snake, is the **slow worm** (*Anguis fragilis*) which, despite the name, is neither a worm nor indeed an eel or snake but a legless lizard. Usually a glossy grey or copper colour, they can be seen on woodland floors and in grassland. They are completely harmless and usually slip away into the leaf litter when they hear footsteps.

TREES

Over the last few hundred years the once-extensive forest cover in southern England has been fragmented into a patchwork of copses and coppiced woodland. Trees were felled for fuel and for shipbuilding and, in the case of the South Downs, to clear land for agricultural needs. In more recent times many of the hedgerows that helped create the familiar patchwork landscape have been grubbed up to create much larger fields.

Nevertheless, there are considerable parts of the Downs that have survived the threat from axe and chainsaw, making up 23% of the entire area of the national park. Half of these woodlands have been there for over 400 years. The main reason for this is that north-facing scarp slope was, and still is, too steep for clearing and too inaccessible for ploughing. Consequently, this is where most of the trees are found. Although there are still areas of semi-natural or ancient mixed woodland, much of the remaining woodland has been coppiced, an old method of promoting growth of more numerous and narrower trunks by cutting a tree at its base. Coppicing was common in hazel stands and the resulting product used in constructing fences and making furniture. Although coppicing is no longer widespread it is still practised in some parts by enthusiasts of old woodland crafts and also by conservationists who recognise that coppiced woodland can be beneficial to certain species.

Most of the woodland on the Downs is mixed deciduous, made up largely of beech and ash but there are many other species to look out for.

Tree species

With its thick, silvery trunk, the **beech** (*Fagus sylvatica*) is one of the most attractive native trees. They favour well-drained soil, hence their liking for the steep scarp slope, and can grow to a height of 40 metres with the high canopies blocking out much of the light. (Indeed, in 2015, a 200-year-old beech tree on the Devil's Dyke estate was measured at 44m and declared the tallest native tree in Britain.) As a result the floors of beech woodlands tend to be fairly bare of vegetation. In autumn the colours of the turning leaves can be quite spectacular.

One species that does survive the shady floor of beech woodland is the distinctive **common holly** (*Ilex aquifolium*) with its dark waxy leaves which have sharp points. Holly varies in size, usually growing as a sprawling bush on the woodland floor or in hedgerows but also as a tree when established in more isolated locations.

Famous for its longevity, lasting for well over a thousand years in some cases, the **common yew** (*Taxus baccata*) is abundant in churchyards but there are also natural stands on the scarp slope and among beech woodland. The dark glossy needles are quite distinctive as is the flaky red bark of the often gnarled and twisted old trunks and branches, and the poisonous bright red berries.

Another tree that's famed for its longevity is the **English oak** (*Quercus robur*); indeed, there's one near Midhurst that's been dignified with a name, the Queen Elizabeth I Oak, and is said to be around 1000 years old.

Usually seen in hedgerows, though it can also grow as a small tree, the hawthorn (*Crataegus monogyna*) has small leaves and, like the yew, produces red berries that provide food for woodland birds, particularly blackbirds.

BUTTERFLIES

The Downs are famous for their butterflies. Many of the national nature reserves in the area were set up specifically because of the variety and number of butterflies. One of the most common is the **meadow brown** (*Maniola jurtina*), which is dusty brown in colour with a rusty orange streak and dark, false eyes. They can be seen in meadows all across the Downs. With deep orange and chocolate-brown markings, the small **gatekeeper** (*Pyronia tithonus*) likes similar habitat and is also widespread throughout the Downs.

The **peacock** (*Inachis io*) is surely Britain's most beautiful butterfly; it's quite common in this area. The markings on the wings are said to mimic the eyes of an animal to frighten off predators. Also common is the impressive **red admiral** (*Vanessa atalanta*). Owing to climate change it is now starting to over-winter in Britain and appears to be thriving.

The **brimstone** (*Gonepteryx rhamni*) is also widespread, though well camouflaged as its wings look very like leaves; the **white admiral** (*Limenitis camilla*), however, is declining in numbers but may still be seen in some woodland sites. Although it has also recently been in decline in other parts of the country, the **small tortoiseshell** (*Aglais urticae*) is still widespread here and also in towns and villages.

Other very common butterflies include the **small white** (*Pieris/Artogeia rapae*) and the **large white** (*Pieris brassicae*); both can travel large distances, some migrating from continental Europe each year.

Along many of the country lanes and tracks the **speckled wood** (*Pararge aegeria*) can be seen basking on hedgerows. It is a small dark butterfly with a few white spots and six small false eyes at the rear.

There are several butterflies that are synonymous with chalk downland, notably the butterflies known as blues. The **holly blue** (*Celastrina argiolus*) and **chalkhill blue** (*Polyommatus/Lysandra coridon*) are similar in appearance, being very small and pale blue in colour, although the chalkhill blue has a dark strip on the edge of each wing. The **common blue** (*Polyommatus icarus*) is even smaller and as the name suggests is the most common of the blues. The underside of its wings is a dusty brown colour with small orange and white spots.

A rare downland butterfly is the **Duke of Burgundy fritillary** (*Hamearis lucina*) which you may be lucky enough to see on Beacon Hill or Old Winchester Hill. It has pale orange spots on small dark wings.

Another rarity that relies on chalk grassland is the **silver spotted skipper** (*Hesperia comma*), a diminutive yellow butterfly with small white flashes on the undersides of the wings.

Finally, the **brown argus** (*Aricia agestis*), a small dark butterfly with distinctive orange spots along the edges of each wing, is another that is restricted to chalk grassland; it can sometimes be seen flying close to the ground.

Common Blue
Polyommatus icarus

Peacock
Inachis io

Small
Tortoiseshell
Aglais urticae

Silver-washed
Fritillary
Argynnis paphia

Small Garden/Cabbage White
Pieris rapae

Chalkhill Blue
Lysandra coridon

Painted Lady
Cynthia cadui

Large
Garden/
Cabbage White
Pieris brassicae

Small
Copper
*Lycaena
phlaeas*

Small
Heath
*Coenonympha
pamphilus*

Red Admiral *Vanessa atalanta*

White Admiral
Limenitis camilla

Meadow
Brown
*Maniola
jurtina*

THE ENVIRONMENT & NATURE

Common Poppy
Papaver rhoeas

Tormentil
Potentilla erecta

Scarlet Pimpernel
*Anagallis
arvensis*

FLOWERS

Many of the flowering meadows that once covered large stretches of downland farmland have been destroyed by modern farming techniques. However, in places, efforts are being made to revive these by encouraging farmers to employ more flower-friendly methods.

Meadows

The dominant grass found in fields all over the Downs is the appropriately named **sheep's fescue** (*Festuca ovina*) which was cultivated specifically for pastureland and is the grass of choice for downland sheep. Of far greater interest are the likes of the **common poppy** (*Papaver rhoeas*) with its spectacular deep red petals. They often colonise arable fields and path edges, preferring well-disturbed soil. Entire fields turn red in the flowering season in late summer.

Earlier in the season walkers are likely to come across the **cowslip** (*Primula veris*) and its head of pale yellow flowers. The flowers flop down in small bunches earning the plant the old nickname 'bunch of keys'.

Perhaps one of the most beautiful of the downland flowers is the **round headed rampion** (*Phyteuma orbiculare*). Its striking dark blue flowers have earned it the local name 'The Pride of Sussex'.

The tiny yellow flower of **tormentil** (*Potentilla tormentilla*) can be seen hugging the ground in short grassland. It gets its name from an age when it was used as a medicinal remedy for diarrhoea and haemorrhoids: the taste is so foul that it tormented whoever took it. Another tiny flower that's found close to the ground is the **scarlet pimpernel** (*Anagallis avensis*), a member of the primrose family. The flowers are just 5mm in diameter but stand out from their grassy background thanks to their light red colour.

Many people assume orchids to be so rare as to be nearly impossible to find. In truth there are several fairly common species that may readily be seen flowering on the Downs,

Rowan (tree)
Sorbus aucuparia

Ramsons (Wild Garlic)
Allium ursinum

Common Hawthorn
Crataegus monogyna

Common Centaury
Centaurium erythraea

THE ENVIRONMENT AND NATURE

Common Ragwort
Senecio jacobaea

Cowslip
Primula veris

Yarrow
Achillea millefolium

Foxglove
Digitalis purpurea

Bird's-foot trefoil
Lotus corniculatus

Meadow Buttercup
Ranunculus acris

Marsh Marigold
(Kingcup)
Caltha palustris

Herb-Robert
Geranium robertianum

Primrose
Primula vulgaris

St John's Wort
*Hypericum
perforatum*

Dog Rose
Rosa canina

Honeysuckle
*Lonicera
periclymemum*

Ox-eye Daisy
Leucanthemum vulgare

Common Knapweed
Centaurea nigra

Red Admiral butterfly (*Vanessa atalanta*) on
Hemp Agrimony (*Eupatorium cannabinum*)

Pyramidal Orchid
Anacamptis pyramidalis

Bee Orchid
Ophrys apifera

usually around mid-summer. These include the **early purple orchid** (*Orchis mascula*) which can be seen in rough grassland. It stands about 10-15cm tall and has an elongated head of pinky-purple flowers. Also quite common are the **pyramidal orchid** (*Anacamptis pyramidalis*) and the **common spotted-orchid** (*Dactylorhiza fuchsii*).

There are of course some species that do fit the rare orchid label including the **fly orchid** (*Ophrys insectifera*) with flowers resembling small insects. These cleverly designed flowers attract wasps which pick up the pollen and take it on to the next insect-shaped flower they see. Another orchid with the same tactic is the **bee orchid** (*Ophrys apifera*) whose flowers are shaped like, well, bees.

Apart from the orchids, one of the most endangered and also one of the most striking flowering plants that may be seen, particularly on the Downs above Eastbourne, is **pheasant's-eye** (*Adonis annua*) with its blood red petals and large seed head.

Bluebell
Hyacinthoides non-scripta

Early Purple Orchid
Orchis mascula

Common Spotted-Orchid
Dactylorhiza fuchsii

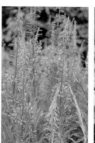

Rosebay Willowherb
Epilobium angustifolium

Gorse
Ulex europaeus

Forget-me-not
Myosotis arvensis

Common Dog Violet
Viola riviniana

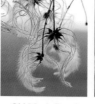

Old Man's Beard
Clematis vitalba

Red Campion
Silene dioica

In overgrown areas thorny **gorse** (*Ulex europaeus*) bushes brighten up the summer with their small yellow flowers that burst open from February until June, filling the air with a coconut-like scent.

Woodland and hedgerows
There are several flowering plants associated with open woods and woodland edges. In May the pink flowers of the slightly inaccurately named **red campion** (*Silene dioica*) come into view along woodland edges and at the foot of hedgerows while deeper into the woods the floor becomes covered with **bluebells** (*Hyacinthoides non-scripta*) in the early spring. Other common woodland flowering plants include the **wood anemone** (*Anemone nemorosa*) with its round white flowers which cover forest floors in a similar way to bluebells. A more isolated flower, although sometimes seen growing in small groups, is the cheerful yellow **primrose** (*Primula vulgaris*).

Bramble (*Rubus fruticosus*) is a common woodland and hedgerow species with small sharp thorns. It spreads rapidly, engulfing everything in its path. In its favour, blackberries appear on the branches in the autumn to provide sustenance for hungry birds and peckish walkers. In hedgerows and along woodland edges you'll see the distinctive feathery climber, **old man's beard** (*Clematis vitalba*), also known as traveller's joy. The feathery part of the plant is actually the fruit. The very tall and graceful **foxglove** (*Digitalis purpurea*) has spires of white or purple trumpet-like flowers. It is commonly spotted along hedgerows, roadside verges and in shady woodland. Other fairly common woodland species that are just as comfortable on hedgebanks include the small blue **forget-me-not** (*Myosotis arvensis*) and tall white **cow parsley** (*Anthriscus sylvestris*).

Perhaps the most unusual and to some the ugliest of plants, found in dark corners of beech woodland, is the pale yellow **bird's nest orchid** (*Neottia nidus-avis*), named for its nest-like root system that intertwines across the ground.

BIRDS

The chalk grassland of the Downs is ideal for a variety of bird species but the grassy hillsides are not the only habitat on the Downs. There are many woodland species in the beech forests on the steep scarp slope, freshwater species on the rivers and seabirds by Cuckmere Haven and the Seven Sisters' cliffs. The following list gives just a few of the birds that may be seen on the Downs.

Scrubland and chalk grassland
One of the most attractive birds the Downs walker might spot, although sadly declining in numbers, is the **lapwing** (*Vanellus vanellus*), also known as the peewit. The name comes from its lilting flight, frequently changing direction with its large rounded wings. Usually seen feeding on open arable farmland, it has long legs, a short bill and a distinctive long head crest, with a white belly, black and white head, black throat patch and distinctive dark green wings.

Towards dusk **barn owls** (*Tyto alba*) hunt for voles along field and woodland edges. To see a barn owl, with its ghostly white plumage, is a real treat but their dwindling numbers make such a sighting increasingly rare.

The colourful little **stonechat** (*Saxicola rubicola*) with its deep orange breast and black head is easily identified by their habit of flitting from the top of one bush to another, only pausing to call out across the fields. The stonechat's call sounds much like two stones being struck together, hence the name.

The **yellowhammer** (*Emberiza citrinella*), also known as the yellow bunting, can sometimes be seen perched on the top of gorse bushes. Some claim that its distinctive song sounds like it is saying 'a little bit of bread and no cheese'. At a push they are right, but it is certainly no talking parrot.

The call of the **skylark** (*Alauda arvensis*) can probably be considered the sound of the Downs. This small, buff-coloured, ground-nesting lark is usually heard but not often seen. The characteristic flight pattern, rising steadily upwards on rapid wingbeats whilst twittering relentlessly, is what makes the skylark so distinctive. However, it is difficult to see against the blue sky but if you look carefully you might just spot one way up high.

Woodland

A common raptor that is often heard before it's seen is the **buzzard** (*Buteo buteo*), a large broad-winged bird of prey that is dark brown in appearance but slightly paler on the underside of its wings. It has a distinctive mewing call and can be spotted soaring ever-higher on the air thermals. Buzzards are less common towards the eastern end of the Downs where the woodland cover is not so great. They are easier to spot above the dense woodland on the West Sussex Downs and around the Meon Valley in Hampshire.

One lovely and fairly recent addition to the number of bird species within the National Park is the **red kite** (*Milvus milvus*), which was hunted to near extinction before a successful reintroduction program that started over 30 years ago saw their numbers, like the birds themselves, soar. Similar in size to a buzzard, the kite is more graceful and acrobatic, with its deeply forked tail a distinguishing characteristic.

The **kestrel** (*Falco tinnunculus*) is much smaller than the buzzard or kite. It hovers expertly in a fixed spot above grassland and roadside verges, even in the strongest of winds, hunting for mice and voles. Similar in size and appearance but rarely seen is the **hobby** *(Falco subbuteo)* which appears in the summer months, often on the margins of woodlands.

The **green woodpecker** *(Picus viridis)* is not all green, sporting a bright red and black head. They are sometimes spotted clinging to a vertical tree trunk or feeding on the ground in open fields. The most common view, however, is as the bird flies away when disturbed. The undulating flight pattern is characterised by rapid wing beats as the bird rises followed by a pause when the bird slowly drops. This is accompanied by a loud laughing call that has earned the bird its old English name of 'yaffle'.

The **woodcock** *(Scolopax rusticola)*, with its long straight beak and plump body, is common in damp woodland where it can hide thanks to its leafy brown plumage. It is most easily sighted in spring at dusk and dawn. This is when the males perform their courtship flight, known as 'roding', which involves two distinct calls, one a low grunting noise, the other a sharp 'k-wik k-wik' call.

Using this guide

This route guide has been divided according to logical start and stop
points. However, these are not intended to be strict daily stages since
people walk at different speeds and have varying interests. The maps
can be used to plan how far to walk each day but note that these are
walking times only (see box below).

On pp32-4 are tables to help you plan an **itinerary**. To provide
further help, **practical information** is presented clearly on the trail
maps. This includes walking times for both directions, places to stay,
camp and eat, as well as shops where you can buy supplies. Further
service **details** are given in the text under the entry for each place.
For an overview of this information see the **village and town facilities table** on pp30-1.

See also the **colour maps** (with **profile charts**) and the cumula-
tive **distance chart** at the back of the book.

TRAIL MAPS   [see key map p208; symbols key p191]
Direction
(See p29 for a discussion of the pros and cons of walking direction.)
If you're doing this walk in an **easterly direction** (**E ➔** ie
towards **E**astbourne having started in Winchester) follow the
maps in an ascending order (from 1 to 42) and the text as below.
If you're walking in a **westerly direction** (**W ←**, ie towards
Winchester having started in Eastbourne), follow the maps
in a descending order (from 42 to 1) and the route overviews in
shaded text. Turn to p178 (or p182 for inland route) to start your
walk in this direction.

Scale and walking times
The trail maps are to a scale of 1:20,000 (1cm = 200m; 3¹/₈ inches =
one mile). Walking times are given along the side of each map and the

---

❏ **IMPORTANT NOTE – WALKING TIMES**
Unless otherwise specified, **all times in this book refer only to the time
spent walking**. You should add 20-30% to allow for rests, photos, checking the map, drinking water etc, not to mention time simply to stop and
stare. When planning the day's hike count on 5-7 hours' actual walking.

arrow shows the direction to which the time refers. Black triangles indicate the points between which the times have been taken. **See box overleaf for important note on walking times**. The time-bars are a tool and are not there to judge your walking ability. There are so many variables that affect walking speed, from the weather conditions to how many beers you drank the previous evening. After the first hour or two of walking you will see how your speed relates to the timings on the maps.

GPS waypoints and what3ways references
The numbered GPS waypoints and what3ways references are listed on pp188-91.

Up or down?
The trail is shown as a **dashed red line**: — — —. An arrow across the trail indicates the gradient; two arrows show that it's steep. Note that the *arrow points uphill*, the opposite of what OS maps use on steep roads. A good way to remember our style is: '**front-pointing** on crampons **up** a steep slope' and 'open arms – Julie Andrews-style – **spreading out** to unfold the view **down** below'. If, for example, you are walking from A (at 80m) to B (at 200m) and the trail between the two is short and steep it would be shown thus: A— — — >> — — — B. Reversed arrow heads indicate a downward gradient.

Other features
Features are marked on the map when pertinent to navigation. In order to avoid cluttering the maps and making them unusable not all features have been marked each time they occur.

ACCOMMODATION

Apart from in large towns where some selection of places has been necessary, almost every place to stay that is within easy reach of the trail is marked. Details of each place are given in the accompanying text.

The number of **rooms** of each type is stated, ie **S** = single bed, **T** = twin beds, **D** = double bed, **Tr** = triple room (for up to three people) and **Qd** = quad (for up to four). Note that most of the triple/quad rooms have a double bed and one/two single beds (or bunk beds); thus for a group of three or four, two people may have to share the double bed but it also means the room can be used as a double or twin.

Rates quoted for a double or twin in B&B-style accommodation are **per person (pp) based on two people sharing a room** for a one-night stay; rates are usually discounted for longer stays and also if three or more people are sharing a room. Where a **single room (sgl)** is available the rate for that is quoted if different from the rate per person. The rate for **single occupancy (sgl occ)** of a double/twin room may be higher. Unless specified, rates are for bed and breakfast; at some places the only option is a **room rate** – this will be the same whether one or two people (or more if permissible) use the room.

The accommodation will either have **en suite** (bath or shower) facilities in the room or **private,** or **shared, facilities** (in either case this is a separate room, with a bath and/or shower, often just outside the bedroom); in some places the

ROUTE GUIDE AND MAPS

facilities may be private if only one room is booked. The text also mentions whether the premises have: **wi-fi** (WI-FI); if a bath (🛁) is available in/for at least one room, for those who prefer a relaxed soak at the end of the day; if **packed lunches** (Ⓛ) can be prepared subject to prior arrangement (though this has not been checked for cities or large towns where there are lots of options); and if **dogs** (🐾) are welcome in at least one room, or at campsites, subject to prior arrangement; see pp193.

If arranged in advance some B&B proprietors are happy to collect walkers from the nearest point on the trail and deliver them back again next morning; they may also be happy to transfer your **luggage** to your next accommodation place. Some may charge for this; check the details at the time of booking.

WINCHESTER   MAP 1, p76

Winchester is a city steeped in history. The area was settled as long ago as 450BC when the nearby **St Catherine's Hill** was inhabited by a Celtic tribe. After the Roman occupation came the Dark Ages of AD400-600 during which time it is believed that **King Arthur** reigned from here. Many romantics today believe the city to be the site of legendary Camelot.

Things brightened up after the Dark Ages when in 871 **King Alfred the Great** (849-899) made the city the capital of Saxon England. He has probably had the greatest influence on the city so it is not surprising that a **bronze statue** of him, constructed in 1901, stands on Broadway. **St Swithun** (see box below) is also inextricably linked with Winchester.

In 1066 **William the Conqueror** arrived in Hastings and made his way to Winchester where he duly took charge and ordered the building of the castle. Soon after, in 1079, work began on the cathedral.

Winchester has had a long and sometimes turbulent history but it is well worth spending an afternoon or the whole day exploring the compact city's many sights.

What to see and do

Winchester Cathedral (☎ 01962-857200, 🖥 winchester-cathedral.org.uk; Mon-Sat 9am-5pm, Sun 12.30-3pm; £12.50) stands elegantly in parkland in the city centre. The spectacular nave is said to be the longest Gothic cathedral nave in the world. The best time to visit the cathedral is during the Sunday morning service when the choir can be heard. The cathedral has witnessed many an historic event: **Henry III** was baptised here in 1207 and it was also the scene of the marriage of **Mary Tudor** to **Philip of Spain** in 1554. In more recent history it became the final resting place in 1817 of **Jane Austen** (see box p74); her grave and memorial are in the north aisle of the cathedral. The ticket price includes the *Kings and Scribes: The Birth of a Nation* (Mon-Sat 11am-4pm, Sun 12.30-2.30pm) exhibition, which features a look at the 12th-century Winchester Bible. There's also a large

---

❑ THE LEGEND OF ST SWITHUN

St Swithun, once Bishop of Winchester, died in AD862. Before his death he asked to be buried outside the old Minster and was duly interred in accordance with his wishes. St Swithun, however, had not counted upon the wishes of Bishop Aethelwold who on 15 July 971 decided to extend the Minster. The expansion plans required the temporary opening of St Swithun's grave before he was carefully re-interred within the new Minster's walls. On the day of the re-interment it began to rain and did not stop for 40 days. To this day the legend says that if it rains on St Swithun's Day it will rain for the next 40 days. Some would say this is not unusual for England in July.

café (Cathedral Refectory, see p77).

Although the cathedral is the centre-piece of the city there are other equally fascinating places such as the extensive **ruins of Wolvesey Castle** (Apr-Sep daily 10am-6pm, Oct-Mar to 4pm; free). The former palace (residence) for the bishops of Winchester, in 1554 the wedding breakfast of Queen Mary and Philip II of Spain was hosted here. Less than a century later the castle was destroyed by Parliamentarians in the English Civil War.

At 8 College St, not far from Wolvesey Castle, is the house where **Jane Austen** died. However, this is a private residence so don't peer through the windows.

Nearby is one of Winchester's hidden gems: tiny **St Swithun-upon-Kingsgate Church**, built, as the name suggests, on top of **King's Gate**, one of Winchester's two surviving city gates (the other being Westgate, see below). Built during the Middle Ages, the church is unusual in that it actually formed part of the fabric of the old city walls.

Also near the cathedral is the **City of Winchester Museum** (⌨ hampshireculture.org.uk/winchester-city-museum; Apr-Dec Mon-Sat 10am-5pm & Sun 11am-5pm, Jan-Mar Mon-Sat 10am-4pm & Sun 11am-4pm; £6.50). The museum traces the history of the city from the Romans to the Victorians.

Next to **Westgate**, the other surviving city gate, is the **Great Hall** (☎ 01962-846476, ⌨ hants.gov.uk/greathall; daily 10am-4pm; £4); Castle Ave, is all that remains of Winchester Castle. Here, on the west wall, hangs, so legend has it, *the* table around which King Arthur and his Knights of the Round Table sat. Carbon dating has quashed that particular story, however, and

the table is actually a few hundred years too young to have been used by Arthur, having been constructed around the end of the 13th century; but it's still a mightily impressive disc of oak, weighing over a ton and elaborately painted during the time of Henry VIII with a beautiful Tudor rose. The Great Hall is also famous for the trial of **Sir Walter Raleigh** for treason in 1603.

In the heart of the city is **City Mill** (☎ 01962-870057, ⌨ nationaltrust.org.uk/visit/ hampshire/winchester-city-mill; **fb**; Wed-Sun 10am-4pm; free), sitting astride the River Itchen, and thought to be the country's oldest working water mill. Although there has been a mill on this site for centuries the present building dates from 1743. Check online or call for times if you're interested in the free-to-watch demonstrations of flour milling. Since 2016 it has been the official start (or end) of the South Downs Way too.

It is possible to visit **Winchester College** (☎ 01962-621209, ⌨ winchester college.org/visit-us; 1hr tours, daily 2.15pm & 3.30pm; tour £10) which was founded in 1382 by William of Wykeham, then Bishop of Winchester; it is said to be the oldest continuously running school in the country. Originally it was home to 70 boys who boarded but it now has over 700 pupils and in 2022 began accepting day pupils in the Sixth Form, including girls. Amongst the 80 listed buildings are the 14th-century chapel, the College Hall, the 17th-century schoolroom and the medieval cloister.

Services

The very helpful **visitor information centre** (☎ 01962-840500, ⌨ visitwinchester.co .uk; Mon-Sat 10am-5pm, May-Aug Sun & Bank Hols 10am-3pm) is on the ground

---

❑ **JANE AUSTEN**

Jane Austen, born near Basingstoke in Hampshire in 1775, is one of the most important English novelists, having written such classics as *Pride and Prejudice*, *Persuasion* and *Northanger Abbey*. In 1816 she began writing *Sanditon* but in the same year she contracted Addison's disease and the novel was never completed. As her condition worsened she moved to a house in Winchester where she spent the last few weeks of her life, dying at the age of 41 on 18 July 1817.

floor of the Guildhall on the High St.

On the pedestrianised High St there are several **banks** and **ATMs,** while inside WH Smith (Mon-Sat 8.30am-6pm, Sun 10.30am-4.30pm) you'll find the main **post office** (Mon-Sat 10am-4pm).

There are several **supermarkets**, including the biggest, Sainsbury's (Mon-Sat 7am-8pm, Sun 11am-5pm), adjoining **Brooks Shopping Centre** on Middle Brook St, and a handy Co-op (daily 7am-10pm) near the railway station. Last-minute hiking equipment (including blister kits) can be found in Mountain Warehouse **outdoor gear shop** (Mon-Sat 9am-5.30pm, Sun 10.30am-4.30pm), on the High St. Boots **Pharmacy** (Mon-Fri 9am-6pm) is towards the top of the High St at Nos 35-39.

There's free **internet access** inside The Arc (formerly the Discovery Centre; Mon-Sat 9.30am-5pm, Sun 11am-5pm), a modern **library** on Jewry St.

Public transport
Both South Western Railway and Cross Country Trains operate **train** services to Winchester (see box p44). The **railway station** is about five minutes' walk from the city centre.

Megabus and National Express **coach** services (Nos 032 & 203; see p45) no longer visit the town itself, stopping instead at St Catherine's Park & Ride, about a 10-15 minute walk from the centre. There are Park & Ride buses to town every 7-12 minutes during the week, every 15 minutes on Saturdays, but none on Sunday.

For Southampton you should take Bluestar's No 1 **bus** while for Petersfield and the villages in between take Stagecoach's No 67. See p46 for details.

Where to stay
Being a popular tourist destination, Winchester is blessed with plenty of hotels and guesthouses. However, the demand on accommodation throughout the year is such that **booking well in advance** is strongly recommended to avoid a night on a park bench by the cathedral.

The nearest **campsite** is the well-equipped *Winchester Morn Hill Caravan*

Club Campsite (off Map 1; ☎ 01962-869877, 🖳 caravanclub.co.uk; camping Mar-end Sep; 🐾 if on a lead), 2¼ miles east of town. In peak season they charge *from* £13.80 per tent plus around £13.30 per adult. Stagecoach's bus No 64 (see p46) goes from the bus station to Winchester Science Centre, which is very close to the campsite, so it is possible to use it as a place to stay, but note they only have six tent pitches. The campsite is also 2 miles north-east of Chilcomb (Map 2) and 1½ miles north of Cheesefoot Head car park (Map 2).

The cheapest accommodation is probably that supplied by the local *Travelodge* (☎ 08719 846552, 🖳 travelodge.co.uk; 62/D or Tr, all en suite; 🛏; wi-fi £3/24hrs; 🐾 £20), on Market Lane. You may gripe at the lack of atmosphere and the complete absence of any personal touch, but you simply can't argue with the location. Rooms start at £40 (if prepaid) but can be double that.

Cathedral Cottage (☎ 01962-878975, 🖳 cathedralcottagebandb.co.uk; 1D en suite), at 19 Colebrook St, is just a stone's throw from the cathedral with a cosy room (from £52.50pp, sgl occ £95) overlooking a pretty cottage garden; your breakfast (full English or continental) can either be served in your room, their dining room or in the garden in the summer. Another room (1D separate bathroom; 🛏; from £40pp, £70g sgl occ) is also sometimes available.

In a beautiful Grade II* listed Queen Anne house at the top of Blue Ball Hill is *St John's Croft* (☎ 01962-859976, 🖳 st-johns-croft.co.uk; 2Tr private bathrooms, 1Tr en suite bathroom but separate toilet; 🛏) with bed and 'Aga-cooked' breakfast from £55pp (sgl occ £80, Tr £47pp). There are comfortable good-sized rooms with views over Winchester.

Winchester Royal (☎ 0330-102 7242, 🖳 winchesterroyalhotel.com; 81D or T plus some suites, all en suite; 🛏) is on St Peter St. This 16th-century townhouse was once a bishop's residence, then a convent, but now offers luxurious hotel accommodation with four-poster beds in two of the rooms. Rates vary widely but expect to pay from £51.50pp (sgl occ full room rate) for

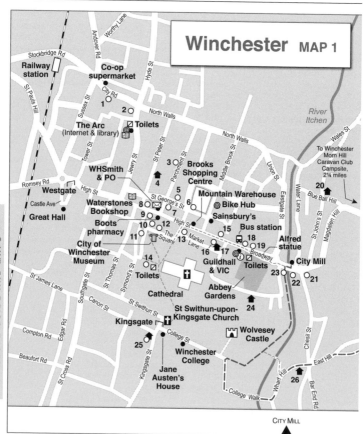

Winchester MAP 1

Railway station

Co-op supermarket

City Rd

1

2

North Walls

River Itchen

The Arc
(Internet & library)

Toilets

North Walls

Wales St

To Winchester
Morn Hill
Caravan Club
Campsite,
2¼ miles

3

Brooks
Shopping
Centre

WHSmith
& PO

4

20

Blue Ball Hill

Westgate

Romsey Rd

High St

Mountain Warehouse
@ Bike Hub

5

6

Sainsbury's

Castle Ave

Waterstones
Bookshop

8

7

9

Great Hall

Boots
pharmacy

10

12

15

Bus station

18

City of
Winchester
Museum

11

13

Market
Lane

16

17

19

Alfred
statue

City Mill

14

Guildhall
& VIC

Toilets

23

21

Toilets

22

Cathedral

Abbey
Gardens

24

St Swithun-upon-
Kingsgate Church

Kingsgate

Wolvesey
Castle

25

College St

Winchester
College

Jane
Austen's
House

26

College Walk

CITY MILL

---

room only, often less if booking more than a week ahead. See their website for special offers, although note that some rates don't include breakfast – check when booking.

At 75 Kingsgate St is *The Wykeham Arms* (☎ 01962-853834, 🖳 wykehamarms winchester.co.uk; 2S/10D/2T, all en suite; 🛑), a cosy inn with quality rooms from £70pp (sgl/sgl occ from £85.50) room only. It's named after William of Wykeham who founded Winchester College (see p74).

Though the name doesn't sound particularly appealing, *The Black Hole* (☎ 01962-807010, 🖳 theblackholebb.co.uk; 10D, all en suite; 🛑; 🐕) is in fact a quality, if somewhat quirky guesthouse with individually designed rooms and a small roof terrace overlooking the city. They charge £47.50-60pp (sgl occ room rate) including breakfast.

Where to eat and drink

Cafés *South Downs Social* (☎ 01962-860220, 🖳 southdownssocial.com, **fb**; Mon-Fri 9am-5pm, Sat 8.30am-5pm, Sun 9.30am-4pm) is a cyclists' café by the shop-

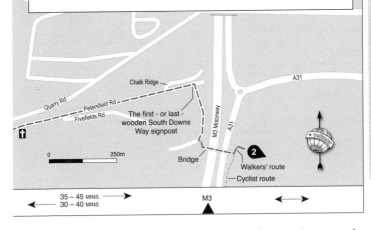

Where to stay
4 Winchester Royal
17 Travelodge
20 St John's Croft
24 Cathedral Cottage
25 The Wykeham Arms
26 The Black Hole

Where to eat and drink
1 Gurkha's Inn
2 Porterhouse Steakhouse
3 Piecaramba!
5 Catch – Fish & Chips
6 South Downs Social
7 Forte Kitchen & The Hatch
8 ASK Italian

Where to eat and drink (cont'd)
9 Winchester Bakery
10 Honey + Harvey
11 The Old Vine
12 The Eclipse Inn
13 Flat Whites
14 Cathedral Refectory
15 Chococo
16 Rick Stein's Fish & Shellfish
18 Gandhi Restaurant
19 Crown & Anchor
21 Chesil Rectory
22 Bridge Patisserie
23 Bishop on the Bridge
25 The Wykeham Arms

ROUTE GUIDE AND MAPS

ping centre, but welcomes all-comers and serves wonderful breakfasts (avocado on sourdough £8.50), toasties, sandwiches and South Downs merchandise. Terrific.

Just a few steps from City Mill, across the road, *Bridge Patisserie* (☎ 01962-890767, 🐾; daily 9am-3pm) is very dog-friendly and does a good line in salads and tasty lunches.

The city centre is dotted with cafés. The large, modern *Cathedral Refectory* (daily 9.30am-5pm) is another dependable option and also has plenty of outdoor seat-

ing for sunny afternoons. A great spot for breakfast, *Honey + Harvey* (☎ 01962-807557, 🖳 honeyandharvey.co.uk/winchester, **fb**; Mon-Fri 8am-4pm, Sat 9am-5pm, Sun 9am-4pm) is a stone's throw away with a clutch of tables spilling out onto the pavement outside. Their blow-out Winchester breakfast (£15.95) will last you all day.

Moving to the High St, upstairs at *Winchester Bakery* (🖳 winchesterbakery.co.uk, **fb**; Mon-Fri 7.30am-5pm, Sat 8am-5pm, Sun 9am-4pm) is a peaceful place to enjoy a coffee and pastry.

For something more quirky, try *Chococo* (🖳 chococo.co.uk, **fb**; Mon-Fri 9am-5pm, Sat to 5.30pm, Sun 10am-5pm) which, as the name suggests, specialises in all things chocolate, including hot-chocolate drinks. They also serve tea, coffee, cakes and soups.

On Parchment St, *The Hatch* (☎ 01962-856840; breakfast daily 9am-noon, lunch Sun-Fri noon-4pm, Sat to 5pm) is the more casual 'café sister' to the upscale *Forte Kitchen* (see Restaurants) where you can choose from light breakfast, hot drinks, sandwiches (from £7.50) and toasties to take away (pre-orders welcome) or eat in.

Serving arguably the best coffee of all, though, is *Flat Whites* (daily 9am-4.30pm), a coffee and snack van with a seemingly-permanent position just off the High St. They do decent cakes here too, and there are tables and chairs scattered beside the van so you don't have to take away.

Pubs There are plenty of pubs to choose from. One of the most attractive and historic is *The Eclipse Inn* (☎ 01962-865676, 🖳 the-eclipse-winchester.co.uk; **fb**; food Mon-Wed noon-2.30pm, Wed-Fri 5.30-8pm, Sat noon-8pm, Sun to 4pm; wi-fi) at 25 The Square. It's a tiny whitewashed, timber-framed house which once served as a 16th-century rectory and is rumoured to be haunted.

Not too far away, across the High St opposite the city clock, and also said to be haunted, is the self-proclaimed oldest pub in Winchester, *The Royal Oak* (☎ 01962-842701, 🖳 greeneking.co.uk; food Mon-Sat noon-9pm, Sun to 8pm), which boasts of parts of the building dating back to 1002! Unfortunately you'll get little sense of its age from the rather bland interior, though the staff are friendly and the food fair value (mains from £11.45 for macaroni cheese).

Opposite the cathedral, on Minster St, *The Old Vine* (☎ 01962-854616, 🖳 old-vinewinchester.com; **fb**; food Mon-Fri 8am-3pm & 6-9pm, Sat & Sun 8am-9pm; 🐕 bar only) is another refurbished old pub that offers hearty and popular breakfasts (full English £12), a traditional ploughman's lunch (£11.50) and sandwiches (from £7.50) as well as more substantial pub fare.

The Wykeham Arms (see Where to stay; daily noon-8pm), south of the cathedral, is friendly, serves top-class fare (main dishes around £18-29) and feels more like a country pub.

Another Fuller's pub, like The Wykeham Arms, and boasting a great location too, *Bishop on the Bridge* (☎ 01962-855111, 🖳 bishoponthebridge.co.uk; Mon-Sat to 9.30pm, Sun to 8pm) is worth visiting for its sun terrace overlooking the River Itchen. They serve a menu of pub classics, including brunch, every day.

Crown and Anchor (☎ 01962-870074, 🖳 crownandanchorwinchester.co.uk; **fb**; food Mon-Thur 12.30-3pm & 5.30-8pm, Fri 11am-8pm, Sat & Sun 11am-5pm; 🐕) is an unpretentious place, cheaper than most (mains from £13.75), friendly and, with a location on the High St just down from the bus station, central too. It also has vegan and gluten-free menus – a big and welcome surprise. The only drawback is that food isn't served in the evening at weekends (Sat & Sun) as, according to one of the bar staff, the place can get a bit rowdy then.

Restaurants & takeaways One of the most enjoyable places to eat is the café-cum-diner *Piecaramba!* (☎ 01962-852182, 🖳 piecaramba.co.uk/winchester, **fb**; Mon & Wed-Sat noon-8.30pm, Tue 5-8.30pm, Sun noon-4.30pm), 11a Parchment St; it's a pie-and-mash specialist with a soft spot for comic books. Superhero stories are plastered across the walls. The menu, meanwhile, is dominated by pies (including beef, chicken, lamb & veggie varieties), which go for just £11.95 as part of a pie-and-mash meal. Great value. Great fun.

On nearby Jewry St, at No 24, is *Porterhouse Steakhouse* (☎ 01962-810532, 🖥 www.porterhouserestaurant.co .uk, **fb**; Sun-Thur noon-10pm, Fri & Sat to 10.30pm) with high-quality steaks (from £27.95) but a cheaper daytime menu (eg 8oz rump £15).

On the High St, *Rick Stein Fish and Shellfish* (☎ 01962-587348, 🖥 rickstein .com; Mon-Sat noon-10pm, Sun to 9pm) was Stein's first restaurant outside Cornwall. Mains cost from £15.95; the two/three-course set lunches (£21.95/ 26.95) are a good deal.

For healthy breakfasts and brasserie-type lunches, the upmarket *Forte Kitchen* (🖥 fortekitchen.co.uk; daily 9am-4pm), at 78 Parchment St, is very popular so booking is recommended. Lunch mains include the likes of roast duck salad (£15.50).

At 1 Chesil St, is *Chesil Rectory* (☎ 01962-851555, 🖥 chesilrectory.co.uk; food Mon-Thur noon-2.30pm & 5.30-9pm, Fri & Sat to 9.30pm, Sun noon-3pm & 6-8.30pm), housed in one of Winchester's best-preserved medieval buildings, which dates from around 1425, and was once owned by Henry VIII. Lunchtime set menus cost £23.95 for two courses or £28.95 for three.

For something more down to earth, grab some pizza or pasta at the Italian food chain, *ASK Italian* (☎ 01962-808986, 🖥 askitalian.co.uk; Mon-Fri 11.30am-10pm, Sat to 11pm, Sun to 9pm), 101 High St, or go for a curry at *Gandhi Restaurant* (☎ 01962-863940, 🖥 gandhirestaurant.com; daily noon-2pm & 5.30-10pm,) at 163 High St. For subcontinental fare with a Himalayan twist there's *Gurkha's Inn* (☎ 01962-842843, 🖥 gurkhasinnwinchester .com; daily noon-2pm, Mon-Sat 5.30-11pm, Sun to 10pm), a popular Nepalese restaurant and takeaway at 17 City Rd.

Alternatively, *Catch – Fish & Chips* (☎ 01962-809602; Mon-Sat 11.30am-9pm) is a good chippy on St George's St.

The route guide

E➔ WINCHESTER TO EXTON   **MAPS 1-6**

These **12 miles (19.5km, 4¼-5¾hrs)** begin at the City Mill in the centre of Winchester and follow the River Itchen south before crossing it to leave the city and enter the rolling East Hampshire countryside.

Until May 2017 the route began at the cathedral in the centre of Winchester and went from the cathedral grounds, along the main shopping street, past the statue of King Alfred then down beside the River Itchen; it's a start that we think is superior. You may prefer to start the route this way.

On crossing the bridge spanning the noisy motorway (M3) spare a thought for the remains of Twyford Down. This once beautiful hill a few miles to the south was, despite vociferous demonstrations, ruthlessly sliced in two as part of a highly controversial road improvement scheme in the early 1990s.

Once away from the noise of the road the path crosses a field before arriving at **Chilcomb** (see p80). The church aside, there's little in the way of shops or services to keep you in Chilcomb so once you have admired the thatched cottages head on up the lane for the gradual but steady ascent to **Cheesefoot Head**

(Map 2) where there are great views to the north over the Itchen Valley. The way then passes close to the pretty village of **Cheriton** (Map 4a; p82). The route continues from here along leafy country lanes and tracks through a typically English landscape of patchwork fields, hedgerows and pockets of woodland; and **Beacon Hill** (Map 6), a National Nature Reserve.

The trail soon reaches the pretty village of **Exton** (Map 6), though there is an alternative route for cyclists (clearly signposted) which skirts around the south of the village. It should also be noted that with accommodation in short supply here at the end of the stage, it's pretty much essential, at least in the high season, to book in advance.

CHILCOMB   MAP 2

Chilcomb is the first of several beautiful Hampshire villages. In fact Chilcomb is one of the older settlements, with a **church** (off the path to the south) that pre-dates Winchester Cathedral.

Campers will find tent pitches at *Winchester Morn Hill Caravan Club*

Campsite (see p75), two miles north-east of here. To get there see Map 2 and at the A31/A272 roundabout turn right and follow this road as far as the big roundabout a mile further east. Keep to the left, continue over the roundabout, then go straight over a second, almost adjacent roundabout, and

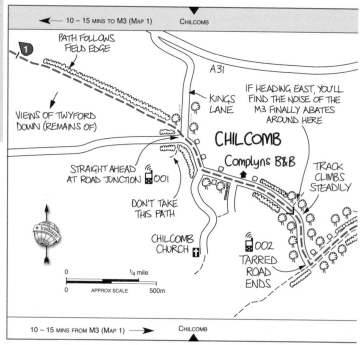

← 10 – 15 MINS TO M3 (MAP 1)   CHILCOMB

PATH FOLLOWS FIELD EDGE

A31

VIEWS OF TWYFORD DOWN (REMAINS OF)

KINGS LANE

IF HEADING EAST, YOU'LL FIND THE NOISE OF THE M3 FINALLY ABATES AROUND HERE

CHILCOMB

Complyns B&B

TRACK CLIMBS STEADILY

STRAIGHT AHEAD AT ROAD JUNCTION 001

DON'T TAKE THIS PATH

CHILCOMB CHURCH

002 TARRED ROAD ENDS

★ trailblazer

0   ¼ mile

0   APPROX SCALE   500m

10 – 15 MINS FROM M3 (MAP 1) →   CHILCOMB

you'll see the campsite in front of you.

There's also a charming **B&B** called *Complyns* (☎ 01962-861600 or ☎ 07890-447982, 💻 complyns.co.uk; 1D/1T, shared

bathroom; 🍽; Ⓛ) in a 17th-century former farmhouse, which charges from £40pp (sgl occ £45). They have a boiler house where you can dry clothes.

CHERITON   MAP 4a, p82

If you're planning on visiting Cheriton, take the path in the corner of the field (see Map 4, p83) rather than following the busy A272. The village is about 35-45 minutes from the Way so unfortunately, unless you are planning on staying the night here, you are likely to miss Cheriton's quaint charms.

On hot sunny days the locals can be seen paddling in the clear waters of the tiny River Itchen, which bubbles out of the chalk about a mile south of Cheriton and runs straight through the village passing beautiful thatched houses and the village green.

Those who do visit should bear in mind that it was not always such a peaceful and charming spot. In 1644, during the English Civil War, the Battle of Cheriton took place just to the east of the village, off Lamborough Lane. The clash between the Parliamentarians and the Royalists resulted in the deaths of 2000 men with the Parliamentarians coming out on top. To this day it is claimed that 'Lamborough Lane ran with the blood of the slain'.

In the village centre is the very useful *Cheriton Post Office & Stores* (☎ 01962-

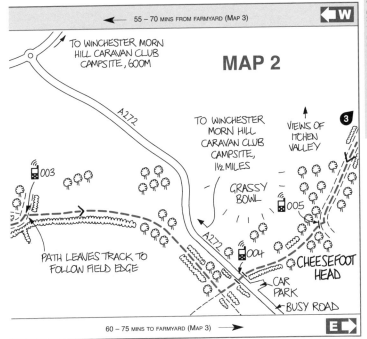

ROUTE GUIDE AND MAPS

55 – 70 MINS FROM FARMYARD (MAP 3) ◀️🚶W

TO WINCHESTER MORN HILL CARAVAN CLUB CAMPSITE, 600M

MAP 2

A272

TO WINCHESTER MORN HILL CARAVAN CLUB CAMPSITE, 1½ MILES

VIEWS OF ITCHEN VALLEY

❸

📱003

GRASSY BOWL

📱005

A272

PATH LEAVES TRACK TO FOLLOW FIELD EDGE

📱004

CHEESEFOOT HEAD

CAR PARK

BUSY ROAD

60 – 75 MINS TO FARMYARD (MAP 3) ➡️ E🚶

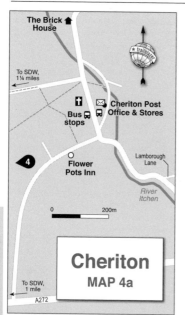

The Brick House

To SDW,
1¼ miles

✞ Cheriton Post
✉ Office & Stores
Bus 🚏
stops

Lamborough
Lane

○ Flower
Pots Inn

River
Itchen

0   200m

Cheriton
MAP 4a

To SDW,
1 mile
A272

771251; Mon-Fri 7am-4.30pm, Sat to 2pm, Sun 7.30am-noon), a combined shop, newsagent, off-licence and part-time **post office** (Mon 1-4pm & Thur 9am-noon).

The charming *Flower Pots Inn* (☎ 01962-771318, 🖳 theflowerpots.co.uk; **fb**; **food** Mon-Thur noon-2.30pm, Fri-Sun noon-4pm & Wed-Sat 6-9pm; 🐾) is a great spot for a meal and a pint. Freshly baked filled ciabattas start from £7, or choose the likes of thyme roasted pork loin steak (£16) or mushroom & ricotta porcini bake with salad and garlic bread (12). The pub has its own **brewery**; their Flowerpots Bitter is definitely worth sampling.

For **B&B,** there's *The Brick House* (☎ 01962-771334, 🖳 brickhousecheriton.co .uk; 2D both en suite; Ⓛ), just past the village centre, which doubles as a bakery school, so hopefully the smell of fresh bread pervades every room 24 hours a day. They charge from £62.50pp (sgl occ £115).

Stagecoach's No 67 **bus** service (Winchester–Petersfield) stops near the church. See p46 for details.

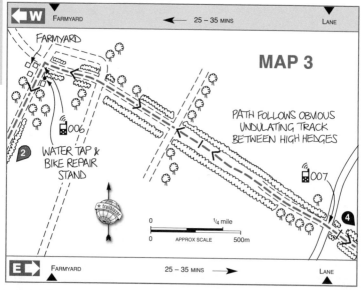

◀ W   FARMYARD   ← 25 – 35 MINS   LANE

FARMYARD

📶006

2   WATER TAP &
BIKE REPAIR
STAND

MAP 3

PATH FOLLOWS OBVIOUS
UNDULATING TRACK
BETWEEN HIGH HEDGES

📶007

4

0   ¼ mile
0   500m
APPROX SCALE

E ▶   FARMYARD   25 – 35 MINS →   LANE

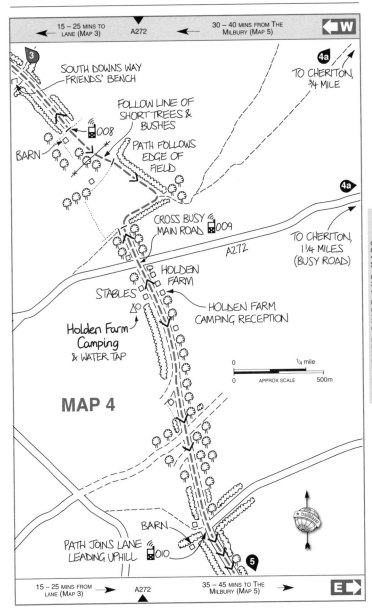

3

SOUTH DOWNS WAY FRIENDS' BENCH

FOLLOW LINE OF SHORT TREES & BUSHES

008

PATH FOLLOWS EDGE OF FIELD

BARN

4a
TO CHERITON, 3/4 MILE

4a

CROSS BUSY MAIN ROAD 009

A272

TO CHERITON, 1 1/4 MILES (BUSY ROAD)

HOLDEN FARM

STABLES

HOLDEN FARM CAMPING RECEPTION

Holden Farm Camping & WATER TAP

MAP 4

0   1/4 mile
0   APPROX SCALE   500m

BARN

PATH JOINS LANE LEADING UPHILL 010

5

ROUTE GUIDE AND MAPS

Holden Farm Right on the Way you'll find *Holden Farm Camping* (Map 4; ☎ 07599-553740, 🖥 holdenfarm.co.uk; 🐾 on lead; Easter to end Sep) with tent pitches (from £20pp, walk-in rate usually around the £15 mark) in a large field opposite the farmhouse. There are showers, toilets and washing-up facilities. They prefer to know people are coming but will always make space for SDW walkers. They also have a **café** now that's open to everyone (Mon-Thur 9am-3pm, Fri to 4pm, Sat & Sun 8am-4pm) operating out of a converted shipping container. It's a lovely spot on a sunny day.

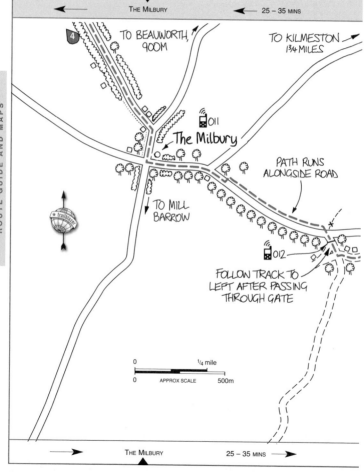

ROUTE GUIDE AND MAPS

Beauworth *The Milbury* (Map 5; ☎ 01962-671300, 🖥 themilbury.co.uk; bar
Wed-Fri from 4pm, Sat & Sun from noon) is a pub full of character, with a 250-
year-old **indoor treadmill** and 300ft-deep (92m) **well** lit all the way to the bottom. At the time of research the bar had recently reopened following an extensive renovation by the new owners, with the kitchen still a work in progress, so
check their website or social media pages to get the latest on their summer opening hours and availability of food. The plans are for a contemporary and locally inspired menu.

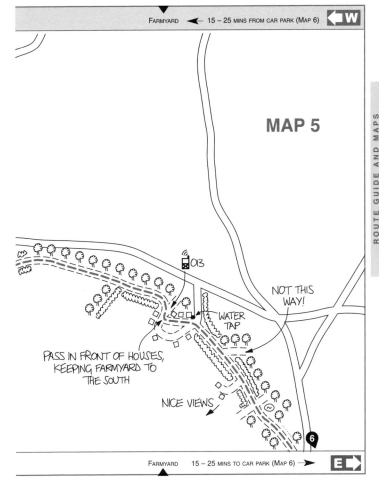

FARMYARD ← 15 – 25 MINS FROM CAR PARK (MAP 6)   W

MAP 5

ROUTE GUIDE AND MAPS

013

NOT THIS
WAY!

WATER
TAP

PASS IN FRONT OF HOUSES,
KEEPING FARMYARD TO
THE SOUTH

NICE VIEWS

6

FARMYARD   15 – 25 MINS TO CAR PARK (MAP 6) →   E

Beacon Hill The highlight of this stage appears rather unexpectedly at the top of Beacon Hill (Map 6), a National Nature Reserve and the first real taste of steep downland scenery. The view over the Meon Valley to Old Winchester Hill is a fine reward. Beacon Hill is one of a number of hills in southern England where beacons or bonfires were lit to warn of invasions, most notably in the 16th century because of the Spanish Armada. It was lit more recently, in June 2012, as part of the celebrations for Queen Elizabeth II's Diamond Jubilee.

W ← EXTON TO WINCHESTER   MAPS 6-1

Though most walkers will probably be eager to get to the end by now, these final **12 miles (19.5km, 4¼-6hrs)** are not without their charms for those prepared to dally awhile. The initial climb out of **Exton** to **Beacon Hill** (Map 6), a National Nature Reserve, is perhaps the stiffest, though the kites and kestrels that follow your progress from above are a welcome distraction. Thereafter the route continues along a combination of hedge-lined paths and country lanes, via the turn-off to the village of **Cheriton** (Map 4a; p82) and straight through **Chilcomb** (Map 2) to the final 'bump' along the trail, **Cheesefoot Head** (Map 2), after which the South Downs Way admirably does its best to avoid schlepping through the suburbs on its way into **Winchester** (Map 1; see p76) – the City Mill – and the end of your adventure.

EXTON   MAP 6

The Meon valley is known for its natural beauty and also for the Meon villages, all of which claim to be the prettiest in the area. Exton is the smallest of them, if you discount the adjoining hamlets of Meonstoke and Corhampton, and dates back to at least AD940 when it was first mentioned in official documents. It also merited an entry in the Domesday Book of 1086, described as a hamlet of one church and two mills.

Several readers have recommended comfortable, walker-friendly *Crossways B&B* (☎ 07904-047679, 🖥 crosswaysb. com; 1D/T or Tr en suite). They charge from £65pp for two in the room (reduction on full rate for sgl occ) for **B&B** in the self-contained annexe which has its own kitchen. Cake on arrival and you make your own breakfast with everything provided – even for a full English!

The Shoe Inn (☎ 01489-877526, 🖥 theshoeexton.co.uk; **fb**; 🐾; food Mon-Fri noon-2.30pm & 6-9pm, Sat noon-3pm & 6-9pm, Sun noon-3pm & 6-8.30pm) is a friendly village pub with real ales and good **food** though it's closed 3-6pm during the week. It offers sandwiches (£9.35), pastries and soups at lunchtime, while the main menu includes lamb shoulder (£19.95); they always have a vegan option too. Booking is advised in the evenings. The pub's name derives from the building next door which was once the village cobbler's.

CORHAMPTON/MEONSTOKE MAP 6

A short distance south of Exton, Corhampton and nearby Meonstoke are useful for a village shop and a good place to stay. If you do stay down here note that there's a shortcut back to the South Downs Way following the disused railway track (see Map 7).

Meonstoke Village Store (☎ 01489-877374, 🖥 meonstokepostofficeandvillage stores.co.uk; Mon-Sat 6am-5.30pm, Sun 7am-noon) incorporates the **post office** (Mon-Fri 9am-5.30pm, Sat to 12.30pm) and is 500m south of Exton. There's a good range of local produce here.

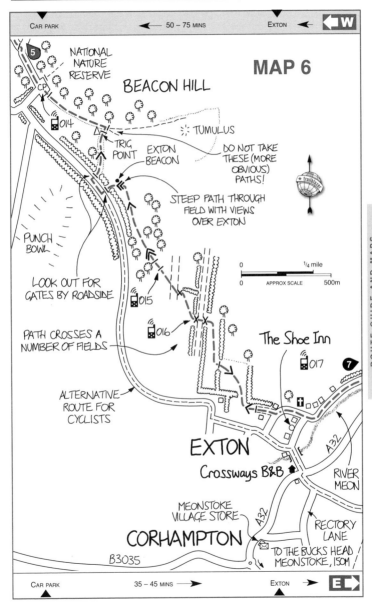

5

NATIONAL NATURE RESERVE

CP

BEACON HILL

MAP 6

014

☀ TUMULUS

TRIG POINT

EXTON BEACON

DO NOT TAKE THESE (MORE OBVIOUS) PATHS!

trailblazer

STEEP PATH THROUGH FIELD WITH VIEWS OVER EXTON

PUNCH BOWL

0 ¼ mile
0 APPROX SCALE 500m

LOOK OUT FOR GATES BY ROADSIDE

015

PATH CROSSES A NUMBER OF FIELDS

016

The Shoe Inn

017

7

ALTERNATIVE ROUTE FOR CYCLISTS

✝

EXTON

Crossways B&B

A32

RIVER MEON

MEONSTOKE VILLAGE STORE

CORHAMPTON

B3035

A32

RECTORY LANE

TO THE BUCKS HEAD MEONSTOKE, 150M

ROUTE GUIDE AND MAPS

The Bucks Head (☎ 01489-877313, 🖥 thebucksheadmeonstoke.co.uk; **fb**; food Wed-Sun noon-3pm, Wed-Sat 6-9pm, Sun to 8.30pm; 🐾), on Bucks Head Hill, is another welcoming pub and they also offer **B&B** (2T/3D, all en suite; 🛏; Ⓛ) from £60pp (sgl occ £95). Follow the A32 south and turn first left onto Bucks Head Hill.

E➔ EXTON TO BURITON   MAPS 6-10

This fine stretch of the Way covering **12½ miles (20km, 4½hrs-6hrs)** takes the walker beside **Old Winchester Hill** (Map 7), the top of which boasts one of the finest Iron Age hill-fort sites in the south. The path skirts around the southern side of the fort – you have to pass through a gate to enter the site itself – but there is a more direct trail (see Map 7) that goes straight to the heart of the fort from the path.

Following a flying visit to the friendly fly-fisherman of **Meon Springs** (Map 8), and after the turn off to the gorgeous village of **East Meon** (Map 8a)

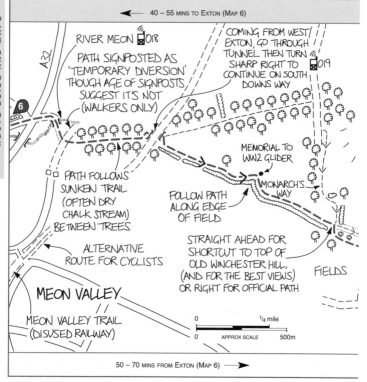

there is a tough pull up the slope for about two miles to **The Sustainability Centre** (Map 9, p92). It is around here that the true line of the Downs begins, stretching east as a high-level ridge, interrupted only by a few river valleys, all the way to Beachy Head near Eastbourne.

The Way continues along the broad ridge with fine views over the Meon valley to the north culminating in the highest point of the South Downs at **Butser Hill** (270m), another National Nature Reserve. From the car park, which has toilets and a **snack shop** (Map 10), the Way slopes down towards the less-than-attractive A3 dual carriageway that slices through the lower flanks.

Once past the din of racing traffic the path climbs steadily back to the top of the downland escarpment above Buriton, passing through **Queen Elizabeth Country Park** (Map 10; see box p94), a magnificent natural mixed woodland that covers the rolling Downs for miles around, just as it has done through the centuries. If the accommodation in **Buriton** is booked up you could head into **Petersfield** (Map 10a, p99), where there are several more places.

ROUTE GUIDE AND MAPS

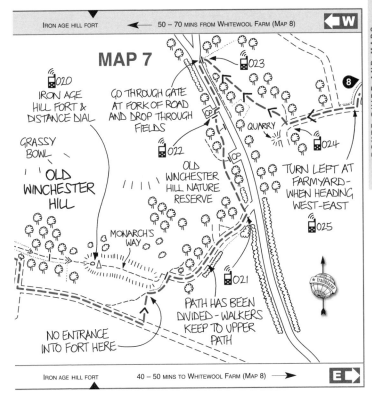

IRON AGE HILL FORT   ← 50 – 70 MINS FROM WHITEWOOL FARM (MAP 8)   ◄ W

MAP 7

☎ 020
IRON AGE
HILL FORT &
DISTANCE DIAL

GO THROUGH GATE
AT FORK OF ROAD
AND DROP THROUGH
FIELDS

☎ 023

8

GRASSY
BOWL

OLD
WINCHESTER
HILL

☎ 022

OLD
WINCHESTER
HILL NATURE
RESERVE

QUARRY

☎ 024

TURN LEFT AT
FARMYARD –
WHEN HEADING
WEST-EAST

☎ 025

MONARCH'S
WAY

☎ 021

PATH HAS BEEN
DIVIDED – WALKERS
KEEP TO UPPER
PATH

★ trailblazer

NO ENTRANCE
INTO FORT HERE

IRON AGE HILL FORT   40 – 50 MINS TO WHITEWOOL FARM (MAP 8) →   E ►

Old Winchester Hill A typical downland hill of chalk grassland and steep ancient woodland and a National Nature Reserve. The top of the hill boasts one of the finest **Iron Age hill-fort** (Map 7) sites in the south. The old earthworks clearly mark the outline of the fort and a display board has an artist's impression of how it once would have looked when the earthy banks were lined with the wooden stakes that formed the walls of the fort. It is clear why it was positioned here since the views in all directions are spectacular, stretching as far as the Isle of Wight on a clear day. Presumably the soldiers of the time also appreciated the views for the strategic advantage it gave them.

Right on the SDW is the welcoming *Meon Springs* (Map 8), where you can stop for sustenance or for the night. There is a **water tap** here.

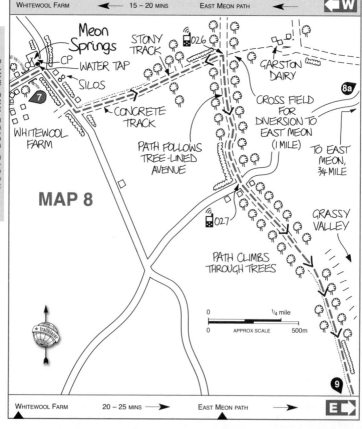

MAP 8

WHITEWOOL FARM ← 15 – 20 MINS EAST MEON PATH ← W

WHITEWOOL FARM 20 – 25 MINS → EAST MEON PATH → E

MEON SPRINGS   MAP 8

Fly-fishery *Meon Springs* (Map 8; ☎ 01730-823134, 🖥 meonsprings.com) plays host to a new café-cum-bistro, *Zed & Bolly's* (🖥 zedandbolly.com; daily 10am-6pm up to 9pm), where you can pick up breakfast baps (from £4.80), coffee, cake, and more hearty fare lunches (around £8-10) throughout the day.

You can also **camp** (phone to book; from £10 per pitch & 2 hikers; 🐾) here with your own tent. There's a toilet and washing facilities but no showers. Campers can just turn up but occasionally they are fully booked so it's worth phoning ahead.

They also have six **yurts** (sleep up to 5) and five **shepherd's huts** (5 x 1D; adults only) too, with complicated pricing but starting from around £90pp (see calendar online; min 2 nights).

EAST MEON   MAP 8a

East Meon is only a half-hour detour from the official path and is well worth the effort for a lunch stop or overnight stay. There are records of a settlement here as far back as AD400 and the whole area was once a royal estate belonging to King Alfred. If in the village, take a look at the 900-year-old **church** at the foot of the hill where you can also admire the 14th-century **courthouse**, once part of a monastery.

The **post office** (Mon-Fri 9am-5.30pm, Sat to 12.30pm) and **East Meon Stores** (Mon-Fri 7am-6pm, Sat to 5pm, Sun 8am-1pm) share premises on the High St.

In the centre of the village, *Ye Olde*

George Inn (☎ 01730-823481, 🖥 yeolde georgeinn.net; 🐾) does upmarket pub **food** (Mon-Sat noon-2.15pm & 6-9pm, Sun noon-3pm & 6-8.30pm: booking recommended at weekends) with prices to match; mains £15-29 and even sandwiches are £12-16. They also offer **B&B** (4D/1T, all en suite; 🍽; (L); 🐾) for £47.50-67.50pp (sgl occ from £85-95). Note, the pub is closed 3-6pm Monday to Friday but open all day at weekends.

The Long House (off Map 8 & Map 8a; ☎ 07889 640353, ☎ 01730-823239, 🖥 thelonghouseeastmeon.co.uk; 2D/1D or T adjacent private bathroom; 🍽; 🐾; (L)) lies

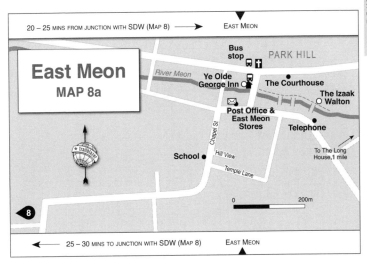

just round the corner from the end of Frogmore Lane, about a mile from the village on the Ramsdean road. **B&B** in this friendly place, with possibly the world's most powerful showers, costs from £45pp (sgl occ £55).

The Izaak Walton (☎ 01730-823252, 🖳 www.theizaakwalton.com; **fb**; pub menu Tue-Sat noon-2pm, Fri & Sat 6-8pm, Sun noon-3pm; café/light menu daily from 10am; 🐾) is named after a famous local angler and has recently undergone a bit of a transformation. The new landlord has divided the entire place in two, with one part now done out as a café, while the other half remains a pub. It doesn't actually matter where you sit, however, for you can drink alcohol in the café and consume coffee and cake in the pub. It's a great place, with a wonderful selection of homemade cakes! Hot food is cheaper than at Ye Olde George Inn, too, with mains starting from just £9.95 (for the homemade lentil cottage pie) and lunchtime paninis from £7.50 – outstanding value.

The No 67 **bus** service (Winchester–Petersfield) stops here. See p46 for details.

The Sustainability Centre (Map 9) Set in 55 acres of woodland, this independent learning and study centre is an award-winning social enterprise charity.

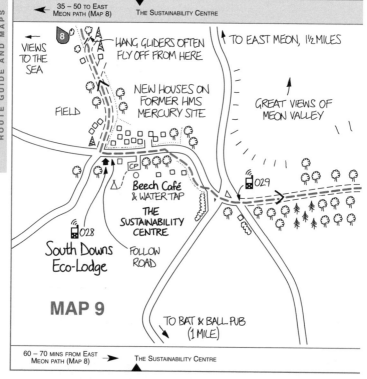

ROUTE GUIDE AND MAPS

35 – 50 TO EAST MEON path (MAP 8)
THE SUSTAINABILITY CENTRE

VIEWS TO THE SEA

HANG GLIDERS OFTEN FLY OFF FROM HERE

↑ TO EAST MEON, 1½ MILES

NEW HOUSES ON FORMER HMS MERCURY SITE

GREAT VIEWS OF MEON VALLEY

FIELD

CP

Beech Café & WATER TAP

029

THE SUSTAINABILITY CENTRE

028

South Downs Eco-Lodge

FOLLOW ROAD

MAP 9

TO BAT & BALL PUB (1 MILE)

60 – 70 MINS FROM EAST MEON path (MAP 8) →
THE SUSTAINABILITY CENTRE

As you'd expect from the name, everything here is environmentally friendly and they use renewable energy. This is also the location of *South Downs Eco Lodge & Camping* (see below), where you can choose from four different **accommodation** options: camping, yurts, hostel or B&B, and the *Beech Café*, right on the Way.

AROUND BUTSER HILL   MAP 9

At *South Downs Eco Lodge & Camping* (☎ 01730-823549, 🖳 sustainability-centre .org) **campers** (£15pp; 🐕 on lead) will appreciate the fact that they allow camp fires in designated areas (and they sell firewood). They also have **yurts** sleeping 2-4 people (Apr-Oct only, booking essential; min 2 nights at weekends; £80-130); bedding is provided and the rate includes a batch of firewood for the heater. The (solar) shower block is open April to October; running water and compost toilets are available all year.

The rate for the **hostel** accommodation (2T/10Tr/1 x 5-bed 'suite', shared facilities) is on a room basis (£60/90/100). Booking (online, see website) is recommended as the hostel is sometimes taken over by groups for sole occupancy use. The hostel has self-catering facilities with a

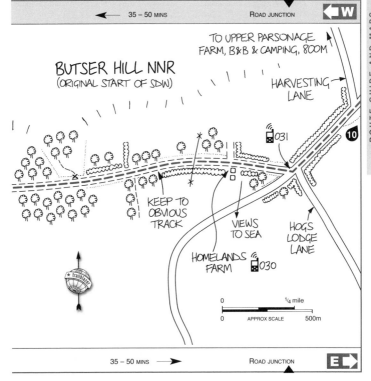

ROUTE GUIDE AND MAPS

← 35 – 50 MINS   ROAD JUNCTION   ◄W

BUTSER HILL NNR
(ORIGINAL START OF SDW)

TO UPPER PARSONAGE
FARM, B&B & CAMPING, 800M

HARVESTING LANE

031

10

KEEP TO OBVIOUS TRACK

VIEWS TO SEA

HOGS LODGE LANE

HOMELANDS FARM   030

0   ¼ mile
0   APPROX SCALE   500m

35 – 50 MINS →   ROAD JUNCTION   E►

well-equipped kitchen, dining area and lounge.

They also now offer **B&B** (1S/4D/4T/ 2Qd, all en suite) in their eco lodge; rates (£75/S, £122/D or T, £157/Qd) are per room and include a continental breakfast. They have deliberately not put TVs in the rooms, in line with the focus of getting guests outside as much as possible!

The Sustainability Centre also has the excellent *Beech Café* (☎ 01730-823755, ☐ thebeechcafe.co.uk; Wed-Sun & Bank Hol Mon 8.30am-4pm, breakfast 8.30-10am, lunches from 11.30am; Ⓛ; 🐾 on lead), a vegetarian and vegan café which can provide packed lunches if pre-ordered.

If you're staying here and need an evening meal, the closest pub that does food is the popular *Bat & Ball* (off Map 9; ☎ 023-9263 2692, ☐ batandballclanfield .co.uk; **fb**; food Mon-Sat noon-9pm, Sun to 8pm; 🐾 bar only), about half an hour's walk to the south, just before the village of Hambledon. Top notch food includes the likes of pan-roasted lamb rump with a sweet potato and chorizo rösti (£28).

If you're walking east, before you reach the car park at the top of the hill, a signpost directs you north towards *Upper Parsonage Farm* (off Map 9; ☎ 01730-823490, ☐ upperparsonagefarm.co.uk, **fb**; Ⓛ), about half a mile from the Way, on Harvesting Lane. This 1400-acre farm has **accommodation** in either a large garden **room** (1D en suite, from £50pp, sgl occ £70, min 2 nights), or in a cosy **shepherd's hut** in the garden (1D, toilet & shower facilities; from £75, sgl occ £50); both are room only, no breakfast. You can also **camp** (£15-20pp) in the garden; each pitch has its own toilets and shower facilities. Dogs are allowed in the shepherd's hut and campsite. And they will even lend you a bike to get you to the pub a bit quicker!

Butser Hill This **National Nature Reserve** earned its status for its fine chalk grassland. It is home to over 30 species of butterfly including the tiny, difficult-to-spot but exquisite chalkhill blue (see p64). It was also the original start/end point for the South Downs Way before it was decided to extend the path all the way to Winchester. There's a snack hut here, *The Roundhouse* (Map 10; Thur-Sun 9am-3pm), that provides a more peaceful alternative to the visitor centre café in Queen Elizabeth Country Park.

Queen Elizabeth Country Park The South Downs Way cuts right through the heart of this vast protected area which includes the chalk downland of Butser Hill. To the east of the hill the park is dominated by one of the largest expanses of unbroken woodland cover in the South-East, comprising both ancient broadleaved wood and beech and conifer plantations.

❑ **QUEEN ELIZABETH COUNTRY PARK**   **Map 10, p96**

The park (open all the time) is popular with daytrippers and picnickers largely thanks to its proximity to the main A3 road. The **Visitor Centre** (☐ hants.gov.uk/qecp; **fb**; Mar-Oct Mon-Fri 10am-5pm, Sat & Sun from 9am, Nov-Feb Mon-Fri 10am-4pm, Sat & Sun 9am-4pm) can provide maps and guides to the park. The centre houses a **shop** and *café* offering cakes and snacks, and there's a water tap outside.

Stagecoach's No 37 **bus** (see p46; Havant–Petersfield) stops on the A3. The northbound stop lies just beyond the slip road under the A3 (the slip road needs to be used with care). Access to the park from the stop on the south side is no problem. Either way this is a **request stop** so make sure you let the driver know you want to stop here and also if you are waiting at the bus stop make sure you can be seen.

BURITON   MAP 10, p97

Buriton is yet another pretty village com-
manding an enviable position at the foot of
the wooded downland escarpment. The
Church of St Mary, by the duck pond, is
of particular interest as the interior dates
back to the 12th century.

Formerly The Village Inn, *The Nest
Hotel* (☎ 01730-233440, 🖳 thenesthotelbu
riton.co.uk; 8D/5T/1Tr en suite; 🍺) is now
a supremely busy hotel and restaurant (food
Wed-Fri noon-3pm & 6-9pm, Sat noon-
9pm, Sun noon-3pm; pub closed Mon &
Tue) that's packing in the punters with its

winning combination of decent pub grub
(mains from £16.50, sandwiches & jacket
potatoes from £12) and a friendly welcome.
Rooms start at £50pp including a continental breakfast (sgl occ full room rate).

The Five Bells (☎ 01730-263584, 🖳
fivebells-buriton.co.uk; food Mon-Sat
noon-3pm & 6-9pm, Sun noon-4pm; 🐾
bar only) is a great pub with friendly staff
and excellent **food** (most mains cost around
£14-24).

AMK's No 94 **bus** operates between
here and Petersfield. See p47 for details.

PETERSFIELD   MAP 10a, p99

This market town still retains pockets of
charm, despite attempts to turn it into
something bland and modern with supermarkets and a small shopping arcade.

An oasis of calm amongst the bustle is
afforded by **Petersfield Physic Garden** (🖳
petersfieldphysicgarden.org.uk; Mon-Sat
9am-5pm, Sun 10am-4pm; free), reached
via an alley off the High St. It features many
of the characteristics and plant varieties of a
17th-century town garden with herbs, topiary and an orchard and plenty of benches to

relax on with your takeaway lunch.

Walkers on a day off might fancy a dip
in Petersfield's **heated open-air swimming
pool** (☎ 01730-265143, 🖳 petersfield
pool.org; open spring to autumn; from
£4/30 mins, £7/1hr) on Tor Way. See the
website for more details on opening times.

The other main tourist attraction in
town, **Petersfield Museum** (☎ 01730-
262601, 🖳 petersfieldmuseum.co.uk; Tue-
Sat 10am-5pm; £8), is largely housed in a
Victorian police station, which before that

W ← BURITON TO EXTON   MAPS 10-6

This fine stretch of the Way covering **12½ miles (20km, 4½-6hrs)** takes in a
couple of notable hills. There's a lengthy perambulation around the perimeter
of the **Queen Elizabeth Country Park** (QECP; Map 10) and a crossing of the
A3 – a metaphorical low point immediately preceding a literal high point, for
Butser Hill (Map 9) is actually the highest point on the entire trail. The path
then meanders to the second major elevation, **Old Winchester Hill** (Map 7),
lying just east of Exton and topped by a fine Iron Age hill-fort. Apparently it's
one of the finest examples in the South according to experts, though I daresay
the average walker will find the gentle bumps in the ground more curious than
jaw-dropping. The official path, incidentally, actually skirts around the fort's
southern side, and descends in a rather circuitous fashion, though there is a more
direct and popular descent (see Map 7) that leaves from the centre of the fort.

Given these hills, it's hardly surprising that there a couple of fairly brutal
ascents on this stage. But mercifully there are also several places to stop, rest
and snack along the way, including cafés at: QECP; the top of Butser Hill; **The
Sustainability Centre** (Map 9); and at the friendly fishing centre of **Meon
Springs** (Map 8).   *[Next route overview p86]*

ROUTE GUIDE AND MAPS

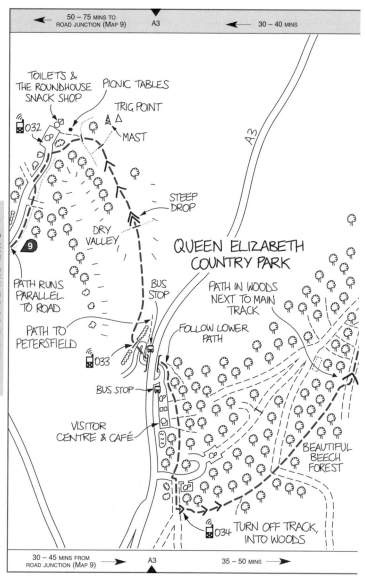

TOILETS & THE ROUNDHOUSE SNACK SHOP

PICNIC TABLES

TRIG POINT

032

CP

MAST

STEEP DROP

DRY VALLEY

QUEEN ELIZABETH COUNTRY PARK

9

PATH RUNS PARALLEL TO ROAD

BUS STOP

PATH IN WOODS NEXT TO MAIN TRACK

PATH TO PETERSFIELD

FOLLOW LOWER PATH

033

BUS STOP

CP

VISITOR CENTRE & CAFÉ

CP

BEAUTIFUL BEECH FOREST

CP

034 TURN OFF TRACK, INTO WOODS

The Nest

The Five Bells

BUS STOP

HANGERS WAY

10 MINS TO BURITON

10a

TO PETERSFIELD, 2½ MILES

NORTH LANE

PITCROFT LANE

CHURCH OF ST MARY

BURITON

CHALK PIT

SOUTH LANE

HALLS HILL

CP

FIELD

036

11

BENCHES WITH GOOD VIEWS

HANGER'S WAY

SUE & KAREN'S TREAT TABLE

037

035

AT END OF LANE CONTINUE ALONG FARM TRACK

MAP 10

★ trailblazer

| 0 | | ¼ mile |
| 0 | APPROX SCALE | 500m |

ROUTE GUIDE AND MAPS

was a court house, and exhibitions include a collection of 175 years of truncheons and handcuffs from Hampshire Constabulary; the former police cells and the court house can be visited. The Flora Twort Gallery houses many of the Petersfield-inspired watercolours and pastels of the late artist.

Services
The **Tourist Information Centre** (☎ 01730-264182, 🖳 visitpetersfield.co.uk; Mon-Fri 9am-5pm) is in the town hall on Heath Rd. They have information about accommodation but can't do any bookings.

The **library** (Mon-Wed & Fri-Sat 9.30am-5pm, Thur to 1.30pm; free WI-FI) has **internet** access plus places where you can charge your laptop or phone.

On the High St there are various **banks** with ATMs, as well as a Boots **pharmacy** (Mon-Sat 9am-5.30pm, Sun 10am-4pm). For a **supermarket** stock-up, the M&S Foodhall (Mon-Fri 8am-8pm, Sat to 7pm, Sun 10am-4pm) is also on the High St, while just off it to the north is a large Waitrose (Mon-Sat 7.30am-8pm, Sun 10am-4pm) and there's a large Tesco south of the town centre (Mon-Fri 8am-10pm, Sat to 9pm, Sun 10am-4pm).

The **post office** (Mon-Fri 9am-5.30pm, Sat 9am-12.30pm) is on the edge of The Square. There are two good bookshops: **Waterstones** (Mon-Sat 9am-5.30pm, Sun 10am-4pm) in Rams Walk, and round the corner on Lavant St the independent **One Tree Books** (Mon-Sat 9am-5pm), which also has a nice *café* (see Where to eat).

On The Square there's a branch of the **hiking store** Mountain Warehouse (Mon-Sat 9am-5.30pm, Sun 10am-4pm).

Public transport
Petersfield is a stop on South Western Railway's London Waterloo to Portsmouth **train** service (see box p44).

Buses leaving from the town centre include: Stagecoach services No 54 (to Chichester); Nos 91, 92 & 93 (to Midhurst); No 67 (to Winchester), No 37 (to Havant), and No 38 (to Alton); and AMK's No 94 (to Buriton). See pp46-8 for details.

For a **taxi** or luggage transfer contact:

14U cars (☎ 01730-300738, ☎ 07795-101895, 🖳 14ucarspetersfield.com).

Where to stay
Campers will have to trudge 1¼ miles (2km) out of town to reach the very basic *Ridge Farm Campsite* (off Map 10a; ☎ 07850-873055; 🐾), where a field and two portaloo toilets await those who wish to pitch their tent (£10pp). The turn-off for the campsite is about 200 metres past *The Cricketers Inn* (off Map 10a; ☎ 01730-261035, 🖳 cricketersinn.com; **fb**; 🐾; food Tue-Sat noon-3pm & 6-9pm, Sun noon-4pm). To get to the campsite, walk north-west along Station Rd, turn right at the roundabout up Bell Hill, and keep walking straight, over the A3 dual carriageway, and past The Cricketers Inn before taking the next left turn down a country track.

At 80 Rushes Rd, just west of the railway station, *Rushes Road B&B* (off Map 10a; ☎ 01730-261638; 1D or T private bathroom; 🖢; ⓛ) is run by a friendly former tour guide. B&B costs from £45pp (sgl occ £70); note that they do not accept card payment. From Swan St, walk under the railway bridge, turn left onto Rushes Rd then take the next right.

The Old Drum (☎ 01730-300208, 🖳 theolddrum.com; 1S/4D/1Qd, all en suite) is a beautiful 18th-century inn, now a boutique hotel with very smart rooms. B&B costs from £62.50pp (sgl from £100).

Where to eat and drink
Petersfield is replete with eating places; some of them are excellent, particularly the town's independent cafés.

Cafés Snug and rightly popular, *Natural Food Deli* (☎ 01730-858183, 🖳 thenatural fooddeli.co.uk; Mon-Sat 8.30am-4pm; 🐾 bar area) is a health-conscious café with rustic décor, wholesome food and great tea, coffee and cakes. Close to the railway station, *Madeleine's Delicatessen* (☎ 01730-260102, 🖳 madeleineskitchen.co.uk; Mon-Sat 8.30am-5pm) is another great place for filled sandwiches and baguettes; you can eat in here too. Nearby, **One Tree Books** (see Services) has a *café* (Mon-Sat 9am-

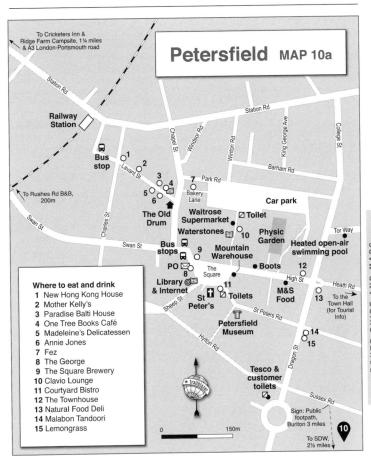

Petersfield MAP 10a

Where to eat and drink
1 New Hong Kong House
2 Mother Kelly's
3 Paradise Balti House
4 One Tree Books Café
5 Madeleine's Delicatessen
6 Annie Jones
7 Fez
8 The George
9 The Square Brewery
10 Clavio Lounge
11 Courtyard Bistro
12 The Townhouse
13 Natural Food Deli
14 Malabon Tandoori
15 Lemongrass

5pm, food until 2.30pm) at the back of the shop. Beside St Peter's Church, *Courtyard Bistro* (daily 8am-5pm) is tiny but has extra seating outdoors, overlooking The Square. There's a good choice of breakfasts here.

Pubs *The Square Brewery* (☎ 01730-264291, ☐ squarebrewery.co.uk; food Mon-Sat 11am-3pm & 6-9pm, Tue-Sat 11am-3pm, Sun noon-3pm; 🐾) is a welcoming, locals-favourite, Fuller's-owned pub, and a popular venue for live music.

Also on The Square, *The George* (☎ 01730-265551, **fb**; food Sun-Thur 10am-8.30pm, Fri & Sat to 8pm; 🐾) is a pub and restaurant which feels more like a city bar than a market-town pub, but is popular nonetheless. Back on High St you'll find award-winning *The Townhouse* (☎ 01730-265630, ☐ townhousepetersfield.co.uk; **fb**; 🐾; food Mon-Tue noon-3pm, Wed-Thur noon-3pm & 5-9pm, Fri & Sat to 9.30pm, Sun noon-4pm) which bills itself these days as a 'Bar & Restaurant' rather than a pub.

The menu is quite pricey though there's no doubting the quality of the food.

Restaurants & takeaways One of the coolest places to eat is tucked away down narrow Bakery Lane: *Fez* (☎ 01730-231266, 🖥 fezpetersfield.com; daily noon-9.30pm) is a Turkish restaurant, meze bar and café rolled into one and is a great place for lunch, an evening meal, or even just a coffee. Mains start at £15.95 for the Turkish equivalent of a pizza, *lahmacun*.

Nearby, on Lavant St, newly refurbished *Annie Jones* (☎ 01730-923110, 🖥 anniejones.co.uk; **fb**) is now a French restaurant and cocktail bar (Tue-Thur 5-9pm, Fri & Sat noon-3pm & 5-9.30pm, Sun noon-3pm) with good food (such as *moules frites* for £18) and a pleasant atmosphere.

Clavio Lounge (☎ 01730-763177, 🖥 thelounges.co.uk/clavio; Sun-Thur 9am-11pm, Fri & Sat to midnight) is in the Rams Walk arcade, off the High St. A typically large, loud and flamboyantly decorated

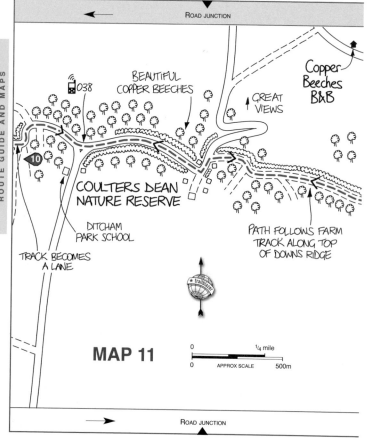

ROAD JUNCTION

ROUTE GUIDE AND MAPS

038

BEAUTIFUL
COPPER BEECHES

Copper
Beeches
B&B

GREAT
VIEWS

10

COULTERS DEAN
NATURE RESERVE

PATH FOLLOWS FARM
TRACK ALONG TOP
OF DOWNS RIDGE

DITCHAM
PARK SCHOOL

TRACK BECOMES
A LANE

trailblazer

MAP 11

0   1/4 mile
0   APPROX SCALE   500m

ROAD JUNCTION

branch of the Lounge chain, there's an extensive menu of tasty, exotic and inexpensive fare (mains from £10.95).

At 16-18 Dragon St, *Lemongrass* (☎ 01730-267077, 🖥 lemongrassrestaurants.co .uk/petersfield; daily noon-2.30pm & 5.30-10.30pm) is a good quality Thai restaurant with dishes such as green curry from £12.95. Next door *Malabon Tandoori* (☎ 01730-268352, 🖥 malabon.co.uk; Sat-Thur noon-2.30pm & 5-10pm, Fri 5-11pm only) serves Indian & Bangladeshi meals to eat-

in or takeaway. For a smarter Indian-food option, try *The Paradise Balti House* (☎ 01730-265162, 🖥 paradisebaltipetersfield .co.uk; Wed, Thur, Sat & Sun noon-2.30pm, daily 5-11pm) at 23 Lavant St. The best Chinese takeaway is *New Hong Kong House* (☎ 01730-265256; Tue-Sun 5-11pm), at 37 Lavant St, while at No 29 there's *Mother Kelly's Famous Fish & Chips* (☎ 01730-265702, 🖥 motherkellys fishandchips.co.uk; Mon 5-9pm, Tue-Sat 11.30am-2pm & 5-9pm).

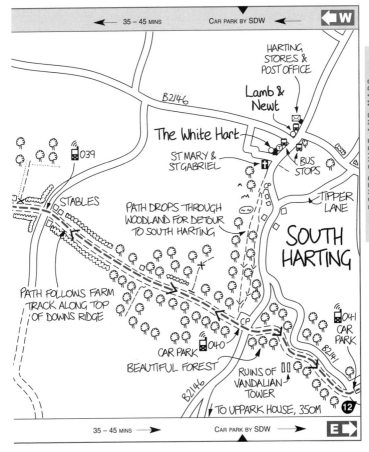

ROUTE GUIDE AND MAPS

❑ **UPPARK HOUSE** (off Map 11, p101)

Uppark House ☎ 01730-825415, 🖥 nationaltrust.org.uk/visit/sussex/uppark-house-and-garden; house Thur-Sun, garden & café daily; £11 house & garden, £8 garden only; café open to ticket holders only) is a magnificent 17th-century country home (though the interior is largely Georgian, ie 18th century) perched high on a hill with extensive views across the Downs and beyond. One of the most remarkable things about Uppark is the near-perfect restoration of the building after it was all but gutted by a rampant fire in 1989.

Note that at the time of going to press **both the house and gardens were closed whilst a major maintenance project is carried out**, so check the website for opening times. The project aims to restore access to previously closed areas of the property.

Stagecoach's No 54 **bus service** calls here (see p46).

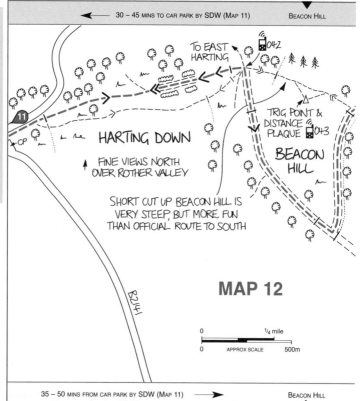

ROUTE GUIDE AND MAPS

E→ BURITON TO COCKING   MAPS 10-14

The route from Buriton follows tracks and lanes along the top of the South
Downs escarpment for **11¼ miles (18km, 3¾-4¾hrs)**. It is very wooded before
reaching **South Harting** (Map 11) so although the views are limited there is
plenty of beautiful shady woodland to enjoy. About 10 minutes south of the Way
where it crosses the B2146 is **Uppark House** (see box opposite).

After South Harting the trees begin to thin out as the Way passes over
Harting Down (Map 12). The views open up over the patchwork fields below
and the path climbs even higher onto **Beacon Hill**, one of two Beacon Hills on
the Way. There then follows another wooded section, the **Monkton Estate**
(Map 13), where it's worth listening out for peacocks, before the path continues
through the pastureland of **Cocking Down**.

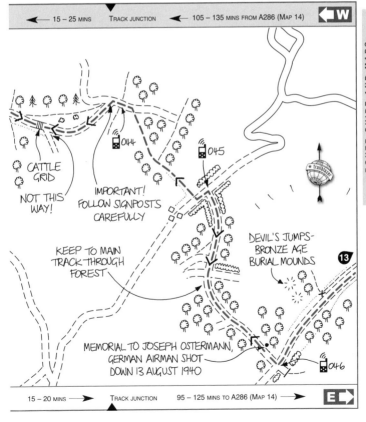

The Way takes you past a large **chalk boulder**, positioned there by the artist Andy Goldsworthy and then down to the main road leading to **Cocking** (Map 14), passing the first of five *Cadence Clubhouses* (see box p107), right on the Way. If the accommodation in Cocking is booked up you could catch a bus to **Midhurst** (p107, off Map 14), where there are other options. There is a bus stop very close to where the Way crosses the A286.

SOUTH HARTING   MAP 11, p101

From the top of Harting Down the village of South Harting, with its distinctive church steeple, is clearly visible and looks very inviting. Note that the road down to the village from the Way has no pavement, so it's much safer, and more pleasant, to use the footpath running parallel to the road and immediately west of it. It's not a long walk but you do have to climb back up the hill through the woods on the return.

The **Church of St Mary & St Gabriel** is interesting and contains an impressive statue of the Archangel Gabriel, by sculptor Philip Jackson, suspended from the ceiling. The **village stocks** are still by the path outside the church.

Harting Stores (☎ 01730-825219, 🖳 hartingstores.co.uk; **fb**; Mon-Fri 7am-6pm, Sat 8am-2pm, Sun to noon) is an excellent village shop, which sells a wide variety of provisions as well as various baked products, wine and beer. It also incorporates the local **post office** (Mon, Tue, Thur & Fri 9am-1pm & 2-5pm, Wed 9am-1pm, Sat 9am-noon).

The upmarket *White Hart* (☎ 01730-825124, 🖳 the-whitehart.co.uk; **fb**; 1T/4D/1Tr/1Qd, all en suite; 🛇; 🐾) offers **B&B** for around £50pp (sgl occ full room rate). It also serves excellent **food** (daily 8am-9pm) such as classic fish pie (£19.75) or pan-fried duck breast (£24).

ROUTE GUIDE AND MAPS

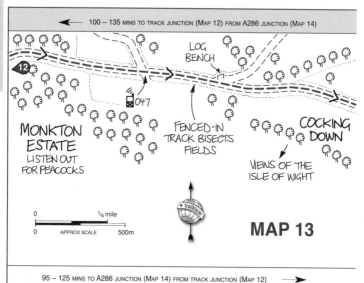

← 100 – 135 MINS TO TRACK JUNCTION (MAP 12) FROM A286 JUNCTION (MAP 14)

LOG BENCH

📱047

12

MONKTON ESTATE
LISTEN OUT FOR PEACOCKS

FENCED-IN TRACK BISECTS FIELDS

COCKING DOWN

VIEWS OF THE ISLE OF WIGHT

0 — ¼ mile
0 — 500m
APPROX SCALE

★ trailblazer

MAP 13

95 – 125 MINS TO A286 JUNCTION (MAP 14) FROM TRACK JUNCTION (MAP 12) →

Visit South Harting church to see Philip Jackson's statue of the Archangel Gabriel.

Near Harting Stores, *Lamb & Newt* (☎ 07787-740254, 🖥 lambandnewt.com; **fb**; Wed-Sat 9am-4pm, Sun 10am-3pm) is a cross between a vintage store and a fine **café**. It's a charming, friendly place where everything, including the furniture, is for sale, and it's a really pleasant addition to the village.

Just over a mile west of South Harting along the Petersfield road (B2146) and directly accessible from the Way (see Map 12), is *Copper Beeches* (☎ 01730-826662, 🖥 copperbeeches.net; 1D/1Qd both en suite; 🍽; Ⓛ; 🐾) with **B&B** from £47.50pp (sgl occ £65, £75 at weekends). The 'quad' has a double bed and bunk beds. During Goodwood events (see box p106) bookings must be for a minimum of three nights.

Stagecoach's No 54 (Petersfield–Chichester) **bus** service calls here as does their No 91 (Midhurst–Petersfield); See pp46-8 for details.

ROUTE GUIDE AND MAPS

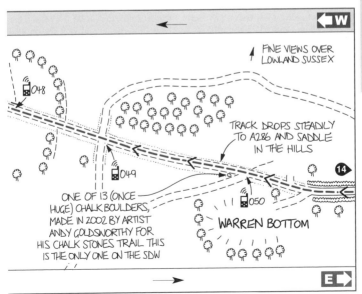

FINE VIEWS OVER LOWLAND SUSSEX

TRACK DROPS STEADILY TO A286 AND SADDLE IN THE HILLS

WARREN BOTTOM

ONE OF 13 (ONCE HUGE) CHALK BOULDERS, MADE IN 2002 BY ARTIST ANDY GOLDSWORTHY FOR HIS CHALK STONES TRAIL THIS IS THE ONLY ONE ON THE SDW

❏ **GLORIOUS GOODWOOD – NOT SO GLORIOUS FOR WALKERS**

Goodwood (🖥 goodwood.com), near Singleton, has long been associated with country pursuits such as horse-racing and shooting but is also host to sports such as flying and motor-racing. The **Festival of Speed**, held every July, celebrates motor sport and is one of many events held here around the year. Other key events are **Goodwood Revival** in early September, and **Glorious Goodwood** horse-racing in late July and early August. Whilst these are probably not of interest to walkers of the South Downs Way, the relevance is that accommodation in the area is often booked up months in advance and significantly pricier at these times so it is worth checking Goodwood's events calendar before you plan your trip.

Compass Travel's No 99 bus service calls here if prebooked (see p47 for details).

COCKING   **MAP 14, p108**

Cocking is pleasant enough but the busy main road that slices the village in two has rather taken the soul out of the place despite one or two pretty, old cottages. The consolation is that it is not too far from the Way. It is best reached by following the farm track (by Manor Farm) down the hill to the village rather than walking along the busy main road, which has no pavement.

Behind The Malthouse you'll find a bronze plinth known as **Cocking History Column**. Containing relief panels detailing the town's history, it was sculpted by local resident Philip Jackson (see also p105) and unveiled in 2005. In the summer Jackson's garden is open to visitors (by appointment only; see 🖥 philipjacksonsculptures.co.uk).

The very small **Cocking Village Shop & Post Office** (☎ 01730-817100, **fb**; shop Mon-Fri 8.30am-5pm, Sat 8am-4pm, Sun 10am-1pm; post office Mon-Fri 8.30am-4pm, Sat 8am-noon), has takeaway sandwiches, pastries and homemade cakes.

The most convenient place to stay, particularly for campers, is on a busy working farm right beside the Way. In addition to rearing sheep, pigs and growing various crops, *Manor Farm* (☎ 01730-814156, 🖥 manorfarmcocking.co.uk; Ⓛ) offers **camping** (Mar/Apr to end Oct; 🐕 on lead) from £10pp for backpackers. If ordered in advance a simple breakfast (eg bacon roll &

W ← COCKING TO BURITON   **MAPS 14-10**

If you've been walking in typically bright South Downs sunshine for the first part of your hike, it may come as a pleasant change to find yourself strolling in some welcome woods (and therefore shade) on this **11¼-mile (18km, 3¾-5hrs) stage**. Though the initial climb out of **Cocking** (Map 14) is on an exposed chalk path – and even takes you past a large **chalk boulder** (Map 13), positioned there by the artist Andy Goldsworthy – thereafter the path plunges into the woodland of the **Monkton Estate**. The first of two **Beacon Hills** on the trail provides some more familiar, open terrain, as does neighbouring **Harting Down** (Map 12), looming above **South Harting** (Map 11), lying to the north of the trail, and **Uppark House**, a short distance to the south of the path. But it's not long before you're back traipsing between the trees of **Coulters Dean Nature Reserve** (Map 11) on the way to the **Buriton** (Map 10; p97) turn-off.

If accommodation in Buriton is unavailable you could head into **Petersfield** (p99), where there are several more options.   *[Next route overview p95]*

hot drink) is available from their farm shop (usually 8-8.30am). They also have accommodation in either a **shepherd's hut** (1D; well-behaved 🐾) or **a log cabin** (1Qd). The cabin has a double bed with a bunk bed above plus a separate sofa bed. Both hut and cabin have private facilities. Rates (from £80/£88/£140 D/T/Qd, from £67 sgl occ) include a continental breakfast. The **farm shop** (Fri-Sun 11am-4pm) sells eggs and home-made sausages as well as sandwiches, drinks and ice-cream.

There's a warm welcome for walkers at *Moonlight Cottage* (☎ 01730-815469, 🖥 moonlightcottage.co.uk; 1D en suite, 3D share bathroom; 🛁; Ⓛ) £57.50-77.50pp. A good continental breakfast is included. There was also once a café here and it may yet reopen.

B&B at the community-owned *The Bluebell Inn* (☎ 01730-239669, 🖥 theblue bellatcocking.co.uk; 1D/2T, all en suite; Ⓛ)

costs from £82.50pp (sgl occ room rate), though they can be as low as £37.50pp if booking on the day – and as high as £165pp during Goodwood events. **Food** (Mon-Sat noon-3pm & 6-8.30pm, Sun noon-3pm) is served most of the day with breakfasts (Mon-Sat 8-10.30am) available in summer too. The menu includes your favourite pub classics (£16-18). Note that if staying here on a Sunday night and you want an evening meal you must arrive and/or order in advance. For cyclists they have an air pump for tired tyres.

If everywhere is booked, you could take Stagecoach's No 60 **bus** to **Midhurst**, about 2½ miles to the north, where there is a wider choice of accommodation. Alternatively, the same number bus southbound goes to **Chichester** where the bus station is opposite the railway station. See pp46-8 for details.

ROUTE GUIDE AND MAPS

> ❏ **CADENCE CLUBHOUSES**
> On the trail, if you're walking from Winchester, Cocking Hill will be your first experience of a *Cadence Clubhouse* (🖥 cadencecycle.club; daily 9am-4pm) – but it won't be your last. A series of five cycle-themed **cafés** – or clubhouses, as they prefer to call them – set right on the trail all along the South Downs Way from here to Eastbourne, the one on Cocking Hill is actually the only permanent structure; all the others are converted shipping containers. The food is great (we love their curried pasties, £5.75), they're dog-friendly, they have wi-fi, basic toilets and water taps, and all in all they're a very welcome addition to the trail.

MIDHURST   off MAP 14, p108

Midhurst (🖥 visitmidhurst.com) has some accommodation options, a good range of places to eat, a Sainsbury's **supermarket** and a Tesco Express **convenience store** (daily 6am-10pm) with an **ATM** outside, and other services should you find yourself here.

The friendly *Pear Tree Cottage* (☎ 01730-817216, 🖥 peartreecottagebandb midhurst.co.uk; 1T or D/1D plus 4ft sofa bed, both en suite) is on Lamberts Lane. B&B costs from £45-47.50pp (sgl occ full room rate); during Goodwood events (see box p106) the rate is from £60pp but they are likely to be fully booked anyhow. The rooms are self-contained and have a fridge,

microwave, toaster and kettle; the twin can sleep an additional child and the double can accommodate up to four people. The ingredients for a continental breakfast are left in the room the night before. Although they don't provide packed lunches there is often enough food in the breakfast for guests to make one, or alternatively stock up at the nearby Tesco Express or **Midhurst Bakery** (fb; Mon-Sat 7am-4pm, Sun to 3pm), opposite the bus station.

Several **bus services** operate from the bus station on North St to: Worthing (No 1), Chichester (No 60), Haslemere (No 70) and Petersfield (Nos 91, 92 & 93), all of which have railway stations. See pp47-8 for details.

❏ THE TWO COWDRAY GOLD CUPS

The Cowdray Estate is probably best known for the Polo Club and the polo matches (both national and international) held there during the year; the main event is the Gold Cup which is held in July.

The second 'Gold Cup' refers to the colour of the paint seen on the window frames and doors of cottages and buildings that are part of the estate, particularly around Midhurst. The 'cowardy custard' yellow, as some locals call it, was first used on the cottages by the 2nd Viscount Cowdray who was a Liberal MP (yellow being the colour particularly associated with the Liberal Party), thus it was a good way of promoting the Liberal Party. The paint was made specially for the Viscount and was originally called 'Cowdray Gold' but is now known as 'Gold Cup', though it is not exactly the same shade as the original colour.

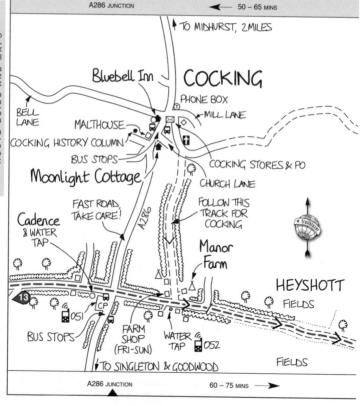

ROUTE GUIDE AND MAPS

E→ COCKING TO AMBERLEY

MAPS 14-18

It is **12 miles (19.5km, 3¾-5¼hrs)** from the Cocking turn off to the Amberley turn off. From the main road south of Cocking, the Way follows a chalk lane, climbing steadily through fields to rejoin the high escarpment.

There is a **water tap** (Map 14) by the farm buildings. Just after that you will notice that the window frames on the cottages here are painted yellow; this shows they are part of the Cowdray Estate (see box opposite). The track here used to be bordered on one side by dense woodland and on the other by a high hedge so the view was somewhat obscured in parts but the former South Downs Joint Committee and Graffham Down Trust created a wildlife corridor in order to link up two rich grassland sites: **Heyshott Down** (Map 14) and **Graffham Down** (Map 15).

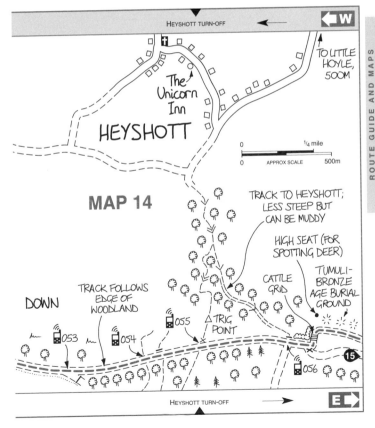

ROUTE GUIDE AND MAPS

The path passes a **Bronze Age burial ground** (Map 14) with **tumuli** clearly visible among the tussocks of grass; it continues on through a mixture of woodland and grassland, passing the turn-off for **Graffham** (Map 15a; see p112).

Climbing back up towards **Bignor Hill** (Map 17) the views open out spectacularly to the south. The rather outlandish-looking tent structure visible by the coast is the Butlins holiday complex at Bognor Regis. Of far greater interest is **Stane St**, the Roman road built around AD50 to connect Noviomagus (Chichester) with Londinium (London). It's well worth going down to **Bignor** (Map 17a; see p115) from here to see the mosaics at **Bignor Roman Villa** (see box p116). Continuing along the Way, there are sensational views to the east along the length of the Downs. Follow the route down into the Arun valley for

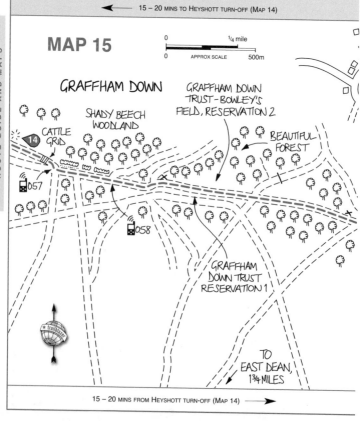

ROUTE GUIDE AND MAPS

← 15 – 20 MINS TO HEYSHOTT turn-off (MAP 14)

MAP 15

0   ¼ mile
0   APPROX SCALE   500m

GRAFFHAM DOWN

GRAFFHAM DOWN TRUST - BOWLEY'S FIELD, RESERVATION 2

SHADY BEECH WOODLAND

CATTLE GRID

14

BEAUTIFUL FOREST

📱057

📱058

GRAFFHAM DOWN TRUST RESERVATION 1

trailblazer

TO EAST DEAN, 1¾ MILES

15 – 20 MINS FROM HEYSHOTT turn-off (MAP 14) →

the villages of **Houghton Bridge** and **Amberley**, both on Map 18. If you have time it is well worth visiting **Arundel** (Map 18a; see p123), about five miles further south along the River Arun. You can reach it by following the riverside footpath but it's quicker to jump on the train (see p44).

Heyshott Down Heyshott Down is one of several nature reserves in this area managed by the **Murray Downland Trust** (see p60). The best view is probably from the **trig point** (Map 14), about 50m off the path.

HEYSHOTT **MAP 14, p109**

It's a steep and sometimes muddy descent from the Way, but Heyshott does have a smart country pub. *The Unicorn Inn* (☎

01730-813486, 🖥 unicorn-innheyshott.co .uk; **fb**; food Mon-Sat noon-2pm, Tue-Sat 6-9pm, Sun noon-2.30pm; 🐕 bar area &

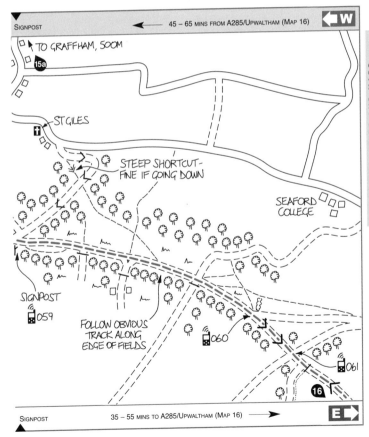

↑ TO GRAFFHAM, 500M

15a

ST GILES

STEEP SHORTCUT–
FINE IF GOING DOWN

SEAFORD
COLLEGE

SIGNPOST
059

FOLLOW OBVIOUS
TRACK ALONG
EDGE OF FIELDS

060

061

16

garden) with excellent food. The menu changes regularly but usually includes some relatively unusual offerings such as pork fillet on potato hash cake and roasted rhubarb with sage cream sauce (£18.50). The views across the hay meadows to the Downs escarpment are lovely. Note, the pub is closed on Sunday evenings.

GRAFFHAM   MAP 15a

There is little to see in Graffham but it has a lazy, peaceful air about it, being well away from any major roads, so makes for a pleasant overnight stay or lunch stop. The very well-stocked **Graffham Village Shop** (☎ 01798-867700, 🖥 graffhamvillageshop .co.uk; Mon-Sat 7am-7pm, Sun & Bank Hol 8-5pm) is more like a mini supermarket than a village store. It also sells hot drinks and baked goods and even has a small *café* area with a few seats and free wi-fi. There's a pop-up **post office** (Tue 8.30am-noon) in the village hall next door.

Campers must head up the road for about a mile to the well-run and welcoming *Graffham Camping & Caravanning Club*

Site (☎ 01798-867476, 🖥 campingandcara-vanningclub.co.uk; limited WI-FI; 🐕 on lead; end Mar to early Nov), set in a peaceful, forested location. The showers are decent and there are laundry facilities. The site has the usual unnecessarily complicated Camping & Caravanning Club prices, but to give you a quick example the price for one backpacker in early July is around £15 (£26 for two).

Brook Barn (☎ 01798-867356, 🖥 brookbarn-graffham.co.uk; 1D/1T shared bathroom; 🍽; 🐕), on Selham Rd, offers **B&B** from £40-45pp (shared bathroom) or £67.50pp (private bathroom; sgl occ from £65) with a continental breakfast.

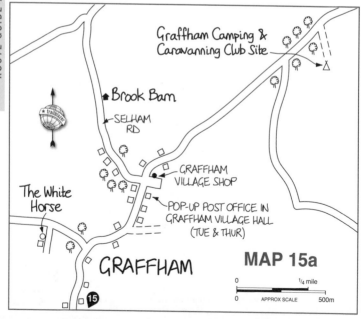

Graffham Camping & Caravanning Club Site

Brook Barn

SELHAM RD

GRAFFHAM VILLAGE SHOP

POP-UP POST OFFICE IN GRAFFHAM VILLAGE HALL (TUE & THUR)

The White Horse

GRAFFHAM

MAP 15a

0   ¼ mile
0   APPROX SCALE   500m

The White Horse (☎ 01798-867331, 💻 whitehorsegraffham.com; **fb**; **food** Tue-Sat noon-2pm & 6.30-9pm, Sun noon-3.30pm; 🐾 bar area only and on lead) itself is now a very upmarket restaurant, boasting a quiet garden and spectacular views onto

the hills. The food's definitely a cut above your average trekker's grub with mains in the region of £19-38.

Compass Travel's No 99 **bus** service calls here if booked in advance. See p47 for details.

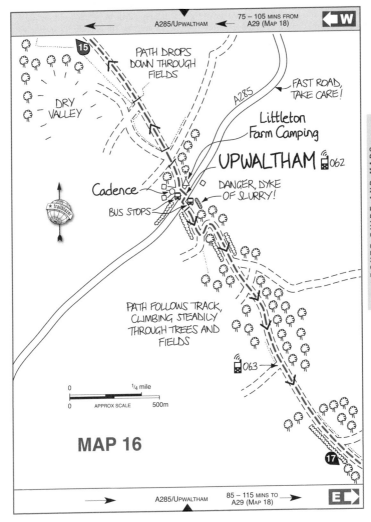

UPWALTHAM   MAP 16, p113

Right by the Way, where it crosses the A285, **campers** can stay at *Littleton Farm Camping* (☎ 07776 274222, 🖳 littleton farm.com; portaloos & showers), a tents-only campsite where a backpacker pitch is £17. Note that because it's a working farm, dogs are not allowed.

Littleton Farm also plays host to *Upwaltham Cadence Clubhouse* (daily 9am-4pm, to 3pm in winter, closed mid-Dec to Easter), another in the series of **cafés**

designed specifically with South Downs Way walkers and cyclists in mind (see box p107). Serving the usual smorgasbord of tasty snacks and drinks, it's a lovely place if the sun is shining, but note that, like several other Cadence cafés, it's in a converted container so there is no indoor area as such although it does offer 'sheltered seating'.

Compass Travel's No 99 **bus** service calls here if booked in advance. See p47 for details.

❑ TUMULI

All along the crest of the Downs are numerous **burial mounds** known as tumuli. These are in the region of 4000 to 4500 years old. Some are overgrown or are not particularly distinct but many are surprisingly well preserved. A glance at an Ordnance Survey map of the area will indicate exactly where they are. Next time you stop for lunch on that nice grassy hump just remember you may be sitting on the grave of someone who has been dead for 4500 years.

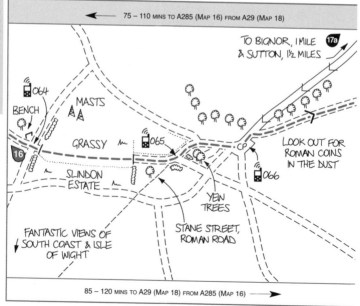

ROUTE GUIDE AND MAPS

← 75 – 110 MINS TO A285 (MAP 16) FROM A29 (MAP 18)

TO BIGNOR, I MILE & SUTTON, I½ MILES   17a

064

BENCH

MASTS

GRASSY

065

CP

LOOK OUT FOR ROMAN COINS IN THE DUST

16

SLINDON ESTATE

066

YEW TREES

FANTASTIC VIEWS OF SOUTH COAST & ISLE OF WIGHT

STANE STREET, ROMAN ROAD

85 – 120 MINS TO A29 (MAP 18) FROM A285 (MAP 16) →

Bignor Hill The Way follows part of the old Roman road over Bignor Hill (Map 17). Look out for the signpost in Latin in the car park (not actually of Roman origin!) and look out, too, for any Roman coins that may be buried among the flint and chalk.

SUTTON & BIGNOR   MAP 17a

The main reason for dropping off the hills to these twin villages is to see the fabulous mosaics at **Bignor Roman Villa** (see box p116) but you can also stay and eat here.

The **church** in Bignor dates from the 11th century; publisher John Murray (1909-95) is buried in the churchyard.

On a quiet corner of the Roman site is *Bignor Farms Camping* (☎ 01798-869259, 💻 bignorromanvilla.co.uk/bignor-farms-camping; 🐕; £15pp); it is a tents only pop-up campsite so the opening dates and the

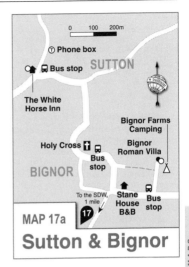

MAP 17a

Sutton & Bignor

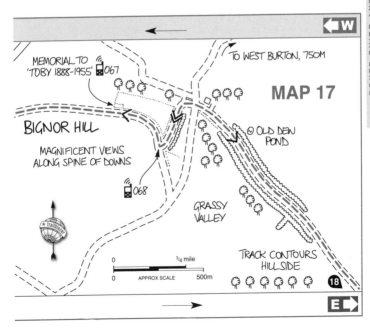

ROUTE GUIDE AND MAPS

number of pitches may vary, but it does have 'shower shacks'.

Very close to the Roman Villa is an excellent **B&B**, *Stane House* (☎ 01798-869454, 🖳 stanehouse.co.uk; 1D/1T both en suite, 1D private facilities; ☻; (Ⓛ)), with rooms from £55pp (£90 sgl occ). They may be willing to drive walkers to a local pub or back up to the trail after a stay.

There's a picnic area at Bignor Roman Villa and the *teashop* (see box below) which is open to the public without an entry ticket.

A mile further on, in **Sutton**, is *The White Horse Inn* (☎ 01798-869191, 🖳 whitehorseinn-sutton.co.uk; 7D/1D or T, all en suite; ☻; 🐾), a magnificent isolated country pub with **B&B** for £60-90pp (sgl occ £90-150). In addition to the five rooms in the main building they also have three rooms in 'lodges' in the garden, one of which has a skylight above the bed, so you can fall asleep while gazing at the stars. They also have a large **restaurant** (food Wed-Sat noon-2.30pm & 6-9pm, Sun noon-4pm) and the food, much of it sourced locally, is exquisite, with treats such as pan-roasted fillet of sea bass and new potatoes with basil, chorizo and olives (£28).

Compass's No 99 **bus service** calls at both Sutton and Bignor if pre-booked. See p47 for details.

❏ BIGNOR ROMAN VILLA　　　　　　　　　Map 17a, p115

Just off the old Roman road of Stane Street are the remains of Bignor Roman Villa (☎ 01798-869259, 🖳 bignorromanvilla.co.uk; *usually* Aug daily 10am-4.30pm, May-Jun & Sep Wed-Fri 10am-2pm, Sat & Sun 10am-4.30pm, Oct weekends only, check website for details; £10). The **teashop** (same hours as Villa) here serves only tea, coffee and cakes; no sandwiches or hot meals.

The villa was discovered by a farmer, George Tupper, while ploughing his field in 1811. Believed to date from the 3rd century AD, Bignor Villa was one of the biggest in England and probably home to a wealthy farmer, considering its enviable position on fertile land close to the main road between Chichester and London. Bignor is most famous for the superb floor mosaics, said to be some of the world's best-preserved examples. Many are in near perfect condition, including a 24-metre length of the 70-metre corridor. It is the longest mosaic on display in Britain.

© Bryn Thomas

BURY   MAP 18, p119

These days, this unassuming village offers only a pub and, if you're here on the right day, a mobile **post office** (Fri 1.15-3.15pm).

The Squire & Horse Inn (☎ 01798-831343, ☐ squireandhorsebury.co.uk; **food** Mon & Tue noon-2pm, Wed-Sat noon-2pm & 5.30-9pm, Sun noon-8pm; ✹ bar area and garden), by the main road, is a free house with a busy restaurant. Main dishes include homemade venison and mushroom suet pudding with roast potatoes (£15.95).

Compass's limited frequency No 69 (Alfold-Worthing) and 71 (Storrington-Chichester) **bus** services call here on certain days. See p47 for details.

HOUGHTON BRIDGE   MAP 18, p119

The village of Houghton Bridge, itself just a short walk from the village of Amberley, can easily be reached from the SDW as the trail almost passes through it.

Southern (see box p44) operates trains to London Victoria and south to Arundel and beyond, from the **railway station** (called Amberley Station). For **buses**, one of Compass's No 74 services continues to Houghton mid afternoon on school days and their **limited frequency** 69 (Tue, Fri) and 71 service (Wed) also drop in. See pp46-8 for details.

Right by the station you'll find the entrance to **Amberley Working Museum** (☎ 01798-831370, ☐ amberleymuseum.co .uk; mid Feb to end Oct Wed-Sun & Bank hols, school hols daily 10am-4.30pm, last entry 4pm, Nov-mid Feb Wed, Sat & Sun 10am-4pm; £15.50), situated in an old chalk pit. This extensive museum features various Victorian industrial processes, including a print shop, clay brick drying shed and pump house. Present day traditional craft businesses also work on-site including a ceramicist and a wood turner. There's a *café* here too. The quarry tunnel at Amberley was used as a film location in the James Bond film *A View To A Kill* in 1984.

Where to stay and eat

Just west of the river, the excellent *South Downs Bunkhouse* (☎ 01798-831100, ☐ southdownsbunkhouse.co.uk; 3 x 4-, 1 x 8-bed dorms, shared facilities; ⓛ; ✹ in utility room) has bunk-bed dormitories and charges from £32.50pp if you bring your own sleeping bag, or you can rent a duvet, sheet and towel (from £6pp). Each bunk has its own power socket and USB charging port, and there's also a communal living room, self-catering and laundry facilities, and even a barbecue you can use in the courtyard outside. Continental breakfast (from £7.50pp) is also available if requested in advance. To access the village you are allowed to cross their fields, which saves you háving to walk on the fast and pavement-less road.

Next door, and run by the same people, *Arun Valley B&B* (same phone number as bunkhouse; ☐ arunvalleybandb.co.uk; 1D or T private bathroom, 1D or T en suite; ☞; ⓛ) has very comfortable rooms from £70pp (sgl occ £90), including a good choice of cooked breakfast options.

At *Riverside* (☎ 01798-831066, ☐ riversidesouthdowns.com; **fb**; summer daily 9am-5pm, winter Wed-Fri 10am-4pm, Sat & Sun 9am-4pm; ✹) you can get breakfasts till noon but they also serve light lunches (hot food to 3pm) and cakes. This café, bar and restaurant is especially popular when the weather is good as they have a riverside garden.

Nearby is *Bridge Inn* (☎ 01798-831619, ☐ bridgeinnamberley.com; **fb**; food Wed-Thur noon-2.30pm & 6-8.30pm, Fri & Sat noon-8pm, Sun noon-4pm; wi-fi; ✹ bar & garden only), a friendly, award-winning pub with real ales and very good food. The pub closes at 5pm on Sunday and all day Monday and Tuesday.

Across the road from them is *Boathouse* (☎ 01243-971880, ☐ theboathouseamberley.co.uk; Wed-Sat noon-3pm and 6-9pm, Sun & bank hols noon-3.30pm), the classy Mediterranean restaurant with mains costing £17-29. Piri piri monkfish tail (£26) is recommended.

ROUTE GUIDE AND MAPS

W ← AMBERLEY TO COCKING   MAPS 18-14

This scenic **12-mile (19.5km, 3¾-5¼hrs)** stage is perhaps the trail at its most typical: a wide chalky track leading up and along the escarpment, with distant views to the sea away to the south and cosy little villages skirting the folds of the downs below to the north. So far, so familiar. But later on in the day there are also several patches of woodland, most notably at Graffham Down, that give those who started their adventure in Eastbourne a taste of things to come, with woodland becoming more prevalent as the trail continues west. All of which makes for a lovely day's walking if the sun's out.

ROUTE GUIDE AND MAPS

▼ ← A29   ← 25 – 35 MINS   ▼ JUNCTION WITH LANE

TO WEST BURTON, 700M
& BIGNOR, 1½ MILES

The Squire &
Horse Inn →

BURY

🚌 🚌 BUS STOPS

0 ___ ¼ mile
0 ___ APPROX SCALE ___ 500m

HOUGHTON →
LANE

TO BURY, 20 MINS
ALONG MAIN ROAD
A29 ↗

⑰

TO BURY, 15 MINS
ALONG COUNTRY
LANE

DANGER! VERY
BUSY ROAD

📱069

📱070

GREAT VIEWS ↓
ACROSS ARUN VALLEY

HOUGHTON

TO ARUNDEL, 3¾ MILES ↘

→ A29   15 – 25 MINS →   JUNCTION WITH LANE

Though the walking may be 'typical' for the South Downs, there are some unique attractions on this stage. To the north of the trail, the mosaics at **Bignor Roman Villa** (see box p116) are really great and always manage to make you feel that the lengthy and steep trudge down to it from the top of **Bignor Hill** (Map 17) was worth doing. It's not surprising the villa was built here, with **Stane Street**, the Roman road built around AD50 to connect Noviomagus (Chichester) with Londinium (London), passing nearby.

The Way continues on through a mixture of woodland and grassland. The track here used to be bordered on one side by dense woodland and on the other

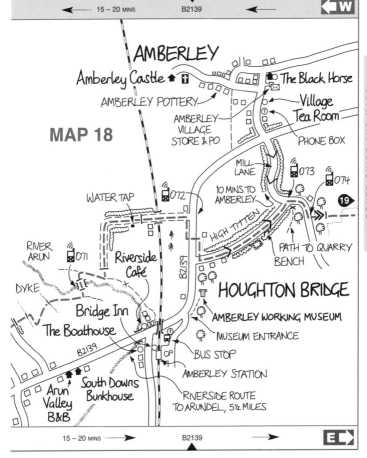

by a high hedge so the view was somewhat obscured in parts, but the former South Downs Joint Committee and Graffham Down Trust created a wildlife corridor in order to link up two rich grassland sites – **Graffham Down** (Map 15) and **Heyshott Down** (Map 14). The path passes a **Bronze Age burial ground** with **tumuli** clearly visible among the tussocks of grass.

There is a **water tap** by Manor Farm's farm buildings and a track from here leads down to **Cocking** (p106). Just after that you will notice that the window frames on the cottages here are painted yellow; this shows they are part of the Cowdray Estate (see box p108).   *[Next route overview p106]*

AMBERLEY   MAP 18, p119

Perched on a sandstone ridge below the chalk Downs with the floodplain landscape of **Amberley Wildbrooks** stretching to the north, Amberley claims to be the prettiest village on the Downs and it would be hard to argue otherwise. The quiet lane leading to the church and castle is lined with thatched cottages; hollyhocks and fox-gloves bloom in the small front gardens in the summer months. Unlike other down-land villages, where local flint is prominent in the architecture, many of Amberley's cottages were built using local sandstone, making the village distinctive. There are records referring to Amberley dating back to AD680.

The pretty **church** was built by Bishop Luffa between 1091 and 1125. Next to the church is the **castle** (now a hotel, see Where to stay) which used to be the bishop's residence until it was recognised as a castle upon completion of the walls in 1377.

More information on the history of the village and the local area can be found at Amberley Working Museum (see p117). **Amberley Village Pottery** (☎ 01798-831876, ☐ amberleypottery.co.uk; Thur-Sun 11am-3pm), housed in an 1867 former chapel on Church St, is open to visitors.

Amberley Village Store (☎ 01798-831171, ☐ avsshop.co.uk; **fb**; Mon-Fri 9am-5pm, Sat & Sun to 4pm) stocks a good range of groceries and also houses the **post office** (Mon, Thur & Fri 9am-1pm, Tue 9am-noon).

Amberley **railway station** is about a mile away in Houghton Bridge; see p46 for details of the No 74A **bus** service that calls

in Amberley and continues to the railway station on school days.

Where to stay and eat
In the **village centre**, if you fancy a splurge, there's every luxury at **Amberley Castle** (☎ 01798-831992, ☐ amberleycastle.co.uk; 15D/4D or T, all en suite; ➥). Gorgeous **rooms** cost from £130pp (sgl occ room rate), though it is always worth enquiring about special offers; there's a minimum two-night stay at weekends. There's a grand **restaurant** (Wed-Sun 12.30-4.30pm & 7-9pm; smart casual) serving a three-course meal for £98pp in the evening. Booking is recommended and note the whole place is closed on Mondays and Tuesdays.

The local pub, the very smart **Black Horse** (☎ 01798-831183, ☐ amberley-blackhorse.co.uk; **fb**; ➥; food Mon-Sat noon-2pm & 6-9pm, Sun noon-6pm) serves top-notch **food** in the bar, or in their Garden Room which boasts excellent views over the South Downs. They also have some charming **bedrooms** (8D/3D or T, all en suite; ➥; ➥) with **B&B** rates £50-85pp (sgl occ £90).

Amberley Village Tearoom (☎ 01798-839196; **fb**; ➥; Apr-Oct Thur-Tue 10.30am-4pm, Mar Thur-Sun only) prides itself on sourcing locally produced food and their cream teas are very popular.

East of the village, about a mile down the lane towards Rackham, is **The Sportsman** (Map 19; ☎ 01798-831787, ☐ thesportsmansussex.co.uk; **fb**), a very pleasant pub with sweeping sunset views across Amberley Brooks from both its beer garden and conservatory. As well as good **food** (Wed & Thur noon-2pm & 6-8pm, Fri & Sat noon-2pm & 6-8.30pm, Sun noon-3pm) and some fine real ales, they offer **B&B** (3D/2T, all en suite; 🛇; 🐾) from £62.50pp (sgl occ £110).

Next door to the pub is *Woody Banks Cottage* (Map 19; ☎ 01798-831295, 🖥 woo dybanks.co.uk; 1T, private shower room) with B&B from £57.50pp (sgl occ £70); the

sitting room for guests now has a 'tea station' so tea can be made and there are biscuits. Another bedroom is available for family and friends.

About 90 metres further along is *Two Farm Cottages B&B* (Map 19; ☎ 01798-831266, 🖥 twofarmcottages.co.uk; 1D/1T private bathroom; 🛇), where guests have their own private lounge. B&B here is £65pp (sgl occ £110).

❑ INTERNATIONAL DARK SKY RESERVE (IDSR)

In May 2016 the South Downs National Park became an IDSR, with 66% of the park being recognised as having Bronze Level Skies. Not only are such dark skies great for star-gazing, they also help nocturnal wildlife such as moths and bats thrive.

Areas with the darkest skies on the South Downs include Old Winchester Hill, Butser Hill, Devil's Dyke, Ditchling Beacon and Birling Gap.

ARUNDEL   MAP 18a, p123
The town of Arundel is about 1½ hours from the South Downs Way via the riverside path from Houghton Bridge or a 5-minute train ride from Amberley Station. Those walking the entire South Downs Way in one trip will find that a visit to this historic town makes an ideal rest day.

Arundel boasts a fine cathedral but it is the perfectly preserved castle with its grand turreted walls that really catches the eye. **Arundel Festival** (🖥 arundelfestival.co .uk) is held over ten days in the castle in August.

What to see and do
The **castle** (☎ 01903-882173, 🖥 arundel castle.org; Easter to late Oct Tue-Sun 10am-5pm, plus bank hols & Mon in Aug; castle & gardens £25, gardens only £14) is the centrepiece of this historical town. Rising grandly from the trees it looms over the Arun Valley and is everything you imagine an English castle to be, complete with imposing walls, turrets and winding stone staircases. Of Norman origin, it is now home to the Duke of Norfolk but is open to the public during the spring and summer. In April the gardens provide one of the largest displays of tulips in the country. The chapel is included as part of the

castle and garden ticket as long as they aren't holding a service there, but it's £2 more to visit the bedrooms.

Arundel's gothic-style **cathedral** (🖥 arundelcathedral.uk; usually Mon-Sat 10.30am-4pm, Sun 12.30-4pm; check website) is somewhat upstaged by the immense castle down the road but is still a fine building in its own right. Founded by Henry, the 15th Duke of Norfolk, the cathedral is relatively new, dating back to 1873. A good time to visit is during the Corpus Christi festivities in late May or early June when the main aisle of the cathedral is covered in a spectacular carpet of flowers.

Arundel Museum (☎ 01903-885866, 🖥 arundelmuseum.org; daily 10am-4pm; £5) is down by the river, opposite the entrance to the castle. The museum's exhibits focus on local history with interesting displays on the castle, the Catholic dukes of Norfolk and their association with the town. The old photographs portraying local life through the years are also rather wonderful.

Arundel Wetland Centre (☎ 01903-883355, 🖥 www.wwt.org.uk/wetland-cen tres/arundel; daily 10am-4.30pm; £14.95, free for WWT members, see p59) is a natural wetland site bordered by ancient woodland and is a perfect diversion for anyone interested in birds. The hides provide opportunities for viewing a variety of warblers and waders as well as the odd buzzard circling above the oak trees.

Swimmers might fancy a dip in **Arundel Lido** (☎ 01903-884772, 💻 arundel-lido.com; mid/late Apr to early/mid Sep daily 6am-8.30pm; £7 per session), a heated open-air swimming pool with views of the castle.

Services

There is no tourist information centre here but for online **information** see 💻 visit arundel.co.uk or 💻 sussexbythesea.com.

If you're looking for the ingredients of a good picnic, **Pallant of Arundel** (☎ 01903-882288, 💻 pallantofarundel.co.uk; Mon-Sat 9am-6pm, Sun 10am-5pm) is the town's excellent **deli** and specialist grocery store. Food supplies can also be found at the small **shop**, McColl's (Mon-Sat 6am-7pm, Sun 7am-7pm), near the bridge at the bottom of the High St, while across the bridge is a Co-op **supermarket** (daily 7am-10pm).

The **post office** (Mon-Sat 9am-5.30pm) lies just across the road from McColl's. Up the hill on High St is the **pharmacy** (☎ 01903-492152; Mon-Fri 9am-6.30pm, Sat 9am-4pm).

There's an **ATM** outside the museum, and another outside the Co-op.

Public transport

The **railway station** is a 10-minute walk from the town centre; services (see box p44) are operated by Southern.

Compass Travel's No 85/85A is the only choice for travel by **bus** to Chichester, though their **limited frequency** No 69 service (Tue & Fri only) calls in on its way between Alford and Worthing; the bus stop is near the bridge. See pp46-8 for details.

For a **taxi** call Castle Cars (☎ 01903-884444, 💻 castlecarsltd.co.uk).

Where to stay

Arundel is popular with tourists so book well in advance. Over some weekends and during local events there may be a two-night minimum stay for some places and prices may increase substantially.

On the road leading from the town centre to the railway station is *Arundel Park Hotel* (☎ 01903-882588, 💻 arundel parkhotel.co.uk; 1S/9D/3T/1Tr/1Qd, all en suite; 🍷; mid Jan to mid Dec); it has plenty of rooms and an unpretentious style. Bed and a full English breakfast costs from £42.50pp (sgl/sgl occ from £75).

Nearby is *Portreeves* (☎ 01903-885392, 💻 portreeves.co.uk; 2D or T, both en suite; 🍷; 🐾). It's a well-run, friendly place offering B&B from £60pp (sgl occ £110) in their two apartments. However, the apartments are often let on a self-catering basis for a week or more, particularly in the summer months, so it is essential to book in advance. Both apartments have a sofa bed so they can sleep three adults or a family with up to two children. Breakfast can be served in your apartment or in the garden.

House Arundel (☎ 07745 526945, 💻 housearundel.co.uk; 5D, all en suite ; 🐾), near the post office at 11 High St, is an intimate little boutique B&B (from £70-90pp, sgl occ room rate). It's in a good location and a gorgeous place to stay.

Nearby is the elegant *Swan Hotel* (☎ 01903-882314, 💻 swanarundel.co.uk; 4T/7D/3Tr, all en suite; 🍷; 🐾) with B&B from £75pp but it can cost around £130pp (sgl occ from £75).

The Town House (☎ 01903-883847, 💻 thetownhouse.co.uk; 4D/1D or T, all en suite; 🍷), opposite the castle at the top of the High St (No 65), is a very attractive place with immaculate and stylish rooms. Expect to pay £57-162pp (sgl occ full room rate).

On Queen's Lane, a few minutes from the centre, is *Arden House* (☎ 01903-884184, 💻 ardenhousearundel.com; 3D/1T/1D or T all en suite, 1D/1T shared facilities; Ⓛ). B&B costs from £47.50-49.50pp (sgl occ £85-89); phone bookings are preferred. They can offer a packed breakfast option for those wanting to leave early and also have room only rates. They also have a lockable garage for up to four bicycles.

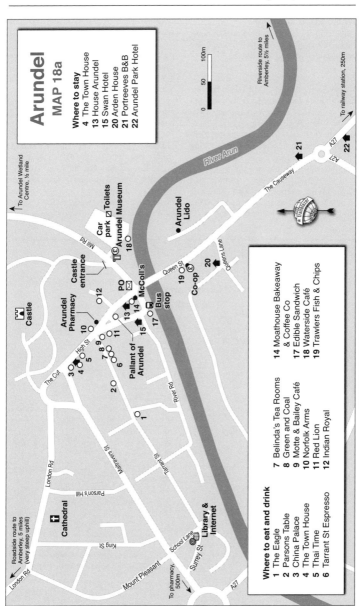

Arundel
MAP 18a

Where to stay
4 The Town House
13 House Arundel
15 Swan Hotel
20 Arden House
21 Portreeves B&B
22 Arundel Park Hotel

To Arundel Wetland Centre, ½ mile

Riverside route to Amberley, 5½ miles

To railway station, 250m

River Arun

The Causeway

● Arundel Lido

Arundel Museum
Car park ⊠ Toilets
Mill Rd
Castle entrance
⊞ⓔ
18 ○
McColl's
PO ⊠
Queen St
19 ○ⓔ
Co-op
20
Queen's Lane

Castle ⚑

Arundel Pharmacy
High St
10 ●
12 ○
7 8 9 ○
5 ○ 4 ●
3 ●
6 ○
11 ○
13 ■ 14 ■
15 ■ 17 ■
Bus stop
Pallant of Arundel

The Cut
2 ○
1 ○

River Rd

Malthevers St
Tarrant St

Cathedral ✚

Roadside route to Amberley, 5 miles (very steep uphill)
London Rd
London Rd
Parson's Hill
King St
Mount Pleasant
Surrey St
School Lane
Library & Internet ⓐ
Thai Time
To pharmacy, 500m
A27

Where to eat and drink
1 The Eagle
2 Parsons Table
3 China Palace
4 The Town House
5 Thai Time
6 Tarrant St Espresso
7 Belinda's Tea Rooms
8 Green and Coal
9 Motte & Bailey Café
10 Norfolk Arms
11 Red Lion
12 Indian Royal
14 Moathouse Bakeaway & Coffee Co
17 Edible Sandwich
18 Waterside Café
19 Trawlers Fish & Chips

0 50 100m

Where to eat and drink
Arundel is bursting with excellent pubs, cafés and restaurants, most of which are centred on or around the High St.

Cafés Starting down by the river, *Waterside Café* (☎ 07779-930236; **fb**; 🐾; daily 9.30am-5pm) is a no-frills café with good-value food including breakfasts, jacket spuds, sandwiches, cream teas and more substantial 'specials' focusing on fish dishes, all of which can be enjoyed while sitting on their simple terrace overlooking the river; a wonderful spot on a sunny day.

Also beside the river, on the other side of the bridge, *Edible Sandwich* (☎ 01903-885969, 🖥 ediblesandwich.co.uk; daily 9am-4pm; 🐾) doesn't have such good riverside seating, but it's friendly and does tasty pastries, cakes and coffee.

Nearby, at 9 High St, is the hugely popular *Moathouse Bakeaway and Coffee Co* (☎ 01903-883297; **fb**; Mon 7.30am-4.30pm, Tue-Thur to 5pm, Fri to 5.30pm, Sat 8am-5.30pm, Sun 8.30am-5pm, winter hours vary; small 🐾), with an excellent range of breakfasts, toasties, filled baguettes and hot drinks.

Heading up the High St, and also very popular, is the bright and modern *Motte & Bailey Café* (☎ 01903-883813, 🖥 motteandbaileycafe.com; **fb**; 🐾; Mon-Sat 8am-4.30pm, Sun 8am-4pm). On summer evenings it moonlights as a tapas restaurant (Thur-Sat 6-9pm) Its status as the smartest café in town, however, is now being chal-

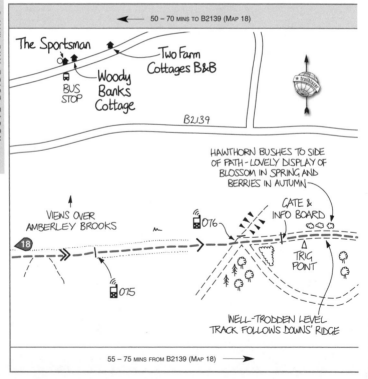

ROUTE GUIDE AND MAPS

← 50 – 70 MINS TO B2139 (MAP 18)

The Sportsman

Two Farm Cottages B&B

BUS STOP

Woody Banks Cottage

B2139

VIEWS OVER AMBERLEY BROOKS

18

O76

O75

HAWTHORN BUSHES TO SIDE OF PATH - LOVELY DISPLAY OF BLOSSOM IN SPRING AND BERRIES IN AUTUMN

GATE & INFO BOARD

TRIG POINT

WELL-TRODDEN LEVEL TRACK FOLLOWS DOWNS' RIDGE

55 – 75 MINS FROM B2139 (MAP 18) →

lenged by the handsome *Green & Coal* (🖥 greenandcoalarundel.com; daily 7.30am-5.30pm), with a small but tasty menu of breakfasts and light lunches (from £6.50 for soup & crusty bread).

Sidling off down Tarrant St will bring you to two more fine cafés: *Belinda's* (☎ 01903-882977, 🖥 belindasarundel.co.uk; fb; daily 9am-5pm; well-behaved 🐾), housed in a charming 16th-century building, has been serving teas and light lunches amongst the wooden beams for several decades now. They also do a great Sunday roast (£15.50, noon-3pm). But for the best coffee beans in town, head next door to the pocket-sized *Tarrant St Espresso* (Tue-Fri 7.30am-4pm, Sat & Sun 9am-4pm; 🐾); they also have filled rolls and salads.

Pubs Popular with locals, and not just because they show the football on the telly, *The Eagle* (☎ 01903-885821; fb; bar Mon-Fri 5-11pm, Sat & Sun 11am-11pm; 🐾), on Tarrant St, serves an impressive array of beers (including Harvey's) and sometimes has live music at weekends. Locals spill out onto the pavement on warm summer evenings even though they don't do food, apart from bar snacks,.

If it's pub food you're after, your best bet is to head to the High St and *The Red Lion* (☎ 01903-882214, 🖥 redlionarundel .com; fb; food daily noon-9pm; 🐾 on a lead). It's a large no-nonsense pub with a rear garden, serving fair value (evening mains from £14.50) huge and filling dishes. There's also a choice of real ales.

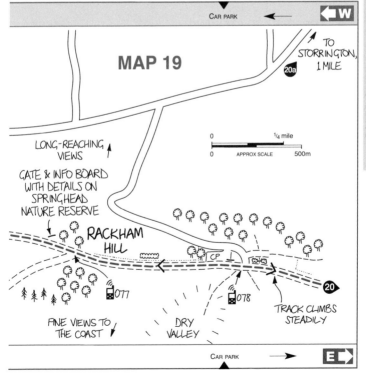

ROUTE GUIDE AND MAPS

Opposite, *Norfolk Arms* (☎ 01903-882101, 🖳 norfolkarmsarundel.com; food Mon-Sat noon-3.30pm & 5.30-8.30pm, Sun noon-3.30pm only; 🐾 bar only) has a traditional restaurant serving English dishes as well as a pub-grub menu in its rather quiet bar.

Restaurants & takeaways The very highly regarded *Parsons Table* (☎ 01903-883477, 🖳 theparsonstable.co.uk; Tue-Sat noon-2pm & 6-9pm; Castle Mews, Tarrant St; booking recommended) is run by husband-and-wife team Lee and Liz Parsons and prides itself on dishes made from locally sourced seasonal ingredients. The results are excellent. A set two-/three-course lunch will set you back £30/36; evening mains start at around £19.50 rising to £39.

For decent Indian food, head to *Indian Royal* (☎ 01903-884224; daily noon-2.30pm & 5.30-11.30pm) at 3 Mill Lane just off the High St. At 67 High St, *China Palace* (☎ 01903-883702, 🖳 chinapalace-arundel.com; Sun, Mon, Wed-Fri noon-2pm & 5.30-10pm, Sat to 10.30pm) is a smarter than average Chinese restaurant which also offers dishes with Malay, Thai and Vietnamese influences. For more flavours of the Far East, round the corner on High St is *Thai Time* (☎ 01444-523424, 🖳 thaitimefood.com; Mon-Fri noon-3pm & 5-10pm, Fri to 11pm, Sat noon-11pm, Sun noon-10pm).

The best chippy in town is *Trawlers Fish & Chips* (Mon-Sat 11.45am-2pm & 4-8pm, Fri & Sat to 9pm, Sun 11.45am-7pm) on Queen St.

E➔ **AMBERLEY TO STEYNING**   **MAPS 18-22**

The first half of this **10-mile (16km, 3¼-4¾hrs)** stretch is an easy stroll along the high crest of the Downs with great views over the swamp-like **Amberley Wildbrooks** nature reserve and the Low Weald. The quickest way to **Storrington** (Map 20a) is along the path leading off the Way at GPS Waypoint 079 (Map 20).

For **Washington** (Map 21; p130) there is an **alternative South Downs Way path** (Maps 20 & 21) which is longer but, in our opinion, superior to the main trail as it both leads the walker directly into this pleasant village *and* allows the walker to pass above the A24 on a bridge, rather than taking your life in your hands trying to cross it as you do on the 'normal' route.

🗌 **DEW PONDS**

The permeability of the chalk on the Downs means there is rarely any standing or free-flowing water available for livestock. To combat the problem farmers have, since prehistoric times, constructed dew ponds. These small, circular ponds are designed to collect and retain water for the sheep and cattle that graze the dry hilltops. Despite their name, dew accounts for very little of the moisture that collects in these man-made bowls; most of it is rainwater. The water is prevented from filtering through the chalk thanks to a base layer of straw and clay, although modern-day dew ponds usually have a layer of concrete instead.

Many dew ponds are hundreds of years old and in a state of disrepair, being overgrown and barely recognisable as ponds. However, in recent years many have been restored, either because of their historic interest or simply to be used again for their original purpose. Good examples of dew ponds can be seen near Chanctonbury Ring and also between Southease and Alfriston.

ROUTE GUIDE AND MAPS

The A24 dual carriageway (Map 21) is something of a blot on the landscape but it is soon forgotten once the steep climb up Chanctonbury Hill (Map 21) begins. At the top, the once storm-ravaged **Chanctonbury Ring** (see box p136) is looking majestic once more.

Acting almost as suburbs of **Steyning** (Maps 22 & 22a), the twin villages of **Bramber** & **Upper Beeding** (Map 22a; see p135) lie either side of the River Adur. They're easily accessed from Steyning, but can also be reached directly from the Way (Maps 22 & 23).

To Steyning The town of Steyning (see p135), 1½ miles north of the path, is well worth the minor detour and not just to replenish supplies and energy. A couple of possible pathways lead down to the village; the best is the more westerly option, between the trig point and the small memorial to a local farmer (Map 22). The descent is a leisurely one with fine views over Steyning Bowl and down to the coastal towns of Worthing and Lancing.

STORRINGTON   MAP 20a

In contrast to many of the other towns and villages along the Downs the busy little town of Storrington is functional rather than attractive. It is a convenient place for topping up on supplies or getting a bite to eat but apart from that there is little reason to make the detour.

There's a small **museum** (🖳 storring tonmuseum.org; Wed, Sat & Sun 10am-4pm; free) covering the local history of the

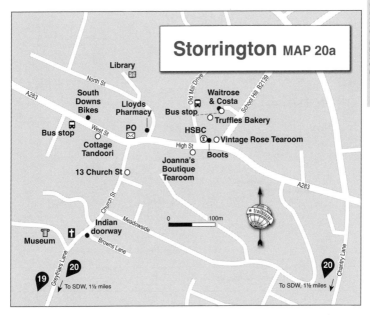

Storrington MAP 20a

area. Near the museum is a wonderfully ornate **Indian doorway**, set into the wall on Browns Lane.

Storrington has the services you would expect in a small but prosperous town. Waitrose **supermarket** (Mon-Sat 8am-8pm, Sun 10am-4pm) is in a small shopping arcade just off the High St. At the other end of the High St there's a branch of the **pharmacy** Boots (Mon, Wed & Fri 9am-5.30pm, Tue & Thur to 6.30pm, Sat to 5pm). The **post office** (Mon-Fri 9am-5.30pm except Wed & Thur closed 1-1.30pm, Sat 9am-1.30pm) is on West St.

For **ATMs** there's an HSBC where Old Mill Drive meets the High St.

If you need **bicycle** parts or repairs, head to South Downs Bikes (🖥 southdownsbikes.com; Mon-Fri 9am-6pm, Sat to 5pm).

There are several cafés and tearooms including the bright and cheery *Joanna's Boutique Tearoom* (☎ 01903-742226, 🖥 joannasboutiquetearoom.com, **fb**; Mon-Fri 9am-4pm, Sat to 5pm, Sun 10am-4pm) at 34 High St, with cream teas and cakes, all-white décor, and a friendly welcome. Booking is advised.

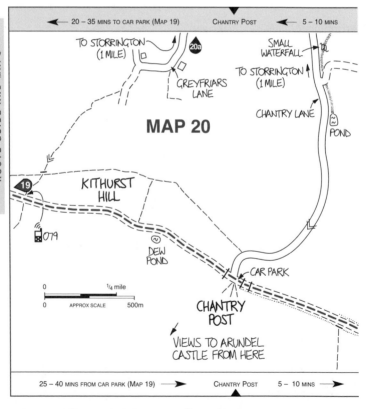

ROUTE GUIDE AND MAPS

20 – 35 MINS TO CAR PARK (MAP 19)   CHANTRY POST   5 – 10 MINS

TO STORRINGTON (1 MILE)

20a

SMALL WATERFALL

20

GREYFRIARS LANE

TO STORRINGTON (1 MILE)

CHANTRY LANE

POND

MAP 20

19

KITHURST HILL

079

DEW POND

CAR PARK

CHANTRY POST

VIEWS TO ARUNDEL CASTLE FROM HERE

0   ¼ mile
0   APPROX SCALE   500m

25 – 40 MINS FROM CAR PARK (MAP 19) →   CHANTRY POST   5 – 10 MINS →

Also very popular, *Vintage Rose Tearoom* (☎ 01903-744100, **fb**; Mon-Sat 9am-4.30pm) is housed in a Grade II-listed building and serves teas and coffees – on interestingly mismatched china – as well as light lunches.

For cheaper, takeaway fare, including tea, coffee, pastries and breakfasts, there's a branch of the family-owned Sussex chain *Truffles Bakery* (☎ 01903-742459; Mon-Sat 7.30am-4pm), near Waitrose.

Two doors down from Waitrose, meanwhile, is a branch of *Costa Coffee* (Mon-Sat 6.30am-5.30pm, Sun 7.30am-4.30pm).

For something a bit fancier, *13 Church Street* (☎ 01903-746964, 🖥 thirteenchurchstreet.co.uk; **fb**; Tue-Sat noon-3pm & 6-11pm) serves high-quality, freshly prepared Thai specialities. Mains cost from £18.

Storrington also has a popular Indian restaurant: *Cottage Tandoori* (☎ 01903-743605, 🖥 cottagetandoori.com; daily noon-2.30pm & 6-11pm).

Stagecoach's No 1 (Midhurst to/from Worthing) **bus** service calls here as do Compass's No 100 (Burgess Hill to/from Pulborough) and their No 74/74A/74B (to Horsham). See pp46-8 for details.

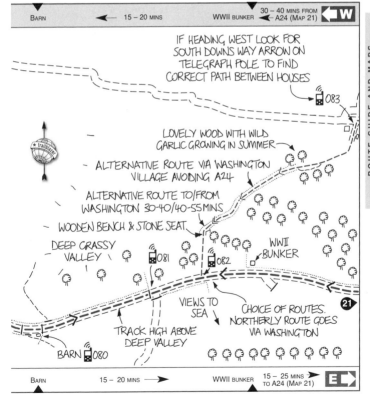

WASHINGTON   MAP 21

Despite the proximity of the busy A24 dual carriageway this village is a peaceful place with most of the traffic noise being absorbed by the trees.

For **camping**, walk a few hundred metres north of the village, on London Rd, to the very welcoming ***Washington Park*** (☎ 01903-892869, 🖥 washcamp.com; 🐕

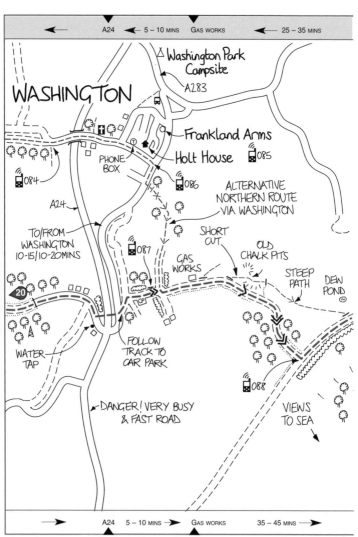

on lead; open all year) which charges walkers from £14 (tent & 1 person, plus £6pp for 2 or more). The rate includes showers and they also have laundry facilities.

There's **B&B** for £40-42.50pp (sgl occ £45-60) at walker- and dog-friendly *Holt House* (☎ 07796-936444, ☎ 01903-893542, or 🖥 annesimmonds_holthouse @yahoo.co.uk; 1D en suite, 1D/1T shared bathroom; ➍; Ⓛ; 🐾). Breakfasts here

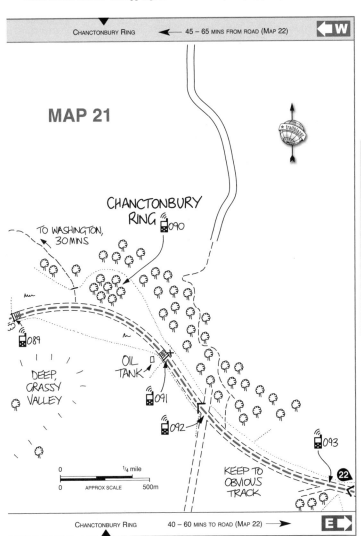

CHANCTONBURY RING ◀— 45 – 65 MINS FROM ROAD (MAP 22)

MAP 21

CHANCTONBURY RING 📱090

TO WASHINGTON, 30 MINS

📱089

DEEP, GRASSY VALLEY

OIL TANK

📱091

📱092

📱093

KEEP TO OBVIOUS TRACK

22

0   1/4 mile
0   APPROX SCALE   500m

ROUTE GUIDE AND MAPS

CHANCTONBURY RING   40 – 60 MINS TO ROAD (MAP 22) —▶

come recommended and laundry services are also available. It is at the end of the path that runs off The Holt.

You can get **food** at nearby *Frankland Arms* (☎ 01903-891405, 💻 thefrankland arms.com; 🐾 on lead; food Mon-Sat noon-8.30pm, Sun noon-5pm) with good value pub grub (lunchtime sandwiches from £5.45, mains such as chilli con carne with

rice from £9.95). You may need to book in the evening at the weekends.

Stagecoach's **bus** No 1 stops here en route between Midhurst and Worthing. Compass's No 100 (Burgess Hill to/from Horsham) also calls here as does the Metrobus No 23 (Crawley to/from Worthing) service. See pp46-7 for details.

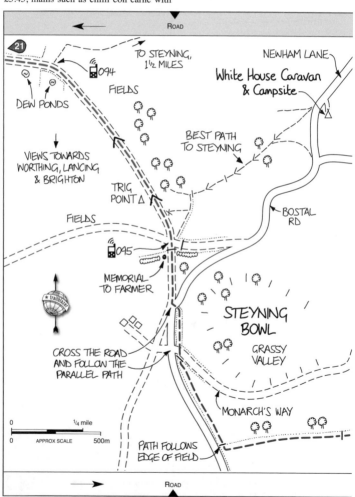

W ← STEYNING TO AMBERLEY   MAPS 22-18

The highlight today occurs fairly early on in this **10-mile (16km, 3¼hrs-4¾hrs)** stage as you tackle the gentle ascent of Chanctonbury Hill to **Chanctonbury Ring** (see p136); it's a magical place that has largely recovered from the devastation caused by a storm in 1987. The **A24** dual carriageway (Map 21) afterwards is both a metaphorical and literal come-down, but a rather

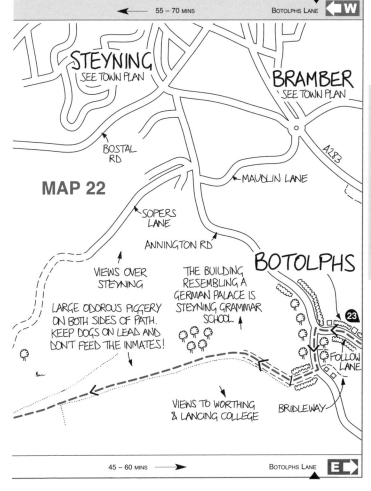

BOTOLPHS LANE

W

STEYNING
SEE TOWN PLAN

BRAMBER
SEE TOWN PLAN

A283

BOSTAL RD

MAUDLIN LANE

MAP 22

SOPERS LANE

ANNINGTON RD

BOTOLPHS

VIEWS OVER STEYNING

THE BUILDING RESEMBLING A GERMAN PALACE IS STEYNING GRAMMAR SCHOOL

23

LARGE ODOROUS PIGGERY ON BOTH SIDES OF PATH. KEEP DOGS ON LEAD AND DON'T FEED THE INMATES!

FOLLOW LANE

VIEWS TO WORTHING & LANCING COLLEGE

BRIDLEWAY

45 – 60 MINS →

BOTOLPHS LANE

E

ROUTE GUIDE AND MAPS

hairy crossing of it can be avoided by a short-but-sweet **alternative trail** via the village of **Washington**. Alternatively, off the trail is **Storrington** (Map 20a; see p127) reached by turning off the trail at Chantry Post car park. As a reward for your exertions the remainder of the stage is an uncomplicated, untaxing stroll along the high crest of the Downs overlooking the **Amberley Wild Brooks** and the Low Weald.

The obvious choice of destination at the end of this stage is either **Amberley** or **Houghton Bridge** (both Map 18); both are beautiful, conveniently situated close to the trail and have some good pubs, cafés and accommodation. But if you can't find what you're looking for in these villages, the even more lovely town of **Arundel** (p123) is just a short train ride away.

[Next route overview p118]

STEYNING   MAP 22a
This small town has retained all the charm of a downland village and it is worth taking an afternoon off to wander around and maybe visit one or two of the sights. There are some beautiful old buildings, particularly along Church St where the **Grammar School (Brotherhood Hall)**, dating from 1614, really catches the eye with its black timber framing. Next to the library is the small **Steyning Museum** (☎ 01903-813333, 🖳 steyningmuseum.org.uk; Wed-Sun 10am-4pm; free) with displays on local history.

Services
For **tourist information** see 🖳 visitsteyning.co.uk.

The High St has several **banks** and **ATMs** and there's a **post office** (Mon-Fri 9am-5pm, Sat 9am-3pm) too. The main **supermarket**, Co-op (daily 6am-10pm) is on the High St; there's also the more expensive Budgens (The Sussex Grocer; Mon-Sat 7am-8pm, Sun 9am-6pm). Steyning also has a good **bookshop** (Mon-Sat 9.30am-5.30pm) that sells maps.

There is **internet access** (free for library card holders, £2.25/hr otherwise; free wi-fi) in the **library** (Mon-Fri 10am-5pm, Sat to 2pm).

Public transport
Bus services calling here are Brighton & Hove Buses' No 2 (to Brighton) and Compass's No 100 (Burgess Hill to

Horsham & Pulborough). See pp46-8 for details.

Where to stay
Campers should head to Newham Lane, where they'll find *White House Caravan and Campsite* (☎ 01903-813737; 🐾; Mar-Oct) which charges £10pp. The walk into town takes about eight minutes; see also Map 22.

For a **room** for the night, walker-friendly *Uppingham B&B* (☎ 07990-532030, ☎ 01903-812099; 1T private bathroom/1D en suite 🛏; Ⓛ; 🐾) is on Kings Barn Villas. B&B costs from £47.50pp (sgl occ £70).

Springwells House B&B (☎ 01903-812446, 🖳 springwells.co.uk; 3D, all en suite; 🛏; 🐾), 9 High St, offers some very smart accommodation. One of the other delights of this lovely place is a seasonal swimming pool in the old walled garden. The prices reflect the quality of the place; they vary throughout the year but in summer you can expect to pay £75-90pp (sgl occ full room rate); weekends are more expensive and there's a two-night minimum stay in summer.

Though the bar can sometimes be noisy, *Chequer Inn* (☎ 01903-814437, 🖳 chequerinn.co.uk; 1T/1D/1Qd, all en suite; limited wi-fi), at 41 High St, offers comfortable B&B from £50pp (sgl occ £60). Note that they cannot offer breakfast before 7.30am but if requested in advance they

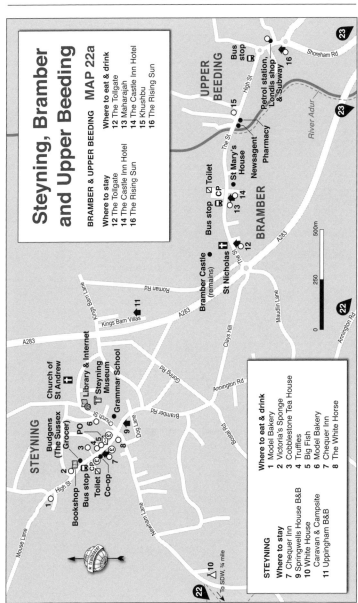

ROUTE GUIDE AND MAPS

may be able to provide a takeaway breakfast.

Where to eat and drink

Baked goods, breakfasts, tea and coffee can be bought at the bakery, *Truffles* (☎ 01903-816140; **fb**; Mon-Sat 7.30am-5pm, café 8am-4pm). It's in the same local chain as the one at Storrington.

For takeaway lunch packs there are filled rolls, buns, cakes and savouries at *Model Bakery* (☎ 01903-813785; Mon-Sat 8am-2pm,), on Church St, with a second branch (☎ 01903-813126; Tue-Sat 8am-2pm) at the northern end of the High St.

For something more intriguing, turn off the High St down Cobblestone Walk, a part-covered alleyway where, amongst a curious collection of boutique shops and gift stalls, you'll find the ever-so charming *Cobblestone Tea House* (☎ 01903-366171; **fb**; daily 9am-5pm; 🐾), housed in a 16th-century timber-framed cottage.

Down the hill a bit further, *Victoria's Sponge* (☎ 01903-814517; **fb**; daily 9am-4pm; 🐾) is very popular, especially with dog owners. The food's good too, with hearty breakfasts, sandwiches, light lunches – and, of course, a good selection of delicious cakes.

For a **pub** with a difference, *The White Horse* (☎ 01903-814084, 🖥 the whitehorsesteyning.com; food Mon-Sat noon-9.30pm, Sun to 9pm; limited WI-FI; 🐾 on a lead) is styled as a 'smokehouse and grill'. It sits at the crossroads on the High St and the food is decent value, especially some of the lunchtime deals (from £8.50). For an evening meal, try their house smoked pork belly with paprika chips (£14.95) or go for one of their sharing boards (from £15.95).

Chequer Inn (see Where to stay; limited WI-FI; 🐾 in certain areas only; food Fri, Sat noon-3pm & 6-8pm, Sun noon-4pm) is a more traditional pub with local ales, good food and occasional live music. They have some good vegan options, including three bean chilli (£12.95).

Finally, at the other end of town, *Big Fish* (Mon-Thur & Sat 5-9pm, Fri noon-2pm & 5-9pm) is the town's chippy.

❑ CHANCTONBURY RING
Map 21, p131

This exposed hilltop is one of the great viewpoints of the South Downs but more significantly it is the **site of an Iron Age hill-fort** believed to date back to the 6th century bc. Today it is equally famous for the copse of beech trees that were planted on the site of the fort by Charles Goring in 1760 and which grew to become one of the

most famous landmarks in Sussex. Not even the infamous storm of 1987 managed to permanently alter the beauty of this place; the replanting programme that took place shortly afterwards to replace the many fallen trees seems to have done the trick, and the copse is looking majestic once more.

Chanctonbury Ring is also known for its folklore, tales of witchcraft, fairies and other mysterious goings-on. Perhaps the most famous story goes that while Satan was digging the nearby Devil's Dyke valley, spadefuls of earth landed here creating the hill you see today. The ring is also said to be haunted. It may be a beauty spot by day but it takes a brave person to spend the night there.

BRAMBER & UPPER BEEDING
MAP 22a, p135

The main attraction is **Bramber Castle** (open dawn to dusk, free), built by William de Broase in 1073 on a prominent knoll behind the village. In truth there is not much left of it, save for a few ramparts and some collapsed sections of wall but the old moat, despite now having no water and having been taken over by trees, is still clearly visible. The only surviving part of the castle that's still in use is the **Church of St Nicholas** which was built around the same time.

St Mary's House (☎ 01903-816205, 🖳 stmarysbramber.co.uk; May-Sep Thur, Sun & bank holidays 2-6pm; £12, garden only £8) is a magnificent place which claims to be the finest example of a 15th-century timber-framed house in Sussex. The perfectly manicured front garden, with its topiary and fish ponds, only adds to the charm. Despite the house being a private residence the owners do allow visitors in to admire the antiques, an Elizabethan *trompe l'oeil* painted room, four-poster beds, a 'mysterious, ivy-clad monks' walk' and octagonal dining-room. It is a popular location for TV dramas, most notably *Dr Who*.

Services

On the main street in Upper Beeding there is a **newsagent** (Mon-Fri 5.30am-5pm, Sat to 1pm, Sun to noon) as well as a **pharmacy** (Mon-Fri 9am-1pm & 2-5.30pm, Sat 9am-12.30pm).

There's a small Londis **shop** (Mon-Sat 6am-11pm, Sun 7am-11pm) that sells hot drinks and snacks; it is in a petrol station on the way out of town.

Public transport

Brighton & Hove Buses' No 2 **bus** service (Steyning–Rottingdean) passes through both Bramber and Upper Beeding. Compass Bus No 100 also calls at both on its way between Horsham and Burgess Hill via Pulborough. See pp46-8 for details.

Where to stay, eat and drink

In **Bramber**, there are two smart options for **meal** and a **room** for the night. *The*

Castle Inn Hotel (☎ 01903-812102, 🖳 castleinnhotel.co.uk; 16D or T/ 4Tr, 1 rm sleeps up to 5, all en suite; ☞; Ⓛ; 🐾) is an olde-worlde pub with B&B in a variety of rooms for around £45 for a single, £35pp in a double or twin. Note there is sometimes a minimum two-night stay at weekends. This is also one of the best places to eat (food Mon-Fri 7-9am, noon-3pm & 6-9pm, Sun noon-4pm; 🐾), which is open for breakfast for non-residents too (full English from £12, bacon & egg muffin £9). They also serve real ale.

If you have cleaned the mud from your boots, a night at the *The Tollgate* (☎ 01903-879494, 🖳 thetollgatehotel.com; 30D/6D or T/4T, all en suite; ☞; Ⓛ; 🐾) could be in order. With lots of pristine rooms, including two with jacuzzis and three dog-friendly rooms, rates are highly variable but start at around £45 for one person, £35pp in a double or twin. For the best rates book well in advance and check their website for special offers. At the time of research their restaurant was temporarily closed – contact them for an update on reopening.

Alternatively, *Maharajah* (☎ 01903-812123, 🖳 maharajahofbramber.co.uk; Wed-Sun noon-2.30pm & 5-11.30pm) claims to be a high-class Indian restaurant, which is fair. Main dishes start at around £9.95, or splash out on their king prawn Chef's Special (£21.95).

In **Upper Beeding**, *The Rising Sun* (☎ 01903-814424, 🖳 risingsunupperbeeding .com; **fb**; 1D/1T en suite ; Ⓛ; 🐾) is a friendly pub with clean rooms, offering B&B from £40pp (sgl occ £60) and decent pub food (Tue-Thur noon-2.30pm & 5.30-8.30pm, Fri & Sat noon-2.30pm & 5.30-9pm, Sun noon-4pm) such as home-baked ham with bubble & squeak (£12.95). While the kitchen is closed on a Monday, the bar is open from 4pm.

There is more Indian food at *Khushbu* (☎ 01903-816646, 🖳 khushbutandoori.co .uk; daily 5.30-10pm) which has an extensive menu. Finally, a branch of the international chain *Subway* (Mon-Fri 8am-7pm, Sat from 9am, Sun 10am-5pm) sits by Londis in the petrol station.

ROUTE GUIDE AND MAPS

E→ STEYNING TO PYECOMBE   MAPS 22-26

After the initial climb the going is easy for most of this **10¼-mile (16.5km, 4-5½hrs, plus 20-30 mins from Steyning to the South Downs Way) section** with a good track leading the way along the level escarpment of the Downs. There are, once again, great views in all directions once you climb out of the Adur Valley to **Truleigh Hill** (Map 23), particularly to the north across the Weald, with the villages of **Fulking** (Map 24; see p140) and **Poynings** (p142) lying hidden at the foot of the Downs below.

Despite the ugly pub and car park at the top of the hill the highlight of this stretch has to be **Devil's Dyke** (Map 24, p141), a spectacular dry valley, 100 metres deep. During Victorian times Devil's Dyke became something of a tourist attraction and even had its own railway station.

After leaving the Dyke the Way drops down to Saddlescombe Farm and then over the flanks of **Newtimber Hill** (Map 25, p143), owned by the National

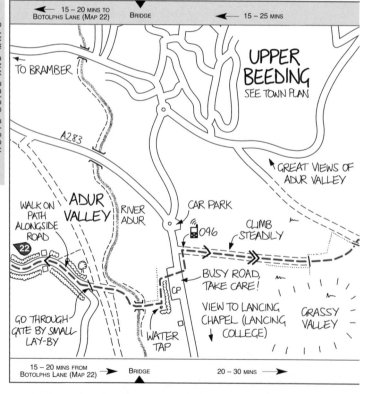

ROUTE GUIDE AND MAPS

Trust and an oasis of calm after the crowds that flock to the Dyke. **Pyecombe** (Map 26; see p144) is perhaps one of the more disappointing villages on the trail, blighted as it is by the constant roar of traffic, but there are accommodation and services here, and buses to Brighton and Crawley, for those tackling the way in stages.

TRULEIGH HILL   MAP 23

Right on the Way, *YHA Truleigh Hill* (reservations ☎ 0345-371 9047, or ☎ 01903-813419, 🖳 yha.org.uk/hostel/yha-truleigh-hill; 6 x 2-, 1 x 4-, 6 x 6-bed rooms; shared facilities; wi-fi communal area; Ⓛ; Mar-Oct) is a tree-shaded, purpose-built hostel with all the usual useful facilities including a drying room. Private **rooms** cost £29-100 for 2-6 sharing; two of

the 6-bed rooms and one of the 4-bed rooms have a double beds so technically they can sleep 7/5.

The *café* (daily 8am-10pm, winter usually weekends only) serves meals (to 8.30/9pm), hot drinks, cold beer and ice-creams and is open to the public too. There's also a small **shop**.

Camping (Mar-Oct; £10pp) is also

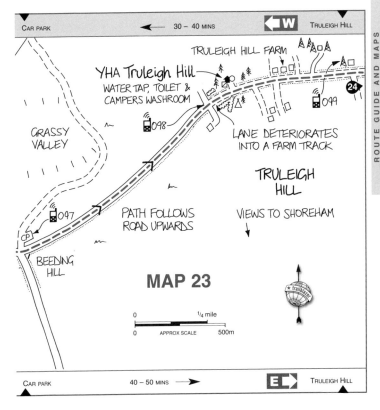

available in the field opposite. There's a 24hr 'campers' washroom' with toilet, shower and changing room beside the **water tap** outside the entrance to the hostel. They also have two **bell tents** (£50-100 for up to 5); each has a double bed, two sin-

gles and a fold-out bed. A further option is provided by some basic **land pods** (£39-100 for up to 4) with two double beds, including bedding and electricity sockets. Dogs on leads are welcome for all camping-type accommodation.

FULKING   MAP 24

This tiny village has little of specific interest to the walker except for the delightful *Shepherd & Dog Inn* (☎ 01273-857382, 🖳 shepherdanddogpub.co.uk; **fb**; food Mon-

Sat noon-8pm, Sun noon-6pm; limited wifi; 🐕 on lead). It's everything a proper country pub should be with plenty of real ales, good **food** (mains from £16) and a

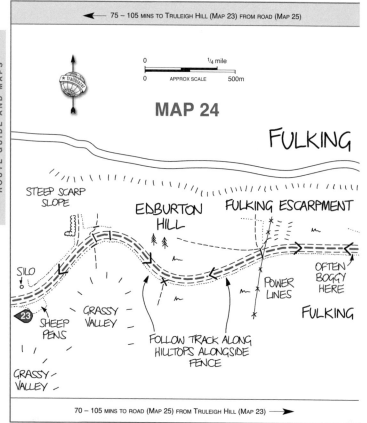

ROUTE GUIDE AND MAPS

← 75 – 105 MINS TO TRULEIGH HILL (MAP 23) FROM ROAD (MAP 25)

0   ¼ mile
0   APPROX SCALE   500m

MAP 24

FULKING

STEEP SCARP SLOPE

EDBURTON HILL

FULKING ESCARPMENT

SILO

23

SHEEP PENS

GRASSY VALLEY

POWER LINES

OFTEN BOGGY HERE

FULKING

FOLLOW TRACK ALONG HILLTOPS ALONGSIDE FENCE

GRASSY VALLEY

70 – 105 MINS TO ROAD (MAP 25) FROM TRULEIGH HILL (MAP 23) →

beer garden with views of the Downs.

The pub gets its name from Fulking's reputation for having a rather large population of sheep: in the early 19th century the village was home to ten times as many sheep as people and the pub was the place where the shepherds would meet after a hard day's shearing to spend their earnings on the local brew.

Next to the pub car park is the locally famous **Victorian fountain**, placed there in memory of John Ruskin, the man responsible for installing the village's water supply.

Devil's Dyke Devil's Dyke (Map 24) is a spectacular dry valley said to have been carved out by Satan himself in order to let the sea flood over the lowland Weald and destroy all the churches. Geologists have blown this theory out of the water by proving that it is in fact a result of folding of the chalk strata due to pressure building between the African and Eurasian plates.

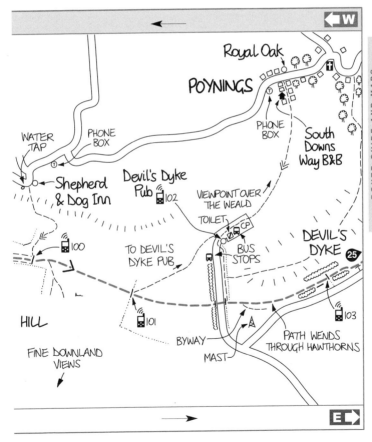

POYNINGS   MAP 24, p141

The hidden leafy village of Poynings sits at the foot of the escarpment away from the hustle and bustle high above at the beauty spot of Devil's Dyke. Poynings is a scenic two-mile walk from the Dyke.

South Downs Way B&B (☎ 01273-857220, 🖳 southdownswaybandb.co.uk; 2D/1D or T all en suite ⒧; 🐾), at Dyke Lane Cottage, is both walker- and cyclist-friendly with free washing and drying facilities for bikes, dogs, clothes and muddy boots! B&B here costs from £55pp with breakfast including locally sourced sausages and eggs from their own hens.

Set in the heart of the village, the *Royal Oak* (☎ 01273-857389, 🖳 royaloakpoynings.pub; food Mon, Thur & Fri noon-3pm & 6-9pm, Sat noon-9pm, Sun noon-6pm; 🐾) serves all the pub-grub classics plus a few less common offerings, such as seafood chowder (£19). Note that the pub is closed on Tuesdays and Wednesdays.

If descending to the Royal Oak does not appeal, the only other choice is the somewhat characterless *Devil's Dyke* (☎ 01273-857256, 🖳 vintageinn.co.uk; food Mon-Sat noon-10pm, Sun noon-9.30pm; 🐾), whose most eye-catching feature is the fabulous views on offer from its benches outside. However, the menu is undeniably extensive with plenty of comfort food on offer, such as fish finger sandwich (£9.95) or mac & cheese (£13.75).

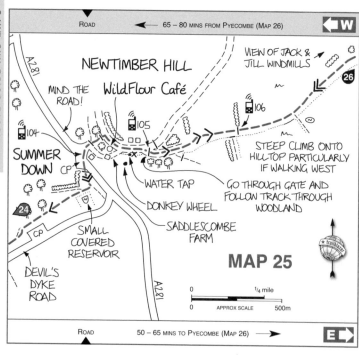

ROUTE GUIDE AND MAPS

ROAD ← 65 – 80 MINS FROM PYECOMBE (MAP 26) ◀W

A281

NEWTIMBER HILL

VIEW OF JACK & JILL WINDMILLS

26

MIND THE ROAD!

WildFlour Café

📱106

📱104

📱105

SUMMER DOWN CP

STEEP CLIMB ONTO HILLTOP PARTICULARLY IF WALKING WEST

WATER TAP

GO THROUGH GATE AND FOLLOW TRACK THROUGH WOODLAND

24

DONKEY WHEEL

SMALL COVERED RESERVOIR

SADDLESCOMBE FARM

MAP 25

DEVIL'S DYKE ROAD

A281

0   ¼ mile
0   500m
APPROX SCALE

ROAD   50 – 65 MINS TO PYECOMBE (MAP 26) →   E▶

NEWTIMBER HILL   MAP 25

Across the A281 from Devil's Dyke is **Saddlescombe Farm**, run by the National Trust. It's here you'll find the quirky, slightly ramshackle, but always great *WildFlour Café* (🖥 wildflourcafe.business.site; **fb**; Mar-Oct Tue-Sun 10am-5pm, Nov Sat & Sun only 10am-4pm, check website for winter hrs), perhaps our favourite eatery on the entire trail. Serving cream teas, cakes and hot food, such as dhals, from a caravan in a courtyard, with only barns for shelter, at the time of writing the café was undergoing a change of ownership, though the outgoing owners are not expecting anything to change.

Nearby is one of the last examples of a **donkey wheel** used to pump water from the well.

W ← PYECOMBE TO STEYNING   MAPS 26-22

It's with little regret that westbound Way walkers finally leave behind the cacophony of traffic at Pyecombe to climb out of the valley and back onto the serenity of the Downs. It's a lovely, straightforward though initially steep **10¼-mile (16.5km, 4¼-5¾hrs, plus 25-35 mins to Steyning)** walk too, as you follow a good track along the level escarpment of the Downs.

Wonderful views once again stretch out on either side, blighted only slightly by the crowds swarming over the trail along here on high days and holidays. Many have made the journey from Brighton, which lies just a few miles to the south, but what brings them here is the scenery surrounding the dry valley of **Devil's Dyke** (Map 24; see p141), a deep, distinctive crumple in the land caused by tectonic pressure. If the weather's on your side a pleasant day can be had meandering along the crest of the Downs, enjoying a lunch at Wildflour Café at **Newtimber Hill** (Map 25) and then perhaps dropping off the trail to visit the twin villages of **Poynings** (p141) or **Fulking** (p140), or remaining on it to eat or stay at the YHA on **Truleigh Hill** (Map 23; p139). While the YHA is in a lovely location and right on the trail, for many the villages of **Upper Beeding** (Map 23 & Map 22a; see p135), and its neighbours **Bramber** and **Steyning** (see p134; both on Map 22 & Map 22a), all just off the trail, provide a natural, logical end to the day.

[*Next route overview p133*]

ROUTE GUIDE AND MAPS

PYECOMBE   MAP 26, p144

Pyecombe, like many a downland village, has some very pretty ivy-clad flint houses but the peace and tranquillity that it evidently once had has been somewhat spoilt by the constant hum of traffic from the A23 which converges with the A273 just below the village. The trees hide the roads from view but struggle to do the same with the constant drone. Nevertheless, it's a convenient place to stay being right on the Way and with a campsite, two B&Bs and a pub.

The Norman **church** (daily 9am-6pm, to 4pm in winter) is very welcoming, allowing you to make yourself a cup of coffee or tea in their kitchen, or use the **toilet**. The former **forge** in the house opposite was once the source of some of the best shepherds' crooks in southern England.

If you're looking for a picnic lunch, the BP petrol station just south of the village has a 24hr **M&S food outlet** stocked with treats, as well as a **Wild Bean Café**.

Camping is available at *Wolstonbury Dreaming* (☎ 07540-350384, 🖳 wolstonburydreaming.com; 🐾 but on leads at certain times of the year) on Chantry Farm. Named after the local hill that's home to several Bronze Age monuments, it's a small eco-friendly place (hot-water tap-and-bucket 'showers'; compost toilets; no mains electricity) with space for half a dozen or so tents (around £20pp) and a couple of cosy **shepherd's huts** (from £120 per night). Conscious of their location next to the Way, they offer both dinner packs (£8) and 'brekkie packs' (£4).

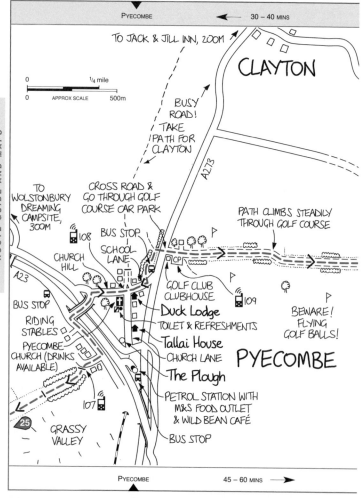

Tallai House (☎ 01273-845848, 🖥 pyecombebb.co.uk; 1D/2D or T, en suite) charges from £82.50pp for B&B (single £145) and is very welcoming.

Alternatively, and right on the trail in the heart of the village, is *Duck Lodge* (☎ 07966-292601, 🖥 duck-lodge.com; 1D en suite) at Stable Cottage on School Lane, offering a rather luxurious wooden cabin with its own hot tub, fridge, microwave and honesty bar. Rates (from £87.50pp; sgl occ £165) include a continental breakfast (freshly baked bread, croissants, cheese, ham, yoghurt & fruit).

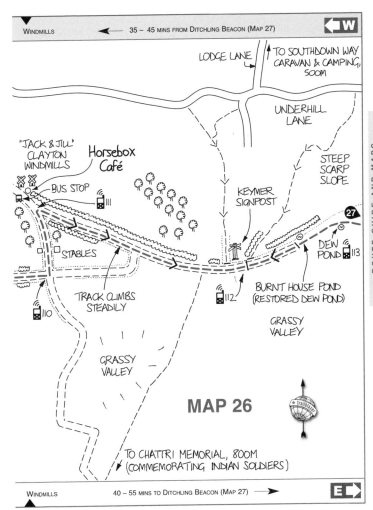

WINDMILLS   ← 35 – 45 MINS FROM DITCHLING BEACON (MAP 27)   ◄ W

LODGE LANE

TO SOUTHDOWN WAY CARAVAN & CAMPING, 500M

UNDERHILL LANE

"JACK & JILL" CLAYTON WINDMILLS

Horsebox Café

BUS STOP

STEEP SCARP SLOPE

KEYMER SIGNPOST

DEW POND 🔋113

STABLES

TRACK CLIMBS STEADILY

🔋112

BURNT HOUSE POND (RESTORED DEW POND)

🔋110

GRASSY VALLEY

GRASSY VALLEY

MAP 26

TO CHATTRI MEMORIAL, 800M (COMMEMORATING INDIAN SOLDIERS)

WINDMILLS   40 – 55 MINS TO DITCHLING BEACON (MAP 27) →   E ►

ROUTE GUIDE AND MAPS

The Plough (☎ 01273-842796, 💻 the-ploughpyecombe.co.uk; food Mon-Fri noon-10pm) commands unenviable views of the traffic hurtling down the A23 to and from Brighton. Despite this it is a good pub with tasty food such as pizzas from £12 and mains from £14; they also do takeaways (10% discount).

Metrobus's No 270 (East Grinstead–Brighton) **bus** stops here as do their 271 and 273 (both Crawley–Brighton). See p47 for details.

E➔ PYECOMBE TO SOUTHEASE   MAPS 26-31

This reasonably long stretch, **15 miles (24km, 5-7hrs)** provides sweeping views north. The high ground in the distance is the High Weald, a large area of sandstone incorporating Ashdown Forest, the home of Winnie the Pooh, while to the south is Brighton and the English Channel.

The high point of this section is **Ditchling Beacon** (Map 27) with its namesake **Ditchling** village (Map 27a; see opposite) within walking distance of the trail. After leaving the hustle and bustle of the Beacon the route continues towards **Black Cap** (Map 28, p149) where the track takes a sharp right-hand turn at the first turn-off point for those wanting to visit **Lewes** (p150).

After the Lewes turn-off the path heads towards, and then across, the A27 dual carriageway (Map 29), then returns to the ridge of the Downs. Having passed the turn-off for the village of **Kingston-near-Lewes** (Map 30, see p159) and crossed the **Greenwich Meridian** (Map 31), the path drops once more, this time to the twin villages of **Rodmell** (see p158) and **Southease** (see p158) where the smell of the sea will probably be prevalent and the chalk cliffs of Seaford Head can be seen in the distance. There are a few accommodation and food options on the way.

CLAYTON   MAP 26, p144

The main attraction of Clayton is not the small village at the foot of the hill but the two **windmills** (see box below) just two minutes from the path.

There's no accommodation in the village itself but out on the bend on the main road, about five minutes' walk away, is *Jack & Jill Inn* (☎ 01273-843595, 💻 thejack andjillinn.co.uk; **fb**; 3T/1D, all en suite; Ⓛ; 🐕 bar only), a family-run pub with good-value **food** (Mon-Fri noon-2pm & 5.30-8pm, Sat noon-8pm, Sun to 6pm), real ale (see box p23) and rooms. **B&B** (4D or T) costs £52.50pp (sgl occ from £75); room-only about £10pp less.

❑ JACK AND JILL WINDMILLS   Map 26, p145

The twin windmills above Clayton, known as Jack and Jill, are famous local landmarks that can be seen for miles around. There is evidence that suggests the first windmill was erected way back in 1765. The names of the windmills are said to originate from the 1920s when tourists first came to visit.

The post mill Jill, the white windmill, has been fully restored and occasionally grinds out some wholemeal flour. It is the only one of the two that is open to the public (💻 jillwindmill.org.uk; May-Sep, most Sun & bank hols 2-5pm; free). There's a small horsebox-cum-**café** here just before the car park, though with highly weather-dependent opening hours.

Ditchling Beacon Ditchling Beacon (Map 27) is a National Nature Reserve and a popular tourist spot. The name refers to the pyres that were burnt here and at other sites along the Downs such as the Beacon Hill (see p86) in Hampshire. The beacons were lit to warn of impending attack, most notably during the time of the Spanish Armada. More recently they were used for celebrating the Queen's Platinum Jubilee in 2022. Access is made easy by the road that winds in hairpins up the escarpment from Ditchling village. Brighton & Hove Buses operate a seasonal and weekend only **bus** service (No 79; see p46) between the car park at the beacon and Brighton.

DITCHLING   MAP 27a

It is about a mile from the Downs to this village but if you are trying to decide on a place to spend the night this is a good choice and worth the short detour. Ditchling is among the prettiest of the pretty, perhaps bettered only by Alfriston and Amberley. There is a multitude of historic buildings centred around the crossroads but the oldest of all is the fine 13th-century Norman **St Margaret's Church**. Opposite the church you can see the house, **Wings Place**, bought by Henry VIII for his fourth wife, Anne of Cleves (see also Plumpton p149 and Lewes p150), as part of a 'pay off' at the end of their marriage.

Not far from the church, in the old Victorian village school, is **Ditchling Museum of Art + Craft** (☎ 01273-844744, 🖳 ditchlingmuseumartcraft.org.uk; mid Jan to mid Dec Wed-Sun & Bank Hols 10.30am-5pm; £8). It's well worth visiting, with impressive collections by famous local artists and craftspeople such as the sculptor and engraver Eric Gill, the printer Hilary Pepler, the weaver Ethel Mairet and the painters David Jones and Sir Frank Brangwyn. They have a small *café* selling hot drinks and cakes.

There is a small village **shop-cum-post office** (☎ 01273-842736; shop & PO daily 8am-1pm) at the crossroads in the centre of the village. Close by is Ditchling **Pharmacy** (Mon-Thur 9am-1pm & 2-5.30pm, Fri 9am-1pm & 2-6.30pm).

Campers should head about a mile west along Clayton Rd to find *Southdown Way Caravan & Camping Park* (off Maps 26 & 27a; ☎ 01273-841877, 🖳 southdown-caravancamping.org.uk; **fb**; 🐾 on lead),

which is exceptionally welcoming for a big caravan park. They charge £10pp for backpackers, the shower block is spotlessly clean and there's a laundry room and a small shop in reception. The campsite can also be reached from the Way, via a footpath from Keymer Signpost (Map 26); at the bottom of the path turn right onto Underhill Lane, left along Lodge Lane and the campsite is opposite the end of the road.

The Bull (☎ 01273-843147, 🖳 thebullditchling.com; 4D/2T, all en suite; 🐾) is a wonderful old pub on the High St. There's very comfortable **B&B** starting from £50pp (sgl occ from £80); at weekends they may have a minimum two-night stay. It's a good place to eat (**food** Mon-Sat 9am-9pm, Sun noon-8.30pm; booking rec-

ROUTE GUIDE AND MAPS

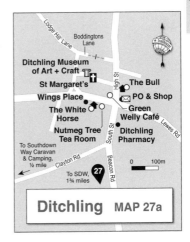

Ditchling   MAP 27a

ommended), though it gets busy at weekends.

There's also ***The White Horse*** (☎ 01273-842006, 🖳 whitehorseditchling.com; **fb**; 3D all en suite, 2D/2D or T private bathroom; ◒; Ⓛ; 🐕 bar only), which charges from £47.50pp (sgl occ from £75) for room only. **Food** (Mon-Thur noon-3pm & 5.30-8.30pm, Fri to 9.30pm, Sat noon-9.30pm, Sun noon-7pm) is available here too, with pub grub mains from £14.

For breakfast, lunch or an afternoon tea try the ***Green Welly Café*** (☎ 01273-841010, 🖳 www.thegreenwellycafe.co.uk; **fb**; Tue-Sun 9am-3pm; 🐕) and either sit indoors or in their pleasant courtyard garden. The menu (eat-in or take away) includes delicious breakfast ciabattas.

Our favourite, however, is just round the corner at the 30s/40s-themed ***Nutmeg Tree Tea Rooms*** (☎ 01273-842708, 🖳 thenutmegtree.co.uk; **fb**; Mon & Wed-Fri 9am-4pm, Sat & Sun 8am-4.30pm; temperamental wi-fi; 🐕), which boasts the best selection of cakes on the entire Way, served to you by traditionally attired waitresses in white aprons. It's very popular with the locals – always a good sign.

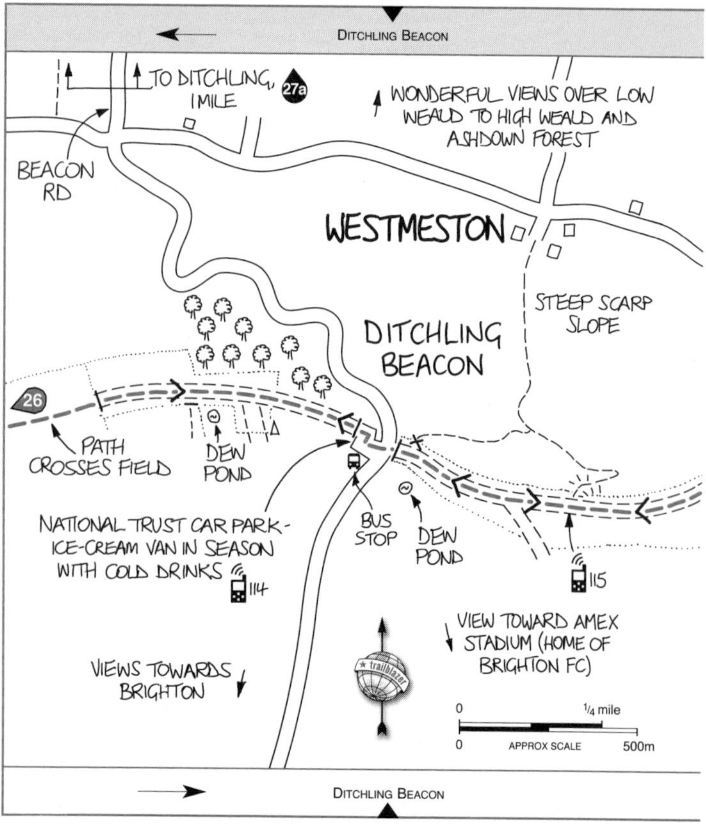

ROUTE GUIDE AND MAPS

Between Ditchling Beacon & Black Cap (Map 27) Right on the Way, about a mile from the Beacon, is the delightful ***Pink Pit Stop*** (**fb**; Mon, Thur & Fri 11am-2pm, Sat & Sun 10am-4pm), serving hot and cold drinks, cakes, toasties and ice cream from a converted van. Their opening hours are highly weather-dependent so check their social media pages for the latest.

PLUMPTON   MAP 27

Famous for its agricultural college, Plumpton is also the location for the privately owned **Plumpton Place**, a 16th-century mansion complete with moat, once owned by Anne of Cleves after it was given to her by Henry VIII. The best view of the mansion is from the Way on the top of the hill, so the only real reason for walkers to come down off the trail here is to visit The Half Moon pub.

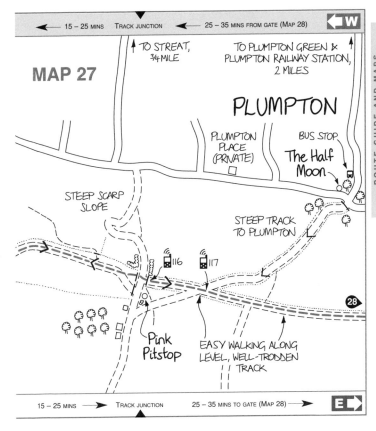

The Half Moon (☎ 01273-890253, 🖳 thehalfmoonplumpton.co.uk; **fb**; **food** Mon-Fri noon-2.30pm & 6-8.30pm, Sat noon-3pm & 6-9pm, Sun to 6pm; 🐾) is an excellent local pub with a wide selection of interesting dishes and real ales on tap. If you're here on a Thursday don't miss their steak nights – £10 for 8oz steak with chips and salad; otherwise, evening mains start at £13.50 for the likes of butternut squash orzotto (similar to risotto but made with pearl barley).

Plumpton **railway station** (see box p44) is actually in Plumpton Green, 2½ miles due north of Plumpton; it's a stop on Southern's London to Eastbourne/Hastings/ Ore line. Compass's **bus** No 166 will take you to Lewes.

To Lewes Those wishing to visit Lewes can either walk or catch public transport. The turn-off from the trail for those walking is at **Black Cap** (Map 28), but note it's at least an hour's walk from here. For those looking to use public transport, there are frequent No 29/29A buses running between Brighton and Lewes along the A27 that stop in front of Housedean Farm (see Map 29 and p156). Also note, it is possible to take a side trip from Lewes to the isolated hill of **Mount Caburn** (see p155-6), the only part of the South Downs that is not covered by the South Downs Way.

LEWES   MAP 28a, p153

'Lewes ... lying like a box of toys under a great amphitheatre of chalky hills ... on the whole it is set down better than any town I have seen in England'   **William Morris**

Lewes, the county town of East Sussex, is an attractive place to visit and one of the most desirable places to live in the South-East. Populated by a vibrant community of independently minded people, Lewes folk tend to like to do things slightly differently from the rest of the country; indeed, they've even issued their own currency (see box p152). It's a lovely place to wander around, there's lots to do and see, and a profusion of places to buy and eat good healthy food; it's well worth spending the night here.

Lewes lies in a strategic position by the River Ouse with Mount Caburn (see p155) rising steeply to the west. This did not go unnoticed by William the Conqueror who had William de Warrene fortify the town soon after the Battle of Hastings in 1066.

The town's focal point is **Lewes Castle** (☎ 01273-486290, 🖳 sussexpast.co .uk; Mar-Oct Tue-Sun 10am-5pm, Jan & Feb Tue-Sun to 4pm, Nov & Dec closed; £10), which sits proudly at the very highest point on a grassy bluff. This Norman castle was built by Lieutenant William de Warenne shortly after the Battle of Hastings in 1066. The well-preserved castle gate and walls can be explored and the ticket also gives access to the **Museum of Sussex Archaeology (Barbican House)** opposite, which has artefacts from the castle, a scale model of 1880s Lewes and a 12-minute video on the history of the town.

You can buy a joint ticket (£15) for both Lewes Castle and the **Anne of Cleves House** (🖳 sussexpast.co.uk; May-Oct Tue-Sun 10am-5pm, Feb-Apr to 4pm, Nov-Jan closed; £6.60), down the hill from the castle. It's well worth dropping in to see the beautiful interior with timber beams and oak furnishings.

Also up near the castle is 15th-century timber-framed **Bull House**, (🖳 sussexpast .co.uk; Mar-Oct Tue-Sun 10am-5pm, Nov-

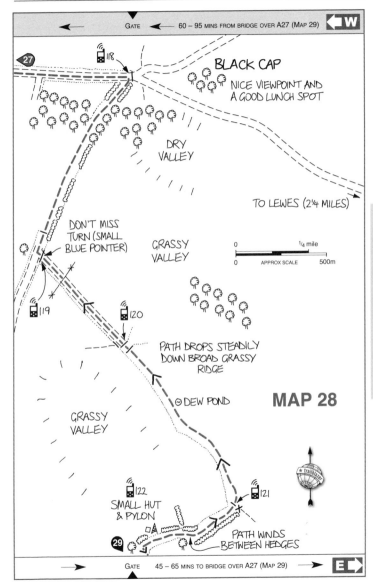

27

118

BLACK CAP

NICE VIEWPOINT AND
A GOOD LUNCH SPOT

DRY
VALLEY

TO LEWES (2¼ MILES)

DON'T MISS
TURN (SMALL
BLUE POINTER)

GRASSY
VALLEY

0   ¼ mile

0   APPROX SCALE   500m

119

120

PATH DROPS STEADILY
DOWN BROAD GRASSY
RIDGE

⊙ DEW POND

MAP 28

GRASSY
VALLEY

122

121

SMALL HUT
& PYLON

PATH WINDS
BETWEEN HEDGES

29

ROUTE GUIDE AND MAPS

Jan closed; free) where Thomas Paine, the founder of American Independence, lived between 1768 and 1774 and now open to the public. During his time in Lewes he acted as the local tobacconist and exciseman.

Lewes still has some excellent book-shops, the oldest of which, **The Fifteenth Century Bookshop** (Sat 11am-5pm, Sun noon-5pm), can be found at the top of the High St near the castle entrance. The timber-framed building that houses the shop is worth a visit in itself.

Priory Park and the ruins of the 11th-century **Priory of St Pancras** are worth visiting and the ruins are well labelled with interesting panels. There's also a little garden of medicinal herbs once grown by the monks. The park and the ruins are always open and there's no entry charge. Between here and the castle are the flower-filled **Southover Grange Gardens**, with a scattering of art sculptures, a 350-year-old mulberry tree and a tulip tree planted in 1951 by Princess Elizabeth before she became Queen Elizabeth II.

Real-ale drinkers cannot go to Lewes without visiting **Harvey's Brewery** (🖳 harveys.org.uk) though with a waiting list of more than a year for guided tours most fans will get no further than the shop. Harvey's is the oldest brewery in Sussex and has been producing real ales (see box p23) for well over 200 years using hops from Sussex and Kent and water from their own spring. The company is still run by the same family that founded it seven generations ago. The **shop** (☎ 01273-480217; Tue-Sat 10am-5pm, Mon & Sun 11am-4pm) sells a vast array of Harvey's products and paraphernalia.

Services

The **tourist information centre** (☎ 01273-483448, 🖳 visitlewes.co.uk; all year Mon-Fri 9.30am-4.30pm, Sat 10am-3pm, to 2pm in winter) is at No 187 High St, on the corner with Fisher St. They can help find local accommodation (although they can't book it for you) and also sell maps, books and guides.

The **post office** (Mon-Sat 9am-5.30pm) is at the lower end of the High St. There is also a Boots **pharmacy** (Mon-Fri 9am-1.30pm & 2.30-5.30pm, Sat & Sun

---

❑ THE LEWES POUND

In 2008, Lewes town took the unusual step of issuing its own currency, to be used alongside sterling. The idea behind the 'Lewes Pound' (🖳 thelewespound.org) is to encourage demand for local goods and services, and the logic behind it is simple: money spent in shops in the town that are merely another branch of a national chain does not stay in the local economy; but money spent in shops owned by locals or on local services does. So while the Lewes Pound would not be accepted in, for example, the local outlet of a nationwide superstore, of which there are several in Lewes, it would be accepted by a local trader – who would then spend it locally with another local trader, and so on. Thus, by ensuring that money is spent locally and so stays within the community, the wealth of the locals is safeguarded.

Lewes Pounds can be bought (with sterling) at one of the issuing points listed on the website, then spent with participating traders.

Whilst the establishing of a new currency may seem like a highly bizarre step to take, it isn't without precedent; indeed, Lewes itself had its own currency for over a century between 1789 and 1895. The issuers of the latest Lewes Pound, however, admit that their currency is not actually legal tender, in that there is no obligation on the part of retailers to accept the pound. Some residents, though, see the Lewes Pound as an unnecessary complication. They argue that they can support local traders by buying from them using good old-fashioned sterling. And it's true that the Lewes Pound doesn't seem to be quite as much in evidence as it was in the past.

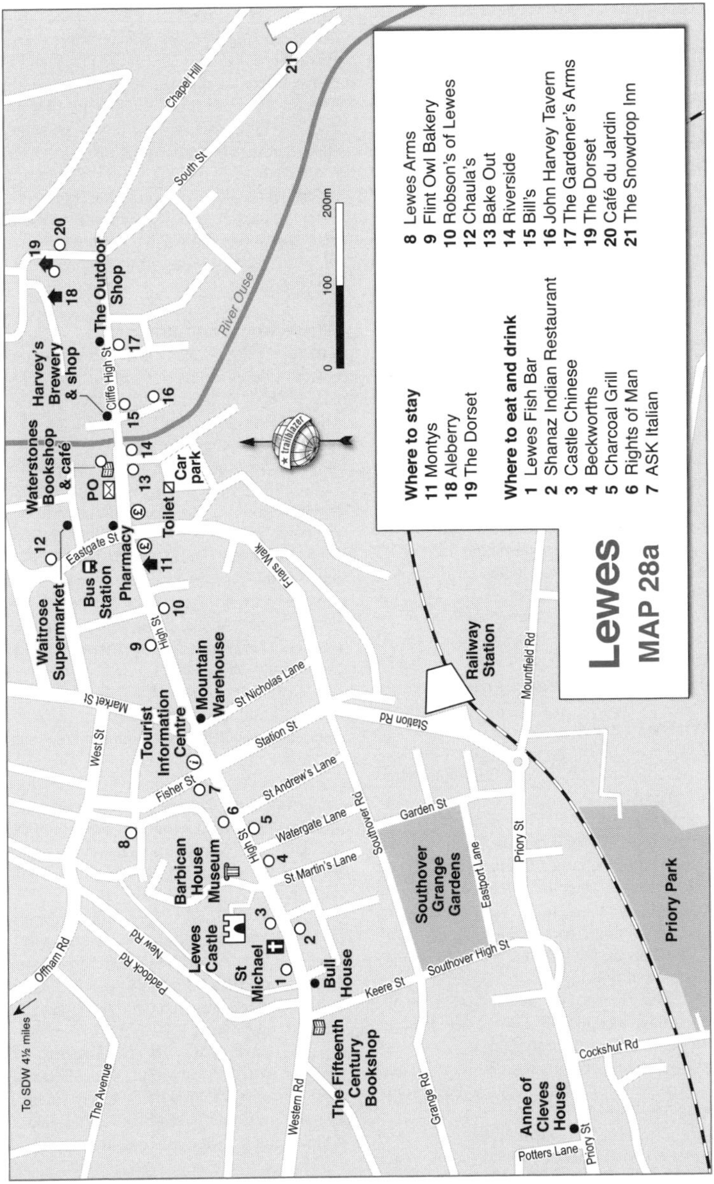

Lewes
MAP 28a

Where to stay
11 Montys
18 Aleberry
19 The Dorset

Where to eat and drink
1 Lewes Fish Bar
2 Shanaz Indian Restaurant
3 Castle Chinese
4 Beckworths
5 Charcoal Grill
6 Rights of Man
7 ASK Italian
8 Lewes Arms
9 Flint Owl Bakery
10 Robson's of Lewes
12 Chaula's
13 Bake Out
14 Riverside
15 Bill's
16 John Harvey Tavern
17 The Gardener's Arms
19 The Dorset
20 Café du Jardin
21 The Snowdrop Inn

Chapel Hill
South St
River Ouse
The Outdoor Shop
Cliffe High St
Harvey's Brewery & shop
Waterstones Bookshop & café
PO
Car park
Toilet
Pharmacy
Eastgate St
Waitrose Supermarket
Bus Station
High St
Market St
Mountain Warehouse
Friars Walk
West St
Tourist Information Centre
Fisher St
St Nicholas Lane
Station St
St Andrew's Lane
Station Rd
Railway Station
Mountfield Rd
Barbican House Museum
Watergate Lane
St Martin's Lane
Garden St
Southover Rd
Southover Grange Gardens
Eastport Lane
Priory St
Lewes Castle
St Michael
New Rd
Bull House
Keere St
Southover High St
Priory Park
Offham Rd
Paddock Rd
The Fifteenth Century Bookshop
Western Rd
Grange Rd
Anne of Cleves House
Cockshut Rd
Potters Lane
Priory St
The Avenue
To SDW 4½ miles
Trailblazer
200m
100
0

ROUTE GUIDE AND MAPS

10am-4pm) and several **banks** with **ATMs**.

Waitrose **supermarket** (Mon-Sat 7.30am-9pm, Sun 10am-4pm) is on Eastgate St while **walking equipment and camping gear** (including fuel for camping stoves) can be found at The Outdoor Shop (☎ 01273-487840; Mon-Fri 9.30am-5pm, Sat 9am-5pm), just past the river, or Mountain Warehouse (Mon-Sat 9am-5.30pm, Sun 10am-4pm) at the top of the hill.

In the same area there's a Waterstones **bookshop** (Mon-Sat 9am-5.30pm, Sun 10am-4pm) and *café* (closes 30 mins before shop).

Public transport
Lewes is a stop on several of Southern's **train** services (see box p44); the **railway station** is on the southern side of town.

The **bus station** is on Eastgate St and there are several useful **bus** services including the No 29/29A (Brighton–Tunbridge Wells). For Rodmell, Southease or Kingston-near-Lewes take the No 123 (to Newhaven); for Eastbourne No 125, or it's No 166 (to Haywards Heath) for Plumpton. See pp46-8 for details.

For a **taxi** try Lewes Town Taxis (☎ 01273-474747, 💻 lewestowntaxis.co.uk) or GM Taxis (☎ 01273-477567 or 01273-473737, 💻 gmtaxislewes.co.uk).

Where to stay
As with any other popular tourist town, it is advisable to book accommodation in advance here.

Aleberry (☎ 01273-480865, 💻 aleberry.co.uk; 1D or T private bathroom; 🛏; min 2 nights) charges £60pp (sgl £100) for B&B with a healthy breakfast of fruit, yoghurt, cereal and toast. They also have an additional single room which is only available when booked with the double as they share a bathroom.

The Dorset (☎ 01273-474823, 💻 the dorsetlewes.co.uk; 5D/1D or T, all en suite; 🛏) is a walker-friendly Harvey's Brewery pub which has rooms for £30-42.50pp (sgl occ room rate). The rate includes a continental breakfast.

Climbing the hill from the river towards the castle, you'll soon reach *Montys* (☎ 017966 818505, 💻 montys accommodation.co.uk; 2D, en suite; 🛏), Broughton House, 16 High St, which charges from £75pp (sgl occ room rate). The lovely room has a kitchenette (but no cooking facilities), a four-poster bed and free-standing bath as well as a shower room. There's also the Courtyard Apartment, comprising a double room with en-suite shower and its own sitting room that opens onto a small courtyard. Note, however, that a two-night minimum stay is preferred.

Where to eat and drink
Cafés At the bottom end of town, on the eastern side of the river, *Café du Jardin* (☎ 01273-480777, 💻 cafedujardin.co.uk; Tue-Sat 9am-4pm, Sun 10am-3pm; 🐾) is a quirky little courtyard café serving lunches and teas. Set amongst an antique shop and a studio, it's right at home here in Lewes.

Overlooking the river is **Riverside** (💻 riverside-lewes.co.uk), a small, market-like food hall with a *café* (☎ 01273-487888; daily 9am-7pm; 🐾), a sweet shop, fishmonger and various other stalls on the ground floor, and a good-value *brasserie* (☎ 01273-472247; Mon-Fri 9am-4.30pm, Sat to 5pm; 🐾) upstairs.

Next door, *Bake Out* (Mon-Fri 7am-4.30pm, Sat 7am-5.30pm, Sun 8.30am-4pm) is a small bakery with some seating for coffee drinkers.

Further up the hill, lovely bakery-cum-café *Flint Owl Bakery* (💻 flintowlbakery .com/pages/lewes; Mon-Fri 8.30am-5pm, Sat 9am-5pm, Sun to 1pm) has more comfortable seating including some in a small back garden.

Across the road, coffee shop *Robson's of Lewes* (☎ 01273-480654, 💻 robsonsof lewes.co.uk; Mon-Sat 9am-5pm, Sun 10am-5pm; 🐾 garden only) serves breakfasts, light lunches, teas and ice-cream to eat in or take away.

For sandwiches, try *Beckworths* (☎ 01273-474502; Mon 10am-4pm, Tue-Sat 9.30am-4pm) which is set in a tiny timber-framed house at 67 High St and is also a deli serving a variety of cold meats.

Pubs With a brewery in town it's not surprising that there's a wide choice of pubs with a cracking selection of real ales.

Harvey's (see p152) owns and serves its ales in several pubs in town. These include *The Dorset* (see Where to Stay; food Mon-Thur noon-3pm & 5-9pm, Fri & Sat noon-9pm, Sun to 4pm; 🐾 bar only), on Mailing St, and *John Harvey Tavern* (☎ 01273-479880, 🖥 johnharveytavern.co.uk; fb; food Mon-Sat noon-8pm, Sun to 4pm; 🐾), opposite the brewery.

Another good spot for a pint of the local brew, and many others since it's a real ale pub, is *The Gardener's Arms* (☎ 01273-474808; bar Mon-Sat 11am-10.30pm, Sun noon-10pm; 🐾) which is conveniently situated a short way down the High St; it is popular with locals wanting a quiet drink.

Tucked away in the side streets behind the castle, *Lewes Arms* (☎ 01273-473152, 🖥 lewesarms.co.uk; food Mon-Fri noon-8.30pm, Sat to 9pm, Sun to 5pm; 🐾) is a lovely traditional pub with snugs and quiet corners where you can enjoy a beer; they offer good pizzas (from £8.50) too.

Below the chalk cliffs that tower above the quiet end of South St, *The Snowdrop Inn* (☎ 01273-471018; fb; food Thur-Sat noon-9pm, Sun to 6pm; 🐾) is named to commemorate the eight people who were killed here in the 1836 avalanche; the deadliest avalanche in British history. The community ties are strong, and it's very friendly with good food, fine ale, some courtyard seating and a menu of pub classics.

Also commemorating the history of Lewes, *The Rights of Man* (🖥 rightsofmanlewes.com; food Mon-Sat noon-3pm & 6-9.30pm, Sun noon-6pm) is named after the seminal work of the town's most celebrated resident, Thomas Paine. A traditional wood-panelled pub at the front with some lovely cosy booths, the back is given over to the restaurant, and there's a roof terrace overlooking the castle too. The comprehensive menu includes such international treats as moules frites (£16.50) or tapas to share (from £5 per dish).

Restaurants & takeaways
There are several decent restaurants down by the river. *Bill's* (☎ 020-8054 5395, 🖥 bills-website.co.uk/restaurants/lewes; Mon-Wed 8am-10pm, Thur-Sat to 11pm, Sun 9am-10pm) is popular, with tables outside on the cobbled street. Now a nationwide chain, the original was here in Lewes (albeit at different premises before they were destroyed in a flood). Wholesome offerings range from seafood linguine and hamburgers to halloumi shawarma and fish pie.

For Italian food you could try *ASK Italian* (☎ 01273-019090, 🖥 askitalian.co.uk; Mon-Thur 11.30am-9.30pm, Fri to 10pm, Sat to 11pm, Sun to 9pm), a reliable chain serving the usual pizza and pasta dishes.

There are several Indian restaurants, of which *Chaula's* (☎ 01273-476707, 🖥 chaulas.co.uk; Tue-Thur noon-2.30pm & 5-9.30pm, Fri & Sat to 10pm, Sun to 9pm), at 6 Eastgate St near the bus station, is amongst the best, with *Shanaz Indian Restaurant* (☎ 01273-488028, 🖥 shanazlewes.co.uk; Sun-Thur 5.30-9.45pm, Fri & Sat 5.30-10.45pm) up at the top end of the High St, proving a worthy rival.

For the flavours of the Orient there's *Castle Chinese* (☎ 01273-473235, 🖥 castlechinese.co.uk; fb; Tue-Thur 5-10pm, Fri & Sat to 10.30pm, Sun to 9.30pm) near the castle, where you can eat in or take away.

For takeaway only there's *Charcoal Grill* (☎ 01273-471126; Sun-Thur noon-midnight, Fri & Sat to 1am) with kebabs and burgers, and *The Lewes Fish Bar* (☎ 01273-472441, 🖥 lewesfishbar.co.uk; fb; Mon-Sat 11.30am-9pm) at the top of the High St.

SIDE TRIP (FROM LEWES) TO MOUNT CABURN

The only part of the South Downs not covered by the South Downs Way is the isolated hill near Lewes, known rather grandly as Mount Caburn. It is something of an anomaly, being the only part of the Downs separated from the main spine of chalk hills. The hill's unique position makes it an excellent vantage point for admiring the rest of the Downs stretched out to the south, as well as the Ouse Valley and the county town of Lewes. The top of the hill is a National Nature Reserve renowned for its butterflies as well as its paragliders.

The hill is best approached from the village of **Glynde** where there is a railway station (trains leave hourly from Lewes; 5 mins). From Glynde station, Mount Caburn (152m/498ft) looms above. Head towards the hill by walking up the road for five minutes. Just past **Glynde Forge** (blacksmith), which is still operating, is a junction that marks the centre of Glynde village. Turn left and look for the stile in the hedgerow opposite the village shop. The path to the top of Mount Caburn follows the obvious route through the fields from the stile and takes about 30-45 minutes. The return is by the same route or via a path further to the north which drops through a small copse to emerge on the lane north of Glynde village.

Around the A27 (Map 29) There is both accommodation (see Housedean Farm, below) and a food option on the Way between the Lewes turn-off and Kingston-near-Lewes.

For sustenance there's no need to divert far from the trail, at least for walkers passing through before 2pm, as *Oscar's* **snack van** (Mon-Fri 7.30am-2pm) parks here in a layby on weekdays. It does huge cooked breakfasts as well as jacket potatoes, bacon baps and hot drinks, and has some tables and chairs on the grass verge alongside.

HOUSEDEAN FARM   MAP 29
Right on the trail, where it crosses the A27, there's *Housedean Farm Campsite* (☎ 07919-668816, 🖳 housedean.co.uk; **fb**; 🐾; Easter-early Oct). In addition to its 25 **pitches** (£15pp) they also have three **camping pods** (2D or T £60, 1Qd £75; bedding not provided). There's also a fully furnished **shepherd's hut** (sleeps 2; £90, min 2 nights) and a **Pig Ark** (1Qd; £90) set in its own private area of the field and with its own cooking shelter and electricity supply and outdoor bath. Note that the double bed

has a duvet and pillows but you'll need your own bedding for the two single beds. For all pitches, pods and the pig ark there is sometimes a two-night minimum stay at weekends from June to August. There are toilets, showers and a fire pit at each pitch.

From outside the farm, on the A27, is the bus stop for **buses** to Lewes (No 29/29A). The stop for buses to Brighton is on the southern side of the road. See p46 for details.

KINGSTON-NEAR-LEWES
**   MAP 30, p159**
This is one of the larger downland villages. From the top of the hill the rather out-of-place housing estate is all too obvious but once you're down in the village it is well hidden. The main street, lined with pretty cottages, comes as a pleasant surprise.

The Juggs (☎ 01273-472523, 🖳 the juggs.co.uk; 🐾; food Mon-Fri noon-3pm, 5-9pm, Sat noon-9pm, Sun to 8pm) is an

excellent pub with a pretty front garden. The unusual name refers to the baskets once used for carrying fish from Brighton to the market in Lewes. A selection from the 'Pie Corner' menu will set you back around £15.50.

The No 123 **bus** service (Lewes–Newhaven) calls here. See p47 for details.

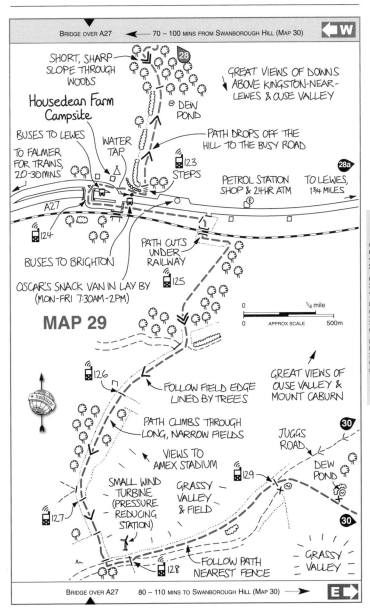

SHORT, SHARP SLOPE THROUGH WOODS

28

GREAT VIEWS OF DOWNS ABOVE KINGSTON-NEAR-LEWES & OUSE VALLEY

Housedean Farm Campsite

DEW POND

BUSES TO LEWES

WATER TAP

TO FALMER FOR TRAINS, 20-30 MINS

PATH DROPS OFF THE HILL TO THE BUSY ROAD

123 STEPS

28a

PETROL STATION SHOP & 24HR ATM

TO LEWES, 1¾ MILES

A27

124

BUSES TO BRIGHTON

PATH CUTS UNDER RAILWAY

125

OSCAR'S SNACK VAN IN LAY BY (MON-FRI 7:30AM-2PM)

MAP 29

0   ¼ mile
0   APPROX SCALE   500m

126

FOLLOW FIELD EDGE LINED BY TREES

GREAT VIEWS OF OUSE VALLEY & MOUNT CABURN

trailblazer

PATH CLIMBS THROUGH LONG, NARROW FIELDS

VIEWS TO AMEX STADIUM

30

JUGGS ROAD

DEW POND

129

SMALL WIND TURBINE (PRESSURE REDUCING STATION)

GRASSY VALLEY & FIELD

30

127

128

FOLLOW PATH NEAREST FENCE

GRASSY VALLEY

ROUTE GUIDE AND MAPS

ROUTE GUIDE AND MAPS

❏ VIRGINIA WOOLF AND THE BLOOMSBURY GROUP

Born in 1882 in London, Virginia Woolf was a highly accomplished novelist, writing such titles as *The Voyage Out*, *Night and Day*, and *Jacob's Room*. In 1912 she married Leonard Woolf. Their links with Sussex began in 1919 when they moved to the 18th-century **Monk's House** in Rodmell. Their friends included a number of famous artists and writers of the time, not least Virginia's sister the artist Vanessa Bell. Along with the poet TS Eliot and the artists Duncan Grant, Roger Fry and Clive Bell they were known collectively as the Bloomsbury Group.

Many of the paintings from the Bloomsbury Group can be seen in the gallery at the former home of Vanessa Bell and Duncan Grant, **Charleston** (see p162), and also in the small church of St Michael and All Angels at **Berwick** (see p165).

Woolf's life was beset by frequent and sometimes enduring spells of mental breakdown. She tried to kill herself through defenestration (ie throwing herself from a window) before finally, on 18 March 1941, filling her pockets with stones and drowning herself in the nearby River Ouse. Her husband was left with a suicide note in which she spelt out the depths of her love for him: 'If anybody could have saved me it would have been you. Everything has gone from me but the certainty of your goodness'.

RODMELL   MAP 31, p160

Rodmell is famous for having been home to Virginia Woolf (see box above) and her husband Leonard. **Monk's House** (☎ 01273-474760, 🖳 nationaltrust.org.uk/visit/sussex/monks-house; summer daily 12.30-5pm, £9), where they once lived, is open to the public.

For general information about Rodmell visit 🖳 rodmell.net.

Opposite the pub is the friendly *Sunnyside Cottage B&B* (☎ 01273-476876; 1T en suite but see note re sitting room; ⓛ; 🐾) with B&B from £50pp (sgl occ also £50) including a good cooked breakfast. The accommodation is like a separate flat though the entrance is through the main house. The sitting room has a single sofa bed so three can sleep here but access to the shower and toilet is through the main bedroom. Note they accept cash or cheques only.

The Abergavenny Arms (☎ 01273-472416, 🖳 abergavennyarms.com; food Mon-Sat noon-8.30pm, Sun to 8pm; 🐾) is a great place to take a break and sit by the log fire if it's cold. The sandwiches (from £7) make a perfect light lunch. The well inside this 15th-century pub was once the main source of water for the entire village.

The No 123 **bus** service also calls here. See p47 for details.

SOUTHEASE   MAP 31, p161

Pretty little Southease is tucked away from any main roads, with a tiny Saxon church, **St Peter's**, incorporating an unusual Norman round tower. This round tower is one of three in Sussex, all in the Ouse Valley and all built in the first half of the 12th century. Inside the church are the remains of some 13th-century wall paintings which once covered the whole church; they were revealed again in the 1930s. There is a **water tap** at the church.

The excellent *YHA South Downs* (☎ 0345-371 9574, ☎ 01273-858780, 🖳 yha.org.uk/hostel/yha-south-downs; 4 x 2-, 2 x 3-, 3 x 4-, 2 x 5-, 4 x 6-bed rooms; ⓛ) is housed in a converted farmhouse near Southease railway station. Some rooms are en suite. Rates start from £15 in a dorm, or

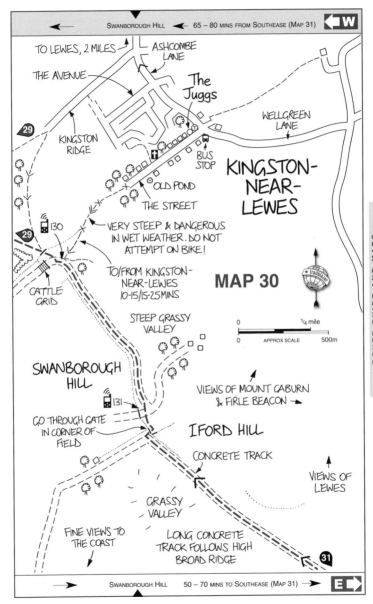

£30 (for a 2-bed room) but vary a lot so check the website for details. **They no longer allow camping** but they do have four heated **camping pods** (from £30/40 for 2/4 people; 🐾); two **land pods** (from £55; sleep 4 in double bunks; 🐾) with table, bench and BBQ firepit outside but no heating inside; and two **bell tents** (sleep 5; from £65; 🐾; Easter to end Sep). Bedding is provided for the pods and bell tents. Other facilities include a self-catering kitchen (closed at the time of research),

drying room and bike shed. The on-site Courtyard **café** (daily 10am-10pm, hot food until 8.30pm) is licensed and is open to the public unless the hostel is booked for sole occupancy.

Because Southease is a stop on Southern's **train** service (see box p44) between Brighton and Seaford it's an ideal place to start or end a day walk. Compass Travel's **bus** No 123 (Lewes–Newhaven) also stops here. See p47 for details.

W ← SOUTHEASE TO PYECOMBE   MAPS 31-26

This stage is long at **15 miles (24km, 5-7hrs)** but with plenty of compensations including views north all the way to the High Weald and Ashdown Forest, the

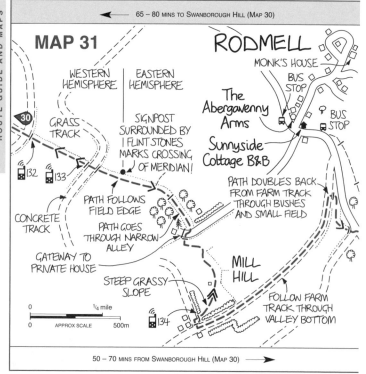

← 65 – 80 MINS TO SWANBOROUGH HILL (MAP 30)

MAP 31

RODMELL

WESTERN HEMISPHERE | EASTERN HEMISPHERE

MONK'S HOUSE

BUS STOP

The Abergavenny Arms

BUS STOP

GRASS TRACK

SIGNPOST SURROUNDED BY 1 FLINT STONES MARKS CROSSING OF MERIDIAN!

Sunnyside Cottage B&B

CONCRETE TRACK

PATH FOLLOWS FIELD EDGE

PATH DOUBLES BACK FROM FARM TRACK THROUGH BUSHES AND SMALL FIELD

PATH GOES THROUGH NARROW ALLEY

GATEWAY TO PRIVATE HOUSE

STEEP GRASSY SLOPE

MILL HILL

0 — ¼ mile
0 — APPROX SCALE — 500m

FOLLOW FARM TRACK THROUGH VALLEY BOTTOM

📱132 📱133 📱134

🔵30

50 – 70 MINS FROM SWANBOROUGH HILL (MAP 30) →

home of Winnie the Pooh. By way of contrast, to the south is Brighton and, glinting beyond, the English Channel, now decorated with military rows of wind turbines. It's because the trail is sandwiched between bustling Brighton and lively **Lewes** (Map 28a; p153; about an hour off the trail via Kingston-near-Lewes), that this stage is, perhaps, the busiest of all. It's possible to take a side trip from Lewes to the isolated hill of **Mount Caburn** (see p155), the only part of the South Downs that is not covered by the South Downs Way. In addition to these large urban centres there are plenty of smaller places on or just off the trail, too.

The highest point, **Ditchling Beacon** (Map 27) is a National Nature Reserve and magnet for dog-walkers, cyclists and horse riders. Those who want to break up this stage will find food and accommodation at **Ditchling** (Map 27a) and **Clayton** (Map 26). The stage ends at **Pyecombe** (p143) which lies right on the trail, although note that the shop and café are about a quarter of a mile south of the village if you are looking to stock up for the next day.

[*Next route overview p143*]

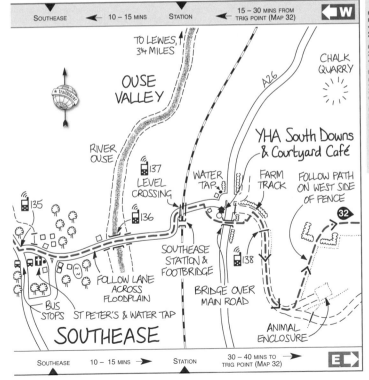

E→   SOUTHEASE TO ALFRISTON   MAPS 31-35

Continuing along the crest of the escarpment, with the high point at **Firle Beacon** (Map 33), this stretch affords easy walking for **7¾ miles (12.5km, 2½-3½hrs)** with fine views to the coast and across the lowlands to **Mount Caburn** (see pp155-6), probably the most grandiose name for any hill of 150 metres' altitude.

Once past **Bostal Hill** the Way passes pathways that lead to **Alciston** and **Berwick** (both off Map 34, p165) before it drops steadily down to pretty, wee **Alfriston** (p168).

WEST FIRLE   off MAP 32

This small village among the trees lies at the foot of the Downs escarpment. **Firle Stores & Post Office** (☎ 01273-858219; Mon-Sat 9am-5.30pm) offers plenty of choice for your lunchbox.

The Ram Inn (☎ 01273-858222, 🖳 raminn.co.uk; **fb**;4D/2D or T, all en suite; 🛉; 🐾) charges £75-97.50pp (sgl occ full room rate) for luxurious **B&B** rooms. **Food** (daily breakfast 9-11am, lunch noon-5pm,

dinner 6-9pm) is served in three rooms, one of which was formerly the Court Room where judges once passed sentence on mis-behaving villagers. The real ales are worth the detour and main dishes will set you back £13-24.

About a 2½-mile walk from the pub is **Charleston** (☎ 01323-811626, 🖳 charleston.org.uk; Wed-Sun & Bank hol Mon 10am-5pm; £18.50) which houses a gallery

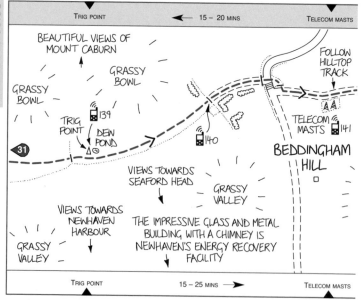

of work by the Bloomsbury group of artists (see box p158). There is now a timed entry system and booking is essential.

Charleston is a stop on Compass's No 125 **bus** service (Lewes–Eastbourne); Cuckmere Community Bus operates the **limited-frequency** No 40 service. See pp46-8 for details.

Around Bostal Hill (Map 33) Turn off here for B&B at *Bo-Peep Farmhouse* (see Alciston, below), about half a mile north-east of the trail.

ALCISTON   off MAP 34, p165

Alciston is yet another beautiful but tiny downland village with little to draw the walker apart from *The Rose Cottage* (☎ 01323-870377, 🖳 therosecottagealciston .co.uk; ♥; 🐾; (Ⓛ)). Formerly a country pub circa 1680, it now offers accommodation in some very charming self-contained flats. The two larger **apartments** (2Qd) boast kitchens, the smaller one (1D) has a microwave and kettle and even one of the smaller **cabins** (2D), known as Hikers' Rests, has a microwave. Rates start at £42.50/57.50pp (sgl occ room rate) in the

cabins/apartments, with breakfast £10pp.

South of Alciston, there's **B&B** at *Bo-Peep Farmhouse* (off Map 33; ☎ 01323-871299, 🖳 bopeepfarmhouse.co.uk; 2D/1T, all en suite; ♥; (Ⓛ)); they charge £75-82.50pp (sgl occ room rate). This was once the home of painter Roger Fry, another member of the Bloomsbury Group. To reach it, turn off the Way at Bo-Peep car park (Map 33).

Alciston is a stop on CCB's **limited frequency** Nos 40, 42 and 44 **bus** services; see pp46-8.

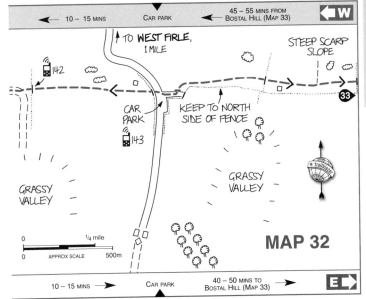

ROUTE GUIDE AND MAPS

❑ **IMPORTANT NOTE – WALKING TIMES**

Unless otherwise specified, **all times in this book refer only to the time spent walking**. You should add 20-30% to allow for rests, photos, checking the map, drinking water etc, not to mention time simply to stop and stare.

ROUTE GUIDE AND MAPS

❑ **ALFRISTON CHURCH AND CLERGY HOUSE**   MAP 35a, p169

The **14th-century flint church** of St Andrew by the river sits in the middle of a well-groomed lawn and is worth a look, as is **Clergy House** (☎ 01323-871961, 🖥 https://www.nationaltrust.org.uk/visit/sussex/alfriston-clergy-house; Easter-Oct; £8) nearby. This beautiful 14th-century, timber-framed thatched house was the first property the National Trust bought in 1896, thanks to the local vicar who suggested the building be safeguarded for the nation. Apart from anything else it's a good spot for a picnic lunch.

BERWICK off MAP 34

Berwick is famous for the Bloomsbury Group of Victorian artists which included Vanessa Bell, Roger Fry and Duncan Grant. Some of Vanessa Bell's work can be seen in the small **church** (St Michael and All Angels) on the edge of the village.

There is a **post office** (Mon, Tue, Thur & Fri 9am-1pm & 2.15-5pm, Wed 9am-noon, Sat 9am-12.30pm) on Station Rd.

For **food** head to *The Cricketer's Arms* (☎ 01323-870469, 🖥 cricketersber wick.co.uk; summer Mon-Sat noon-9pm, Sun to 5pm; booking recommended; winter kitchen hrs vary, see website; 🐕 on lead). Their menu generally includes such pub favourites as ham, eggs & chips (£13.50).

Berwick has useful transport links, making it a good place to start or end a day walk. It is a stop on Southern's **railway** line (see box p44).

Although several **bus** services call here, some are **limited frequency** and/or **seasonal** services so check timetables carefully. There's the No 125 (Eastbourne–Lewes), CCB's No 26 (Sun only), No 47 (Cuckmere Valley Rambler, summer Sun only) and Nos 40, 42, 43 & 44 (1 or 2 a week) services also call here. Some services connect with train arrivals. See pp46-8 for more details.

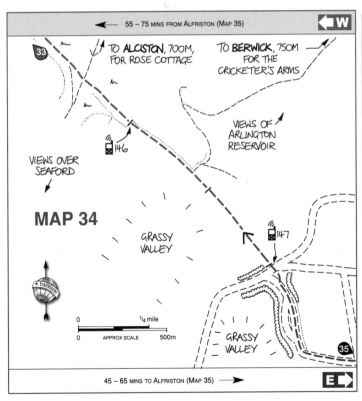

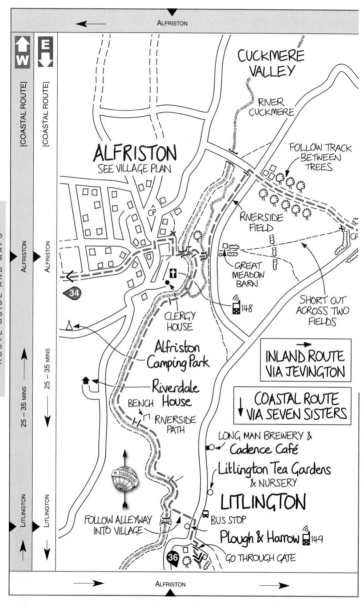

W E

[COASTAL ROUTE]

[COASTAL ROUTE]

ALFRISTON

ALFRISTON

25 – 35 MINS

25 – 35 MINS

LITLINGTON

LITLINGTON

ALFRISTON

CUCKMERE VALLEY

RIVER CUCKMERE

FOLLOW TRACK BETWEEN TREES

ALFRISTON
SEE VILLAGE PLAN

CP

34

RIVERSIDE FIELD

GREAT MEADOW BARN

148

SHORT CUT ACROSS TWO FIELDS

CLERGY HOUSE

Alfriston Camping Park

Riverdale House

BENCH

RIVERSIDE PATH

★ trailblazer

INLAND ROUTE VIA JEVINGTON

COASTAL ROUTE VIA SEVEN SISTERS

LONG MAN BREWERY & Cadence Café

Litlington Tea Gardens & NURSERY

LITLINGTON

BUS STOP

Plough & Harrow 149

FOLLOW ALLEYWAY INTO VILLAGE

36

GO THROUGH GATE

ALFRISTON

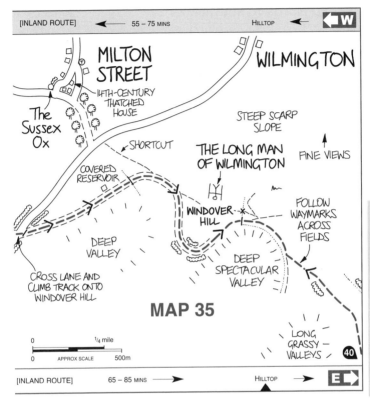

MILTON STREET

WILMINGTON

The Sussex Ox

14TH-CENTURY THATCHED HOUSE

STEEP SCARP SLOPE

SHORTCUT

THE LONG MAN OF WILMINGTON

FINE VIEWS

COVERED RESERVOIR

WINDOVER HILL

FOLLOW WAYMARKS ACROSS FIELDS

DEEP VALLEY

DEEP SPECTACULAR VALLEY

CROSS LANE AND CLIMB TRACK ONTO WINDOVER HILL

MAP 35

0   ¼ mile

0   APPROX SCALE   500m

LONG GRASSY VALLEYS

40

ROUTE GUIDE AND MAPS

❑ THE LONG MAN OF WILMINGTON   Map 35, above

No-one is quite sure when or why this large chalk figure appeared on the side of Windover Hill above Wilmington.

Best viewed from the lane leading out of the village, he stands 70m tall and holds a vertical rod in each hand. Although it was only in 1969 that the white blocks were placed along the lines of the figure, suggestions as to when the original was made range from the prehistoric era or the Roman age to just a few hundred years ago.

As for the question of why, well that is even harder to answer. Some say he is a fertility symbol robbed of his genitalia; others claim he was carved out for fun by monks from the nearby Wilmington Priory. Or could it be that a real giant collapsed and died on that very spot?

Though the site is easily accessible on the Inland Route, those who took the Coastal trail will miss out. However, there is the Cuckmere Community **Bus** (CCB) No 26 that stops at Wilmington village, at the foot of the Long Man, as well as the **limited frequency** Nos 40 & 44; see pp46-7.

W ← ALFRISTON TO SOUTHEASE   MAPS 35-31

It's not easy to tear yourself away from Alfriston. It's not just the pull of the place itself, but the steep ascent out of the village that begins this **7¾-mile stage (12.5km, 2½-3½hrs)**. The villages of **Berwick** and **Alciston** (both off Map 34) provide reasons to drop right back down again, but if you're staying on the trail you'll find the walking does get easier, at least once you get over **Bostal Hill** (Map 33) and as you hike around the stage's high point at **Firle Beacon** (Map 33).

Your destination on this stage, **Southease** (Map 31), lies hidden in a valley but you can get an approximation of its location by drawing a line south from **Mount Caburn**, the isolated hill to the north of the trail and a near-permanent presence on this stage.

[Next route overview p160]

ALFRISTON   MAP 35a

Alfriston is another candidate for 'prettiest village on the South Downs Way'. However, this small collection of Tudor wood-beamed buildings slung higgledy-piggledy along a narrow main street is far from a well-kept secret. In high season coachloads of tourists come to 'ooh' and 'ahh' at the sights and have cream teas. Nevertheless, it is worth planning on spending a few hours to take it all in at a leisurely pace. Whilst here make sure you take a look around the **church** and the **Clergy House** (see box p164) which is by the church and the village green.

Services

The beating heart of Alfriston is the **village store/deli** (☎ 01323-870201; Mon-Sat 9am-6pm, Sun 10am-6pm; deli closes daily at 4.30pm), where it's worth a visit just to take in its almost authentic 'Olde Worlde' atmosphere. The now-forgotten 'Lamson' system of moving cash to a single cashier, whereby cannisters containing the money were shot along wires and tubes, is still in place though no longer used. The deli here is a great place to pick up the ingredients for a top-class picnic. There's also a small exhibition upstairs of the local history with the shop featuring prominently, having been here since 1793.

There's an excellent independent **bookshop**, Much Ado Books (☎ 01323-

871222, 🖳 muchadobooks.com; Thur-Mon 10.30am-5pm) with an interesting stock of old and new books, maps and guides.

For **information** about the village see 🖳 alfriston-village.co.uk. However, note that getting a wi-fi signal can be a problem here.

Public transport

The No 125 (Lewes–Eastbourne) & 126 **bus** services (Berwick–Seaford) call here as do the **limited frequency** CCB services Nos 25, 26, 47 (seasonal, Sun/bank hol Mon only), as well as their No 42 (Wed only). See pp46-8 for details.

Where to stay

Campers will find plenty of room at the family-friendly *Alfriston Camping Park* (Map 35; ☎ 07591-880129, 🖳 alfriston-camping.com; wi-fi patchy at best; 🐾; Mar-Oct) on Pleasant Rise Farm. It's situated in three large fields surrounded by woods, a couple of minutes' walk from the village centre. There's a laidback atmosphere, so it can get noisy. They charge from £12pp, including use of the toilets and showers.

For **B&B** there's comfortable *Riverdale House* (Map 35; ☎ 01323-871038, 🖳 riverdalehouse.co.uk; 3D/1D or T/1Tr, all en suite; ☛; (Ⓛ; 🐾), which is peacefully located on the edge of the village, off Seaford Rd. Rates range from £47.50 to £72.50pp (sgl occ rates on request). Luggage transfer is available by prior arrangement: to/from Lewes and Eastbourne (from £20 per trip).

Wingrove House (☎ 01323-870276, 🖳 wingrovehousealfriston.com; 16D, all en suite; ☕) is a restaurant with rooms in a 19th-century colonial-style building. The rooms are luxurious and the food good (see Where to eat). B&B costs £65-135pp (sgl occ room rate).

The village's historic **pubs** also have rooms. ***The George Inn*** (☎ 01323-870319, 🖳 thegeorge-alfriston.com; **fb**; 5D, all en suite; ☕; Ⓛ; 🐕) is a magnificent old building with oak beams. B&B costs £60-85pp (sgl occ full room rate; min 2 nights at weekends).

Ye Olde Smugglers Inne (aka **The Market Inn**; 🖳 smugglers-alfriston.co.uk; 1T/2D/1D, T or Tr, all en suite; ☕; 🐕) charges £67.50-72pp (sgl occ full room rate) including continental breakfast. The name is derived from a famous gang of smugglers who once used the pub to plan smuggling ventures at Cuckmere Haven. Note, they only take accommodation bookings through 🖳 booking.com (to which they have a link on their own website).

The third in the triumvirate of great, ancient pubs in Alfriston, ***The Star Inn*** (☎ 01323-870495, 🖳 thepolizzicollection.com/the-star; 30D or T inc 4 'junior suites', all en suite; ☕; 🐕) re-opened in 2021 after extensive (and televised) refurbishment. Some rooms connect to provide accommodation for families/groups and many are in a separate 1960s building behind the inn. B&B costs from £110-250pp (sgl occ room rate; min 2 nights on summer weekends).

At the southern end of the village is the large ***Deans Place Hotel*** (☎ 01323-870248, 🖳 deansplace.co.uk; 3S/28D or T/4Tr, all en suite; ☕; 🐕), a smart 14th-century country house hotel set in a big garden with manicured lawns and an open-air (heated) swimming-pool (May-Sep). B&B costs from £61pp (sgl/sgl occ from £104.50); contact them to enquire about special deals.

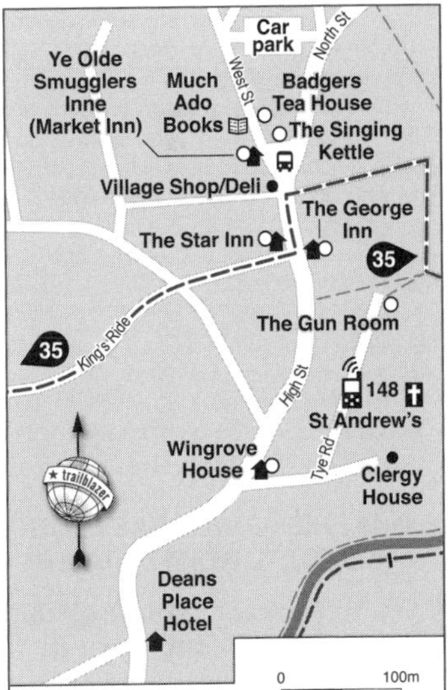

Alfriston MAP 35a

Where to eat and drink

For such a small village Alfriston does well for pubs and cafés, many of which have long histories.

Badgers Tea House (☎ 01323-871336, 🖳 badgersteahouse.com; Tue-Sat 9.30am-4pm, hot food until 2pm; 🐕) is a traditional English tearoom. Housed in a building dating back to 1510, the café has long been a favourite of walkers thanks to its delicious scones and with a pleasant walled garden to sit in. A cream tea costs from £9.25 and afternoon tea from £20.95.

Just off the trail and occupying an enviable location across the green (known as The Tye) from the church, ***The Gun Room*** (🖳 thegunroomalfriston.co.uk; daily 10am-4pm; 🐕) sells soup, toasties, pastries, cakes and hot drinks and is very dog-friendly.

Right in the centre of the village, ***The Singing Kettle*** (☎ 01323-870723; **fb**; daily

9am-4.45pm; 🐾) does a good range of breakfasts, plus sandwiches, cakes and good strong coffee.

One of the best **pubs** is undoubtedly *The George Inn* (see Where to stay; food Mon-Sat noon-9pm, Sun to 8.30pm), which was first licensed way back in 1397. The menu changes seasonally but mains such as game casserole with braised red cabbage tend to start from £17, and there's a good selection of vegetarian options, such as roasted beetroot risotto (£18). The pub also serves some cracking real ales.

Ye Olde Smugglers Inne (☎ 01323-870241; see also Where to stay; food Mon-

Sat noon-2.30pm & 6-8.30pm, Sun noon-7pm; 🐾) has friendly staff and an attractive conservatory at the back. They serve good-value pub grub (mains from £13) with daily specials, Harvey's ales and Long Man Brewery beer (see box p23).

Wingrove House (see Where to stay; Mon-Sat noon-4pm & 6-9pm, Sun noon-3pm & 6-8pm) is a stylish **restaurant** and the contemporary British menu top notch. Mains will set you back £20-30. The wine list is extensive, and there's garden and terrace seating. Non-residents can eat here but booking is recommended.

E→ALFRISTON TO EASTBOURNE (COASTAL ROUTE VIA CUCKMERE)

MAPS 35-39

These **10¾ miles (17.5km, 4¼-5¾hrs)** to the end of the Way – plus another **1½ miles (2.4km) to Eastbourne**; see Map 42) are arguably the highlight of the whole walk, including a stretch through the beautiful **Cuckmere Valley** (Maps 35 & 36) which culminates in wide meanders leading to what is one of the few undeveloped river mouths in the South-East.

The final assault on Eastbourne is a spectacular roller-coaster ride over the **Seven Sisters** (Map 37), a line of chalk cliffs that are less famous than The White Cliffs of Dover, but far more spectacular and, ironically, given the names, far whiter due to more constant erosion. If that was not enough the path continues, past the popular shingle beach at **Birling Gap** (Map 38), to reach the final high point of the whole walk: **Beachy Head** (Map 39), a spectacular chalk cliff jutting into the English Channel with 360° views. Even the sprawling mess of Eastbourne is worth admiring from here.

The path finishes at the foot of the hill where it meets abruptly with Eastbourne's suburbs. There are both accommodation and refreshments in the neighbourhood of **Meads Village** (see p178), but if you want to go into **Eastbourne** (see p183) there is a bus from there or a half-hour coastal walk along pavements to the town centre.

[For inland route via Jevington see pp180-2]

LITLINGTON   MAP 35, p166
Sitting on the eastern bank of the Cuckmere River, Litlington is yet another oh-so-charming downland village complete with flint cottages. On the other side of the valley is a chalk-horse figure carved into the hillside in 1924.

The local pub is *Plough and Harrow* (☎ 01323-870632, 🖥 ploughandharrow litlington.co.uk; **fb**; summer food Mon-Sat noon-8pm, Sun noon-5.45pm; winter hrs vary, check online; 🐾) which serves a variety of bar meals ranging from sandwiches

cont'd on p174

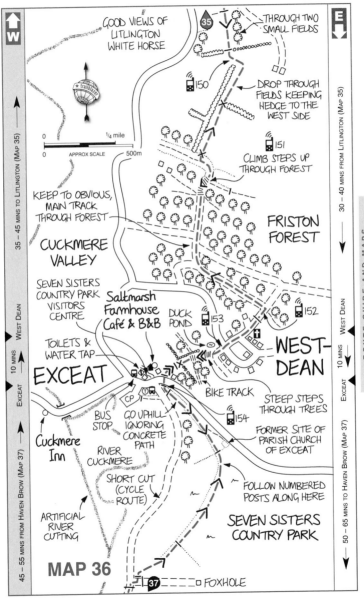

W

GOOD VIEWS OF LITLINGTON WHITE HORSE

THROUGH TWO SMALL FIELDS

35

E

trailblazer

0   ¼ mile
APPROX SCALE
0   500m

📱150

DROP THROUGH FIELDS KEEPING HEDGE TO THE WEST SIDE

📱151

CLIMB STEPS UP THROUGH FOREST

KEEP TO OBVIOUS, MAIN TRACK THROUGH FOREST

FRISTON FOREST

CUCKMERE VALLEY

SEVEN SISTERS COUNTRY PARK VISITORS CENTRE

Saltmarsh Farmhouse Café & B&B

DUCK POND

📱153

📱152

TOILETS & WATER TAP

WEST-DEAN

EXCEAT

BIKE TRACK

STEEP STEPS THROUGH TREES

BUS STOP

CP

GO UPHILL IGNORING CONCRETE PATH

📱154

FORMER SITE OF PARISH CHURCH OF EXCEAT

Cuckmere Inn

RIVER CUCKMERE

SHORT CUT (CYCLE ROUTE)

FOLLOW NUMBERED POSTS ALONG HERE

SEVEN SISTERS COUNTRY PARK

ARTIFICIAL RIVER CUTTING

MAP 36

37   FOXHOLE

35 – 45 MINS TO LITLINGTON (MAP 35)   WEST DEAN   10 MINS   EXCEAT   45 – 55 MINS FROM HAVEN BROW (MAP 37)

30 – 40 MINS FROM LITLINGTON (MAP 35)   WEST DEAN   10 MINS   EXCEAT   50 – 65 MINS TO HAVEN BROW (MAP 37)

ROUTE GUIDE AND MAPS

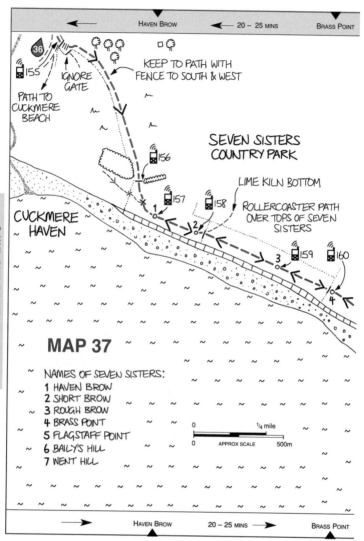

MAP 37

NAMES OF SEVEN SISTERS:
1 HAVEN BROW
2 SHORT BROW
3 ROUGH BROW
4 BRASS POINT
5 FLAGSTAFF POINT
6 BAILY'S HILL
7 WENT HILL

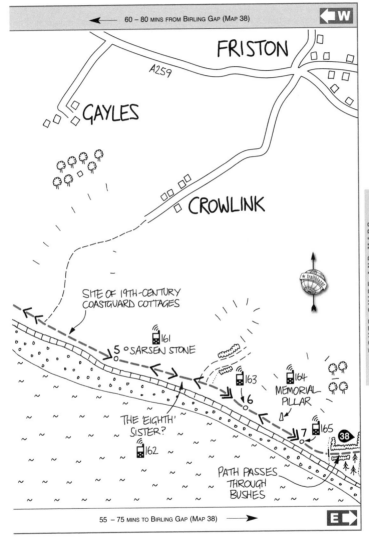

60 – 80 MINS FROM BIRLING GAP (MAP 38)

FRISTON

A259

GAYLES

CROWLINK

SITE OF 19TH-CENTURY
COASTGUARD COTTAGES

161
5 SARSEN STONE

163
6

164
MEMORIAL
PILLAR

THE EIGHTH
SISTER?

162

7 165

38

PATH PASSES
THROUGH
BUSHES

55 – 75 MINS TO BIRLING GAP (MAP 38)

ROUTE GUIDE AND MAPS

(continued from p170) (from £9) to classic pub-grub mains (from £14). The bar is open all day and there's a beer garden at the back.

The village is also home to the delightful ***Litlington Tea Gardens & Nursery*** (☎ 01323-870222; **fb**; mid Mar-end Oct Tue-Sun & bank hols 11am-5pm; 🐾), which claims to have been around since 1870. Their lovely tree-shaded garden is the per-

fect spot for a cream tea. Note they accept cash only. If they're shut, a couple of hundred metres north of here in the grounds of the Long Man Brewery is yet another branch of the ***Cadence*** coffee chain (see box p107; Mon-Fri 9am-4pm, Sat & Sun 8am-4pm).

Litlington is a stop on CCB's **limited frequency** No 47 and No 40 **bus** services. See pp46-8 for details.

WESTDEAN & EXCEAT
MAP 36, p171

On the northern side of the small wooded ridge of chalk is the wonderfully secluded and secret **Westdean**, a tiny collection of beautiful cottages complete with duck pond, nestled in a wooded fold.

On the other side of the ridge is the deserted medieval village of **Exceat**, now more a collection of tourist facilities than a village but with a very good information and visitor centre. This is the gateway to

Seven Sisters Country Park and the spectacular Cuckmere Valley and beach. If Exceat is an overnight stop on your walk, try to arrive here early in the day to give yourself time to enjoy the area around the beach.

The excellent **Visitor Centre** (🖥 sevensisters.org.uk; Easter-Oct daily 10-5pm, Nov-Easter to 4pm only) has information on wildlife and conservation efforts in Seven Sisters Country Park. It also sells

---

❏ SEVEN SISTERS COUNTRY PARK

This extensive country park of rolling coastal downland includes the spectacular Seven Sisters chalk cliffs over which the South Downs Way passes.

Apart from the obvious attraction of the chalk cliffs and downland the park also includes Cuckmere Haven and estuary, one of the only river mouths in the south-east of England that has not been spoilt by development. That is not to say that the estuary is untouched. The natural meanders of the river, seen so spectacularly from the ridge above Exceat, have been left to sit as idle ponds thanks to the man-made channel dug in 1847 that diverts the flow of the river more swiftly to the sea. Plans were underway to restore the Cuckmere Estuary to its natural state by filling in the man-made channel and allowing the blockade to gradually deteriorate. This would have restored the flow of the river through the meanders and encouraged the natural restoration of the saltmarsh and mudflats. However, by 2006 this plan had been suspended after a 'modelling miscalculation' by the project's environmental consultant was found.

The country park covers an area steeped in history. Some of the most fascinating stories involve the numerous shipwrecks that litter the seabed below the Seven Sisters' cliffs. The most significant of these is that of the Spanish ship *Nympha Americana* which, in 1747, ran aground halfway along the line of chalk cliffs, resulting in the deaths of 30 crewmen.

❑ SMUGGLING

Smuggling of wool, brandy and gin was rife along the Sussex coast with Cuckmere Haven and Birling Gap being favourite places for gangs of smugglers to load and unload their contraband in the late 18th and early 19th centuries. One of the most infamous groups was the Alfriston Gang who would smuggle goods to and from Cuckmere Haven along the Cuckmere River.

The leader of the Alfriston Gang was Stanton Collins who owned the now aptly named Ye Olde Smugglers Inne from where the group plotted their exploits. These included a raid on a Dutch ship wrecked at Cuckmere Haven. The figurehead of the ship, a red lion's head, still stands next to the Star Inn in the village. Stanton Collins was eventually arrested in 1831 for sheep rustling and was shipped off to Australia.

souvenirs, cold drinks and snacks; there's a **water tap** by the toilet block behind the visitor centre.

You can **stay** and **eat** here too: *Saltmarsh Farmhouse* (☎ 01323-870218, 🖥 saltmarshfarmhouse.co.uk; 3D/1T/1Qd, all en suite; 🐾) has extremely smart rooms (with the 2-bedroom suite from £340 a night), but **B&B** in some rooms can be from around £70pp (sgl occ phone for discounts). They also have an upmarket *café* (usually daily 9am-5pm but weather dependent) with some courtyard seating.

By the bridge, the large *Cuckmere Inn* (☎ 01323-892247, 🖥 vintageinn.co.uk; **fb**; food daily noon-9.30pm; 🐾 certain areas only) has a big garden overlooking the River Cuckmere. Their menu includes standard pub fare (mains £11.75-16.95). It gets very busy during the summer due to its great location. If staying at Saltmarsh Farmhouse and visiting the pub in the evening, take a torch as the road between the two is unlit.

The Nos 12, 12A, 12X and 13X **bus** services provide regular links to Brighton and Eastbourne. CCB's **limited frequency** No 47 stops at Seven Sisters Country Park (seasonal, weekends only) and their No 40 (Tue & Fri only) calls at both Westdean and Exceat. See p47 for details.

See p47 for details.

BIRLING GAP   MAP 38, p176

All that's in this gap is a small line of terraced houses that are falling into the sea, plus a visitor centre and café of sorts. Considering the beautiful position of the hamlet on a low saddle along the line of chalk cliffs, it's a shame that some of the buildings are so ugly and out of place. The huge steel staircase leading down to the stony beach is also an eyesore, although the beach is a popular spot on sunny summer days. For further information see 🖥 nationaltrust.org.uk/visit/sussex/birling-gap-and-the-seven-sisters.

The *National Trust Birling Gap Café* (☎ 01323-423197; Apr-Oct Mon-Fri 10am-5pm, Sat & Sun to 5.30pm, Nov-Mar to 4pm) is currently undergoing a fairly extensive 'remodelling', with the former café being demolished owing to its proximity to the unstable cliff edge. Despite this upheaval they still offer sandwiches and hot paninis, snacks, drinks, cakes and ice-creams, and in the same building is the **visitor centre** and **souvenir shop** (both daily Apr-Oct 10am-5pm, Nov-Mar to 4pm). In a separate building are some **toilets** (daily Apr-Oct 9.30am-6pm, Nov-Mar 10am-4pm).

A 15- to 20-minute walk from Birling Gap, *Belle Tout Lighthouse* (Map 38; ☎

ROUTE GUIDE AND MAPS

01323-423185, ⌨ belletout.co.uk; 6D, all en suite; 🛏; adults only) is now a luxury B&B with incredible coastal views. They charge from £105-155pp (sgl occ £140-264), with prices higher on summer weekends. There's usually a two-night mini-

mum-stay policy but it's worth contacting them at short notice for a single-night stay.

Birling Gap is a stop on the No 13X **bus** service (Sun & Bank hol Mon only). See pp46-8 for details.

BEACHY HEAD   MAP 39, p179

The highlight here is the **Beachy Head Story** (daily 10am-5pm), a visitor centre with some surprisingly excellent archeological exhibits telling the story of the area, including Anglo-Saxon brooches, 4500-year-old Bronze Age pots, and Beachy Head Woman, a skeleton dating back to the Roman era. Next door is a pub, ***The Beachy***

Head (☎ 01323-728060, ⌨ vintageinn.co .uk/thebeachyheadeastbourne; food summer Mon-Sat noon-10pm, Sun to 9.30pm, winter daily noon-9pm; 🐕), which isn't really the best place to celebrate the walk's end but is useful if you need to shelter from the weather, and does have a sun-trap beer garden. The food is good value too.

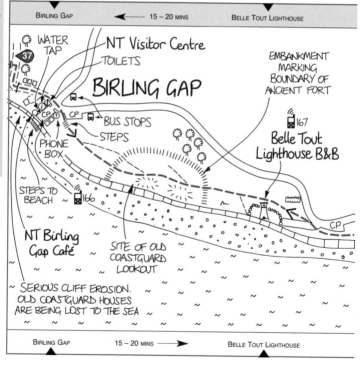

ROUTE GUIDE AND MAPS

❑ LULLINGTON HEATH
MAP 40, p180

This hidden **National Nature Reserve** near Jevington is a short detour from the South Downs Way and is a good place to escape the crowds who tend to congregate around the tourist traps of Alfriston, Jevington and Wilmington. The rough chalk grassland is a fine place to see a variety of species of butterfly including the chalkhill blue. In summer the shallow valley is often ablaze with the yellow flowers of gorse and broom. To the south of Lullington Heath is the expansive cover of **Friston Forest**, another good place to get lost and explore countless forest tracks.

Across the car park, there's another 'hub' of the *Cadence* café chain (see box p107; Mon-Fri 10am-3pm, Sat & Sun 9am-4pm) that, when the sun's out at least, proves more of a draw for walkers and cyclists.

The No 13X (Sun/Bank hol Mon only) **bus** service calls here; Stagecoach's Nos 3/3A services call at the foot of Beachy Head (end of South Downs Way). See p46 for details.

ROUTE GUIDE AND MAPS

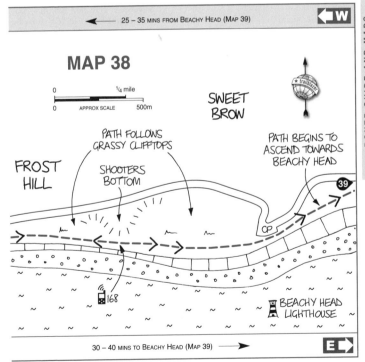

25 – 35 MINS FROM BEACHY HEAD (MAP 39) ← **W**

MAP 38

0   ¼ mile
0   APPROX SCALE   500m

SWEET BROW

★ trailblazer

PATH FOLLOWS GRASSY CLIFFTOPS

PATH BEGINS TO ASCEND TOWARDS BEACHY HEAD

FROST HILL

SHOOTERS BOTTOM

39

OP

168

BEACHY HEAD LIGHTHOUSE

30 – 40 MINS TO BEACHY HEAD (MAP 39) → **E**

MEADS VILLAGE   MAP 39

Meads Village is actually the most westerly suburb of Eastbourne. It is a quiet, well-to-do part of town with a genuine village feel and a couple of options to stay the night. More importantly for South Downs Way walkers, it is positioned right at the official end (or start) of the walk, making a stop here a more appealing prospect than the half-hour walk into the more hectic centre of Eastbourne. The village lies on Holywell Rd, to the north of the start/end of the trail.

Everything you might need is centred along one short stretch of Meads St. There is a **Co-op** (daily 7am-10pm) on the corner of Matlock Rd which also incorporates the **post office** (daily 8am-7pm). There's also a **Tesco Express** (daily 7am-11pm) and a **pharmacy** (Mon-Fri 9am-5.30pm, Sat to noon).

To the south of the village, the *Cadence* café chain have yet another hub (daily 9am-4pm), this time in the thatched pavilion in Helen Garden, at the foot of the Downs.

If it's **B&B** you're after, *Beachy Rise* (☎ 01323-639171; book online via 🖳 booking.com; 2D/1T/1Tr, all en suite; 🛏; (L̃)), on Meads Rd, has rooms from £45pp.

The Pilot Inn (☎ 01323-723440, 🖳 pilot-inn.co.uk; **fb**; 4D, all en suite; 🛏; 🐾 bar only), on a bend on Meads St, is the first pub reached after leaving the end of the South Downs Way. The bar is open all day (Mon-Sat 11am-11pm, Sun to 8pm), which makes it convenient for a celebration drink. And the **food** (Mon-Sat noon-9pm, Sun to 6pm) is well-priced (toasted ciabatta rolls £9, mains £15-28). **Room only** costs around £45-55pp (sgl occ room rate); a cooked breakfast (£12pp) is available.

Stagecoach's No 3/3A **bus** services go to central Eastbourne from here as well as from the foot of the hill at the end of the South Downs Way. See p46 for details.

W← EASTBOURNE TO ALFRISTON   [MAPS 39-35]
(COASTAL ROUTE VIA CUCKMERE)

It is this initial **10¾-mile stage (17.5km, 4½-hrs** – plus another **1½ miles (2.4km) from Eastbourne** station to the official start; see Map 42, p185) on the South Downs Way that perhaps provides the main reason why most people choose to walk the trail from west to east. For while they have left the best – and toughest – section to the end, having used the rest of the path to toughen up their feet and improve their fitness, those who begin at Eastbourne are instead plunged straight into the deep end, and have to tackle the hardest and most scenic stage first. It's true, too, that the best views are reserved for those who are looking east – so those walking from Eastbourne will often find themselves looking over their shoulder to glimpse the best of the panoramas.

Still, if you are walking the South Downs Way in this direction, at least you'll have the satisfaction of knowing that, once you've tackled **Beachy Head** (don't forget to look behind you for views of the lighthouse) and the ever-undulating chalk cliffs of the **Seven Sisters Country Park**, you've got the toughest section of the trail out of the way, and will find the rest of the hiking, by comparison, a mere walk in the (National) park.

What's more, the lovely villages of **Westdean** (Map 36) and **Litlington** (Map 35), and the views over beguiling Cuckmere Valley towards **Birling Gap** (Map 33), are all certainly easier on the eye than parts of Eastbourne.

[Next route overview p168]

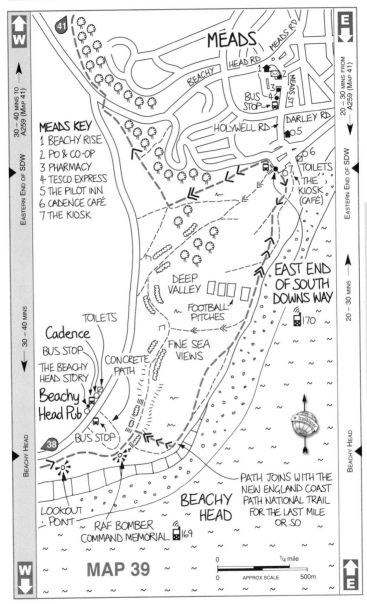

MEADS

MEADS RD

BEACHY HEAD RD

MEADS ST

BUS STOP

HOLYWELL RD

DARLEY RD

MEADS KEY
1 BEACHY RISE
2 PO & CO-OP
3 PHARMACY
4 TESCO EXPRESS
5 THE PILOT INN
6 CADENCE CAFÉ
7 THE KIOSK

TOILETS
THE KIOSK (CAFÉ)

EAST END OF SOUTH DOWNS WAY

170

DEEP VALLEY

FOOTBALL PITCHES

FINE SEA VIEWS

TOILETS

Cadence
BUS STOP
THE BEACHY HEAD STORY

CONCRETE PATH

Beachy Head Pub

38

BUS STOP

PATH JOINS WITH THE NEW ENGLAND COAST PATH NATIONAL TRAIL FOR THE LAST MILE OR SO

LOOKOUT POINT

RAF BOMBER COMMAND MEMORIAL 169

BEACHY HEAD

MAP 39

0 — 1/4 mile
0 — 500m
APPROX SCALE

41

30 – 40 MINS TO A259 (MAP 41)

EASTERN END OF SDW

30 – 40 MINS

BEACHY HEAD

W

20 – 30 MINS FROM A259 (MAP 41)

EASTERN END OF SDW

20 – 30 MINS

BEACHY HEAD

E

trailblazer

ROUTE GUIDE AND MAPS

E→ALFRISTON TO EASTBOURNE   MAP 35, MAPS 40-41 & MAP 39 (INLAND ROUTE VIA JEVINGTON)

This inland **alternative route** is geared towards horse-riders and cyclists but walkers are welcome to use the bridleway too. Although these **8¼ miles (13.5km, 2¾-3¾hrs – plus another 1½ miles (2.4km) to Eastbourne** centre) are not as spectacular as the coastal route there are still plenty of fine downland

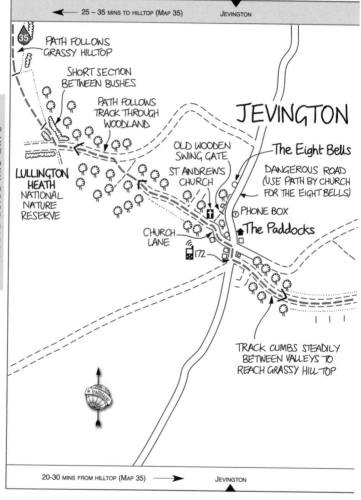

views to enjoy high up on **Windover Hill** (Map 35), while a detour to see the famous **Long Man of Wilmington** (see box p167) is strongly recommended and the sweet little villages/hamlets of **Milton Street** (Map 35) and **Jevington** (Map 40) are right on the trail.

It is a good idea to keep an extra day spare for this section even if you have already walked the coastal route.

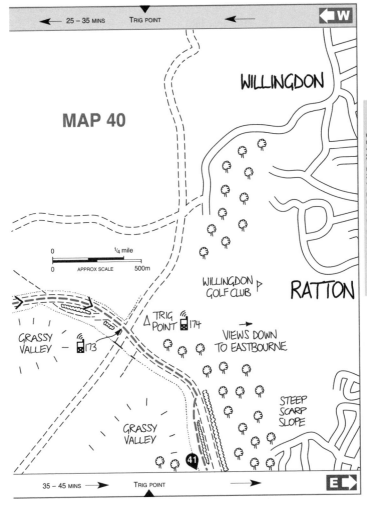

ROUTE GUIDE AND MAPS

MILTON STREET   MAP 35, p167

Milton Street is nothing more than a small collection of scattered houses. There is, however, a good pub here; *The Sussex Ox* (☎ 01323-870840, 🖥 thesussexox.co.uk; **fb**; food Mon-Sat noon-2.30pm & 6-9pm, Sun noon-4pm & 5-8pm; 🐾). The menu is varied and changes daily but favourite lunchtime mains might include the Ox beef burger (£18) or a lamb shank (£25), with the meat from their own organic farm in Jevington. Their draught lagers and ciders are all from Sussex including the Long Man Brewery at Wilmington and Burning Sky in Firle.

JEVINGTON   MAP 40, p180

Jevington, sitting comfortably in the Cuckmere valley, is another beautiful village that provides a potential alternative stop to the somewhat exploited streets of Alfriston. In the centre of the village is a plaque commemorating the former Hungry Monk Restaurant, which claimed to be the birthplace in 1971 of banoffee pie.

For accommodation in the village there is *The Paddocks* (☎ 01323-482499, 🖥 the paddockstables.co.uk; 1D/1T, both en suite; 🛏; (L); 🐾), a comfortable **B&B** charging from £42.50pp (sgl occ £55). Breakfast is a help-yourself buffet.

The only place to eat is at the village pub, *The Eight Bells* (☎ 01323-484442, 🖥 eightbellsjevington.com; **fb**; bar Tue & Sun 10am-8pm, Wed-Sat 10am-11pm; food Tue noon-3pm, Wed-Sat noon-3pm & 6-9pm, Sun noon-6pm; 🐾 on lead). It's a 5-minute walk up the lane; note the blind bend on the road is very dangerous as there is no pavement for pedestrians – it is safer to use the path by the church. They have a a pleasant garden, with views over the Downs and serve a wide range of pub meals including their ploughman's lunch with a choice of scotch egg, sausage roll or cheese & pickled onion tart (£12), or mains such as Pie of the Week (from £18) or 'push-the-boat-out' treats such as pan-fried seabass with white bean cassoulet (£26) . It's a freehouse and has a variety of Sussex ales. Note that the pub is completely closed on Mondays all year round, and also on Tuesdays and Wednesdays in winter.

W ← EASTBOURNE TO ALFRISTON   MAP 40, MAPS 39-8, MAP 35 (INLAND ROUTE VIA JEVINGTON)

It seems a shame to miss the most iconic, and certainly the most photographed, stage of the South Downs Way (I'm pretty sure, for example, that the Seven Sisters or Beachy Head has featured on the cover just about every edition of this guide). But the truth is that if you're tackling the walk from east to west, you may simply not feel ready to do the toughest section, along the coast, straight out of the starting blocks. Thankfully this picturesque **8¼-mile alternative (13.5km, 2¾-3¾hrs)** plus another **1½ miles (2.4km) from Eastbourne centre** where most people will start their walk, is easier – though, it must be said, still fairly challenging.

There is interest aplenty on this route too, including a couple of cute villages (**Jevington**, Map 40) & **Milton Street** (Map 35), the views from **Windover Hill** (Map 35) and, if you take the recommended detour, a visit to the **Long Man of Wilmington** (see box p167).

[*Next route overview p168*]

ROUTE GUIDE AND MAPS

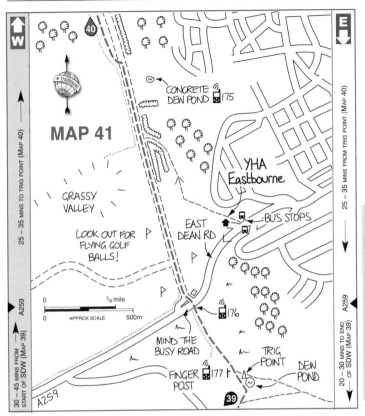

EASTBOURNE   MAP 42, p185

Eastbourne is a typical English seaside resort, complete with a grand Victorian pier, though it does have something of a reputation as a retirement town.

Having received a lot of criticism over the years as being one of the least adventurous resorts, particularly when compared to its upbeat neighbour Brighton, Eastbourne has undergone something of a revival. The signs on the edge of town shout out 'Welcome to the Sunshine Coast' and certainly this is one of the sunnier corners of the UK. However, parts of the centre, particularly the area around the railway

station, are far from appealing, and not the sort of places to linger. It certainly doesn't have the history and charm of Winchester at the other end of the South Downs Way, although nearby Beachy Head, at least, makes for a fitting end to a long walk.

You can walk along the long, stony **beach** on either side of the 300m-long **pier** which was built between 1866 and 1872 on stilts sitting in cups on the sea-bed allowing it to shift a little in stormy weather. It's a good spot for arcades, fish & chips, coffee and ice-cream.

On College Rd is an interesting gallery

of contemporary art, **Towner** (☎ 01323-434670, 🖳 towner eastbourne.org.uk; Tue-Sun & Bank Hol Mons 10am-5pm; free).

Right on the seafront, the **Wish Tower** (🖳 wishtower.org.uk), officially Martello Tower 73, is maintained by volunteers who occasionally open it to the public in summer; see the Events page on their website for more details.

Services

Terminus Rd is both the commercial and tourist centre, with most of the shops up at the railway station end of the road, and the restaurants, cafés and souvenir shops at the beach end. It's about 30 minutes' walk from the foot of the South Downs and the end of the Way. The smart, purpose-built **Visitor Centre** (☎ 01323-415415, 🖳 visiteastbou rne.com; Mon-Sat 9am-5pm, Sun 10am-4pm) is in The Welcome Building on Compton St. There is plenty of free information here, not only for Eastbourne but also for south-east England and London.

The **post office** (Mon-Sat 9am-5.30pm) is inside WH Smith on Terminus Rd, where you'll also find several **banks**. Also on Terminus Rd is a **pharmacy**, Boots (Mon-Sat 8.30am-6pm & Sun 10.30am-4.30pm), and inside the vast Beacon Shopping Centre there's big Sainsbury's **supermarket**. There's also a Tesco Express on Seaside Rd. Most open daily from around 7am to 11pm.

You'll also find branches of the **outdoor shops** Millets (Mon 10am-5pm, Tue-Sat 9am-6pm, Sun 10am-4pm) and Trespass (Mon-Sat 9am-5.30pm, Sun 10am-4pm) on Terminus Rd, plus a Waterstones **bookshop** (Mon-Sat 9am-5.30pm, Sun 10am-4pm).

Back near the Visitor Centre on Compton St is Hudson's (**fb**; Mon-Sat 7.30am-5pm), a quality **deli** with great-value made-to-order sandwiches.

For sticks of rock, jars of humbug mints, boxes of Eastbourne fudge and other traditional teeth-rotting souvenirs, head to **Ye Olde Fashioned Humbugge Shoppe** (Mon-Sat 9am-5pm, Sun 10am-4pm, but stays open until 9pm in summer), a family-run business that's been here for more than 70 years.

Public transport

Eastbourne is connected by Southern Railway's **train** (see box p44) services to places along the south coast as well as to Gatwick Airport and London Victoria.

There are several local **bus** services. The No 3/3A runs to Meads Village at the end of the South Downs Way; the Nos 12/12A/12X & 13X call at Birling Gap and Beachy Head); the No 125 goes to Lewes on weekdays while the CCB No 25 covers the same route on Saturday. CCB also run several **limited frequency** services including No 26 to Seaford and Nos 43 & 44 which call here on certain days of the week. See pp46-8 for details.

For a **taxi** try Eastbourne 720 Taxis (☎ 01323-720720, 🖳 720taxis.com).

Where to stay

As a major seaside resort Eastbourne is overflowing with accommodation. That said, much of it is rather similar – impersonal seafront high rises catering mainly to coach parties and with a certain sort of faded charm. The following, therefore, is not in any way a complete list of accommodation options in the town, but a brief guide to some of the smaller and more personal independent B&Bs and guest houses. Note that for most seafront hotels, rates are higher for rooms with a sea view.

At the time of research, *YHA Eastbourne* (Map 41, p183; ☎ 0345-371 9316, 🖳 yha.org.uk/hostel/eastbourne; sleeps 30) was available only to groups hiring the entire hostel. As such, it's probably not an option for most hikers.

For a similar style of accommodation, *Citrus Hotel* (☎ 01323-722676, 🖳 citrus hoteleastbourne.co.uk; 50 rooms, all en suite; 🛏; 🐾), on King Edward's Parade, is a cross between a hostel and a hotel. Rooms range from single, double and triple to self-catering 'studios' (the only option with wi-fi) sleeping up to six people; their suites have a sea view. The hotel is packed with facilities including a recreation area with table tennis, dartboard and pool table; there's also a bar serving snacks. Prices can be very reasonable, starting at £40pp (sgl/sgl occ from £65/75) including a

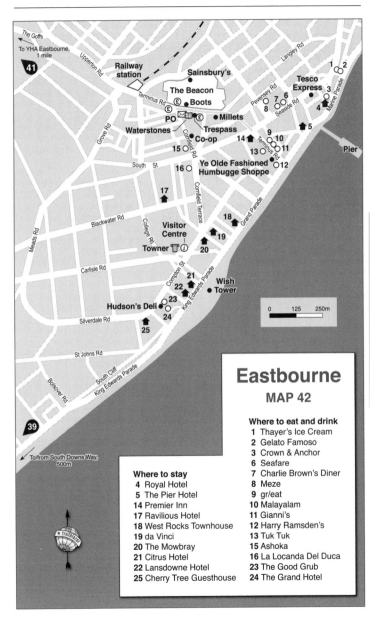

ROUTE GUIDE AND MAPS

Eastbourne

MAP 42

Where to eat and drink
1 Thayer's Ice Cream
2 Gelato Famoso
3 Crown & Anchor
6 Seafare
7 Charlie Brown's Diner
8 Meze
9 gr/eat
10 Malayalam
11 Gianni's
12 Harry Ramsden's
13 Tuk Tuk
15 Ashoka
16 La Locanda Del Duca
23 The Good Grub
24 The Grand Hotel

Where to stay
4 Royal Hotel
5 The Pier Hotel
14 Premier Inn
17 Ravilious Hotel
18 West Rocks Townhouse
19 da Vinci
20 The Mowbray
21 Citrus Hotel
22 Lansdowne Hotel
25 Cherry Tree Guesthouse

cooked breakfast. If not requested at the time of booking breakfast costs £7.99.

Near Citrus Hotel you'll find a couple of good **B&B**s. At 15 Silverdale Rd, *Cherry Tree Guesthouse* (☎ 01323-722406, 🖳 cherrytree-eastbourne.co.uk; 3S/2T/5D/1Tr, all en suite; �¤; 🐾) is an Edwardian townhouse with B&B for £45-60pp (sgl/sgl occ from £55). Very efficiently run with varied and delicious breakfasts, they are also very dog-friendly and even have towels by the front-door to use for any dogs caught in a downpour.

Nearby, *da Vinci* (☎ 01323-727173, 🖳 davinci.uk.com; 4S/10D/5D or T/ 2Tr, all en suite; ➤), on Howard Sq, has an **art gallery** downstairs and 'art-themed' rooms. It's a friendly, comfortable place and B&B is from around £40-62.50pp (sgl/sgl occ from £50). Phone for the best prices.

Right opposite the pier and appropriately-named, *The Pier Hotel* (☎ 01323-728313, 🖳 thepierhotel.co.uk; 12S/11D/8T, all en suite; ➤) is not without its charms and is in a great location. Rooms cost from £39pp (sgl from £48, sgl occ rates on request) though can easily be double that in high season.

At 8-9 Marine Parade, the *Royal Hotel* (☎ 01323 649222; 🖳 eastbourneroyal.co.uk, 3D/1D or T/1T/3S all en suite/1S private facilities; 🐾; no under 12s) describes itself as 'the only certified eco-friendly guest accommodation in Eastbourne'. They provide fresh homemade breakfasts, homemade muesli, bread & preserves, from their vegetarian kitchen and can cater for vegans. The good value rooms (from £50pp, sgl from £49) are available in a range of sizes, some with sea views.

Moving along to King Edward's Parade, although somewhat larger *The Lansdowne Hotel* (☎ 01323 725174; 🖳 lansdowne-hotel.co.uk, 98 rooms inc D, T, Tr & Qd, all en suite) has been family owned since 1912. Rates are highly variable depending on whether you choose a courtyard or sea view, but start from around £52.50pp inc breakfast.

There are several options on (or just off) Grand Parade, such as the dog-friendly *West Rocks Townhouse* (☎ 01323 920800; 🖳 westrockshotel.com; 44 rooms inc S, D, T & family rooms, all ensuite; 🐾) at Nos 44-46. Rates start from £43pp for room only (note there is no restaurant or bar here).

Set back a little from Grand Parade is contemporary guest house *The Mowbray* (☎ 01323 720012; 🖳 themowbray.com; 1S/12 D or T) at 2 Lascelles Terrace. They operate a flexible self-check in (noon-midnight) so the reception is unmanned overnight but this could be a good option if you expect to arrive late.

Moving further inland, at 16 Blackwater Rd, *Ravilious Hotel* (☎ 01323 733142; 🖳 ravilioushotel.com; FB; 1S/7D all en suite; ➤) is a smart, family-run boutique hotel in a beautifully refurbished Victorian house. Rates are from £60pp although note they usually require a minimum booking of two nights.

Finally, the chain *Premier Inn* (☎ 0333-321 9323, 🖳 premierinn.com; 65D, all en suite; ➤) has a hotel on Terminus Rd. Book online rather than calling the high-rate phone number. Saver rates can be as low as £35 per room if booked and paid well in advance or more than twice for late bookings. The rooms have very comfortable beds and there's a restaurant: a cooked breakfast costs £9.99pp.

Where to eat and drink
You'll find a surprisingly eclectic mix of restaurants and cafés on or around busy **Seaside Rd** and **Terminus Rd**.

Cafés & pubs
On Terminus Rd, the Greek café and deli *.gr/eat* (🖳 gr-eat.co.uk; Jan-Oct Tue-Sat noon-3pm & 5.30-9pm; Nov & Dec hrs vary) has a good selection of Mediterranean fare.

On Seaside Rd, at No 54, *Charlie Brown's Diner* (☎ 01323-726588, 🖳 charliebrownsdiner.co.uk; Tue-Thur 6-10.30pm, Fri & Sat to 11pm) is good for burgers and the like, and the portions are, as they describe, American-sized (ie huge!).

For something more refined, and away from the holiday-maker hordes, *The Good Grub* (🖳 thegoodgrub.co.uk; fb; Thur 5-10pm, Fri-Sat 10am-10pm, Sun 10am-

4pm), 12 Compton St, is an award-winning vegan restaurant with a nice line in vegan takes on classic dishes such as (seitan) steak and fries (£15.95) or plant-based salmon fillet (£15.95). Booking is recommended.

There are many **pubs**, some friendlier than others. *Crown & Anchor* (☎ 01323-642500, ▣ crownandanchoreastbourne.co .uk; food daily 10am-9pm; ⚒), on the seafront at 15 Marine Parade, often has live music at weekends and is one of the more welcoming places.

As with any British seaside town, **ice-cream** is a big seller in Eastbourne. Between Marine Parade and Seaside Rd are two particularly popular competing outlets; both very good. The cheaper of the two, *Thayer's Ice Cream*, (☎ 01323-641906; Mar-Oct Mon-Fri 1-9pm, Sat & Sun noon-9pm, winter closed) is a small family-run business with dozens of different flavours. Bigger, brasher *Gelato Famoso* (☎ 01323-722138, ▣ gelatofamoso.co.uk **fb**; Mon-Fri 9am-5pm, Sat & Sun to 6pm), nearby, also has a sit-down café selling hot drinks, sandwiches and cakes.

Restaurants & takeaways

At the seafront end of Terminus Rd, friendly pizzeria *Gianni's* (▣ giannieastbourne.co .uk; Mon-Fri 11am-9pm, Sat & Sun to 10pm) also sells Italian ice-cream. There are various pizza chains around town, but for something a bit classier, *La Locanda Del Duca* (☎ 01323-916011, ▣ la-locanda-del-duca.com; Sun-Thur noon-2.30pm & 5.30-10pm, Fri & Sat to 11pm), 26 Cornfield Terrace, is an authentic Italian place offering set menus for £25.90/28.90 for two/three courses and traditional favourites à la carte.

Staying by the Mediterranean, *Meze* (☎ 01323-731893, ▣ meze-restaurant.co .uk; daily noon-midnight), at 15 Pevensey Rd, is a good Turkish restaurant.

For decent Indian cuisine, head to *Ashoka* (☎ 01323-733344, ▣ ashokaeast bourne.com; daily noon-2pm & 5.30-11.30pm), at 28-30 Cornfield Rd. It's been in business since the 1980s. But the best Indian in town is probably *Malayalam* (☎ 01323-722227, ▣ malayalamrestaurants .com; Mon-Thur noon-2.30pm & 5.30-9pm, Fri & Sat to 10pm, Sun noon-4.30pm) at 229 Terminus Rd, serving South Indian fare with mains starting at just £8.25. A third subcontinental restaurant, *Tuk Tuk* (☎ 01323-430210; ▣ tuktukrestaurant.co.uk; Tue-Sun 5.30-10pm), across the road at No 240, serves what it describes as Indian street food with mains £12-14. To be honest, the menu isn't vastly different from your average Indian restaurant, but the food is undeniably good.

But for something more traditionally English, it has to be **fish and chips**. There are plenty of options here, including a branch of the *Harry Ramsden's* chain (☎ 01323-417454, ▣ harryramsdens.co.uk/ locations/eastbourne; summer Sun-Thur 11.30am-8pm, Fri & Sat to 8.30pm), on the seafront at the end of Terminus Rd. For a more down-to-earth chippy, try *Seafare* (☎ 01323-641893; **fb**; Tue-Sun noon-9pm, winter days/hours variable), at 66 Seaside Rd.

ROUTE GUIDE AND MAPS

❏ AFTERNOON TEA AT THE GRAND

If your walk ends at about tea-time (or if you're starting tomorrow) and you wish to celebrate in style there can be no better place for a top-of-the-range cream tea than *The Grand Hotel* (☎ 01323-412345, ▣ grandeastbourne.com). You should phone ahead to book. It's served every day (Mon-Thur 2-5.30pm, Fri-Sun 2.30-5.30pm; booking essential) and for £30-34.50 you get a full spread including sandwiches, scones and cakes. You could push the boat out even further with the Grand Champagne Tea (£38.50-43).

The hotel is easy to find: you walk right past it on the way into Eastbourne from the end of the South Downs Way. Splash out – you deserve it!

APPENDIX A: GPS & WHAT3WORDS WAYPOINT REFERENCES

Each waypoint (WPT) below was taken on the route at the reference number marked on the maps in the route guide. **GPS coordinates** and **what3words references** that correspond to these waypoints are listed here and may be particularly useful in an emergency (see p56). Gpx files for waypoints can be downloaded from 🖥 trailblazer-guides.com.

WPT	COORDINATES	DESCRIPTION	///WHAT3WORDS
001	N51° 03.228' W01° 16.749'	Road junction	///unfilled.marathon.excuse
002	N51° 02.862' W01° 16.146'	Tarred road ends/starts	///card.loans.cocoons
003	N51° 03.006' W01° 15.865'	Path/track junction	///adding.surreal.majoring
004	N51° 02.813' W01° 14.842'	Road crossing (A272)	///equipping.mute.airbrush
005	N51° 02.997' W01° 14.437'	Gate (Cheesefoot Head)	///refrained.splints.convinced
006	N51° 03.433' W01° 14.089'	Track junction at farmyard	///loafer.firebird.feasting
007	N51° 02.955' W01° 12.769'	Cross road	///parading.handover.increment
008	N51° 02.727' W01° 12.399'	Gate to field	///deals.objecting.fussed
009	N51° 02.346' W01° 12.081'	Cross A272 road	///node.dispenser.fruits
010	N51° 01.586' W01° 11.793'	Path junction	///replaying.leopard.reassured
011	N51° 01.041' W01° 11.358'	The Milbury	///soldiers.quote.gaps
012	N51° 00.821' W01° 10.521'	Gate	///smokers.examine.banquets
013	N51° 00.580' W01° 09.631'	Track passes houses	///heavy.aspect.candidate
014	N51° 00.059' W01° 08.913'	Beacon Hill car park	///foal.nicely.windows
015	N50° 59.555' W01° 08.413'	Kissing gates to cross fields	///blunt.vacancies.icicles
016	N50° 59.342' W01° 08.227'	Track between stiles	///airports.elbowing.delay
017	N50° 59.040' W01° 07.728'	The Shoe Inn, Exton	///organ.additives.ankle
018	N50° 59.252' W01° 07.208'	Bridge over River Meon	///leathers.glove.dawn
019	N50° 59.186' W01° 06.720'	Go through tunnel	///shops.half.tortoises
020	N50° 58.854' W01° 05.328'	Hill fort, Old Winchester Hill	///slant.audibly.positions
021	N50° 59.009' W01° 04.712'	Turn off/onto track	///twit.butterfly.emulated
022	N50° 59.279' W01° 04.827'	Car park	///pigtails.badly.conveys
023	N50° 59.443' W01° 04.934'	Gate at fork in road	///bigger.universal.froth
024	N50° 59.238' W01° 04.546'	Join/leave track	///pints.mills.gold
025	N50° 59.296' W01° 04.200'	Farmyard	///excellent.hotspot.incurs
026	N50° 59.446' W01° 03.153'	Tree-lined avenue	///decays.tensions.sandpaper
027	N50° 59.066' W01° 03.085'	Road crosses track	///thrilled.cracker.giraffes
028	N50° 58.079' W01° 02.373'	South Downs Eco Lodge	///wiggles.comical.headlines
029	N50° 57.939' W01° 01.698'	Road junction	///backtrack.playfully.balanced
030	N50° 58.051' W01° 00.110'	Homelands Farm	///cosmic.bump.sprayer
031	N50° 58.026' W00° 59.794'	Jctn with Hogs Lodge Lane	///lasts.books.stance
032	N50° 58.465' W00° 59.274'	Butser Hill car park	///streamers.stays.rush
033	N50° 57.891' W00° 58.866'	Gate by A3 road crossing	///fussed.essays.massaging
034	N50° 57.450' W00° 58.658'	Track into/out of woods	///clotting.positions.tablets
035	N50° 58.095' W00° 57.775'	Track junction	///unfocused.marathons.equal
036	N50° 58.372' W00° 57.375'	Road crossing	///fidelity.dined.agent
037	N50° 58.206' W00° 56.546'	Track junction	///stub.proper.cape
038	N50° 58.153' W00° 55.787'	Road junction	///generals.episodes.ghost
039	N50° 57.980' W00° 54.137'	Road crossing	///register.curvy.truckload
040	N50° 57.611' W00° 53.213'	Car park, B2146 road crossing	///thrashing.farm.violinist
041	N50° 57.435' W00° 52.672'	Car park, B2141 road crossing	///spouse.bandaged.react
042	N50° 57.659' W00° 51.469'	Turn-off to East Harting	///legal.campfires.flashback
043	N50° 57.547' W00° 51.119'	Trig point, Beacon Hill	///healers.banquets.informer

WPT	COORDINATES	DESCRIPTION	///WHAT3WORDS
044	N50° 57.535' W00° 50.447'	Junction of several paths	///avoiding.unloads.reset
045	N50° 57.267' W00° 49.981'	Track junction	///appetite.quoted.diver
046	N50° 56.760' W00° 49.665'	Track crossroads	///butternut.adapt.burying
047	N50° 56.999' W00° 48.587'	Track crossroads	///earplugs.spot.arriving
048	N50° 56.873' W00° 47.494'	Path junction, Cocking Down	///impressed.cadet.plots
049	N50° 56.759' W00° 47.002'	Track crossroads	///discount.expel.flute
050	N50° 56.660' W00° 46.360'	Junction near chalk boulder	///redefined.removals.bongo
051	N50° 56.571' W00° 45.338'	Car park at A268 crossing	///clouds.described.countries
052	N50° 56.544' W00° 45.002'	Water tap	///reshaping.odds.glad
053	N50° 56.440' W00° 44.226'	Fork in track	///swimsuits.beyond.cringes
054	N50° 56.463' W00° 43.706'	Track junction	///gets.twilight.surnames
055	N50° 56.466' W00° 43.258'	Turn-off to Heyshott	///brilliant.shortens.novelists
056	N50° 56.457' W00° 42.857'	Path junction	///unpacked.foster.pasta
057	N50° 56.378' W00° 42.375'	Track junction	///career.birthdays.treatment
058	N50° 56.353' W00° 42.128'	Track junction	///upwards.cropping.remote
059	N50° 56.239' W00° 40.938'	Signpost	///aware.handsets.removal
060	N50° 56.016' W00° 39.082'	Track junction	///learning.bins.raced
061	N50° 55.902' W00° 39.598'	Track crossroads	///purifier.hats.motor
062	N50° 55.307' W00° 38.925'	Cross A285 road	///crawler.burglars.verb
063	N50° 54.803' W00° 38.488'	Track junction	///examples.tucked.opposites
064	N50° 54.441' W00° 37.926'	Track junction	///ahead.relishing.absorbs
065	N50° 54.402' W00° 37.319'	Track junction	///branch.protrude.object
066	N50° 54.464' W00° 36.968'	Bignor Hill car park	///send.dignify.every
067	N50° 54.587' W00° 36.157'	Memorial to Toby 1888-1955	///rated.defends.segregate
068	N50° 54.470' W00° 35.814'	Track junction	///siesta.dancer.conquests
069	N50° 53.884' W00° 34.403'	Cross A29 road	///intrigues.muddy.spurted
070	N50° 53.837' W00° 33.310'	Cross country lane	///festivity.pumps.thousands
071	N50° 53.952' W00° 32.927'	Bridge over River Arun	///remind.waltz.bristle
072	N50° 54.025' W00° 32.358'	Cross B2139 road	///freely.entertainer.official
073	N50° 54.195' W00° 31.927'	Road junction	///ventures.stunts.stub
074	N50° 54.188' W00° 31.839'	Leave/join road	///convert.exonerate.stand
075	N50° 54.158' W00° 31.215'	Gate	///rocky.charts.workshops
076	N50° 54.190' W00° 30.413'	Join/leave track	///unlocking.indulgent.opened
077	N50° 54.145' W00° 29.540'	Track junction	///lollipop.headrest.trophy
078	N50° 54.111' W00° 28.747'	Track junction	///lines.towel.powerful
079	N50° 54.051' W00° 28.347'	Turn-off to Storrington	///sponge.crisp.marketing
080	N50° 53.656' W00° 26.641'	Barn	///spins.outfitter.fades
081	N50° 53.755' W00° 26.032'	Gate on track	///bandaged.sits.expiring
082	N50° 53.791' W00° 25.812'	Washington path jctn (alt route)	///walled.pepper.performed
083	N50° 54.262' W00° 25.039'	Join/leave track (alt route)	///december.fade.desiring
084	N50° 54.251' W00° 24.885'	Road/track meet (alt route)	///foggy.insert.tempting
085	N50° 54.304' W00° 24.306'	Frankland Arms, (alt route)	///united.distanced.waistcoat
086	N50° 54.189' W00° 24.382'	Road jct, Washington (alt route)	///chairing.glosses.dumpling
087	N50° 53.807' W00° 24.344'	Steep section of track	///swimsuits.project.swells
088	N50° 53.617' W00° 23.643'	Track junction	///confining.flamenco.dummy
089	N50° 53.757' W00° 23.351'	Gate on track	///list.privately.sideboard
090	N50° 53.779' W00° 22.928'	Chanctonbury Ring	///nicknames.coffee.purifier
091	N50° 53.637' W00° 22.612'	Gate on track	///chuckling.test.diverged
092	N50° 53.409' W00° 22.421'	Track junction	///rather.slimmer.listen
093	N50° 53.269' W00° 22.001'	Track junction	///courier.nips.compacts
094	N50° 53.219' W00° 21.675'	Turn-off to Steyning	///responded.custodian.ducks
095	N50° 52.669' W00° 20.972'	Track junction	///conspire.ghost.thumbnail

WPT	COORDINATES	DESCRIPTION	///WHAT3WORDS
096	N50° 52.403' W00° 17.958'	A283 road	///luxury.define.thud
097	N50° 52.430' W00° 17.094'	Car park	///eventful.comedians.corded
098	N50° 52.881' W00° 15.991'	Road by YHA Truleigh Hill	///slippery.character.union
099	N50° 52.919' W00° 15.461'	Communications tower	///bikes.chatted.piled
100	N50° 53.063' W00° 13.763'	Turn-off to Fulking	///tango.changed.folk
101	N50° 52.937' W00° 13.213'	Gate	///hazy.exams.qualify
102	N50° 53.092' W00° 12.744'	Devil's Dyke pub	///easels.guidebook.stamp
103	N50° 52.978' W00° 12.254'	Gate on path	///whispers.files.knowledge
104	N50° 53.309' W00° 11.663'	Road crossing (A281)	///agreeable.carrots.label
105	N50° 53.349' W00° 11.466'	Gate by woodland	///hurry.reseller.measure
106	N50° 53.410' W00° 10.968'	Gate on path	///streetcar.index.jams
107	N50° 53.743' W00° 10.001'	Gate by road	///exonerate.pastels.inserted
108	N50° 53.923' W00° 09.837'	Crossroads, Pyecombe	///rattled.snoozing.haunt
109	N50° 54.056' W00° 09.593'	Car park at golf club	///self.establish.probably
110	N50° 54.026' W00° 08.687'	Track crossroads	///radio.bulge.loses
111	N50° 54.227' W00° 08.718'	Track junction	///feel.tracks.scorched
112	N50° 54.027' W00° 07.845'	Gate by Keymer signpost	///commended.bliss.pass
113	N50° 54.146' W00° 07.327'	Dew pond	///amuses.arise.replace
114	N50° 54.046' W00° 06.278'	Car park, Ditchling Beacon	///eventful.cactus.relay
115	N50° 53.940' W00° 05.814'	Turn-off to Ditchling	///desktop.worthy.speedy
116	N50° 53.910' W00° 04.709'	Track between gates	///founding.liberated.sheep
117	N50° 53.876' W00° 04.387'	Turn-off to Plumpton	///goodbyes.progress.handed
118	N50° 53.759' W00° 03.198'	Junction with path to Lewes	///developed.completed.cabbies
119	N50° 53.259' W00° 03.666'	Gate at track junction	///decide.octagonal.simmer
120	N50° 53.000' W00° 03.295'	Gate at track/path junction	///probable.jungle.computers
121	N50° 52.505' W00° 02.808'	Through gate by stile	///infuses.appoints.glides
122	N50° 52.426' W00° 03.190'	Small hut and pylon	///browsers.powerful.scan
123	N50° 51.977' W00° 03.268'	Steps	///quietly.tins.unsecured
124	N50° 51.977' W00° 03.487'	Bridge over A27 road	///blackouts.exam.crest
125	N50° 51.872' W00° 02.952'	Path cuts under railway	///palms.golden.degree
126	N50° 51.548' W00° 03.227'	Through gate	///recovery.weeds.embedded
127	N50° 51.224' W00° 03.463'	Through gate	///condensed.jump.ready
128	N50° 51.025' W00° 03.266'	Through gate, follow fence	///suitcase.passports.clays
129	N50° 51.278' W00° 02.526'	Gate by dew pond	///ruling.leaflet.them
130	N50° 51.032' W00° 01.876'	Path joins/leaves track	///safe.cars.slowly
131	N50° 50.673' W00° 01.557'	Track, Swanborough Hill	///method.zoom.pink
132	N50° 50.086' E00° 00.479'	Leave/join track through gate	///layers.corrode.unlocking
133	N50° 50.009' E00° 00.149'	Track between gates	///powder.wealth.herbs
134	N50° 49.566' E00° 00.315'	Through gate onto/off track	///guess.boomed.butlers
135	N50° 49.795' E00° 01.061'	Road junction, Southease	///slurs.swims.advances
136	N50° 49.805' E00° 01.562'	Bridge over River Ouse	///distract.unfit.hooks
137	N50° 49.888' E00° 01.849'	Level crossing	///restore.behalf.tailing
138	N50° 49.804' E00° 02.228'	Gate on track east of A26 bridge	///dummy.circulate.collision
139	N50° 49.875' E00° 03.090'	Trig point & dew pond	///bullion.brick.guests
140	N50° 50.092' E00° 03.667'	Gate onto track	///raven.hesitate.cuter
141	N50° 50.063' E00° 04.114'	Telecom masts, Beddingham Hill	///silks.samplers.teamed
142	N50° 50.069' E00° 04.468'	Gate on path	///column.alright.receiving
143	N50° 50.018' E00° 04.987'	Car park, Firle Beacon	///aquatics.whizzing.deform
144	N50° 50.029' E00° 06.497'	Trig point, Firle Beacon	///conveying.raced.download
145	N50° 49.527' E00° 07.208'	Gate, Bo-Peep	///amounting.repair.reports
146	N50° 49.108' E00° 07.823'	Gate on path	///shocks.lawns.organ
147	N50° 48.659' E00° 08.550'	Gate by track junction	///olive.paddle.liquid

WPT	COORDINATES	DESCRIPTION	///WHAT3WORDS
148	N50° 48.405' E00° 09.581'	Church, Alfriston (coast route)	///asked.kingpin.wades
149	N50° 48.689' E00° 09.581'	Plough & Harrow, Litlington	///surfacing.laying.treatment
150	N50° 47.440' E00° 09.628'	Path goes round the hedge	///clattered.distracts.boring
151	N50° 47.098' E00° 09.471'	Steps through forest	///studs.fled.obeyed
152	N50° 46.707' E00° 09.699'	Track junction	///topples.rezoning.uptown
153	N50° 46.605' E00° 09.566'	Crossroads, Westdean	///inspects.fired.installs
154	N50° 46.499' E00° 09.244'	Road crossing, Exceat	///tastier.luring.denoting
155	N50° 45.905' E00° 09.085'	Track end	///pebble.informer.across
156	N50° 45.909' E00° 09.508'	Gate on path	///segmented.expecting.detriment
157	N50° 45.376' E00° 09.578'	Haven Brow	///brands.jungle.signed
158	N50° 45.310' E00° 09.793'	Short Brow	///snails.seemingly.playfully
159	N50° 45.198' E00° 10.139'	Rough Brow	///known.behaving.resettle
160	N50° 45.143' E00° 10.376'	Brass Point	///promise.overture.husbands
161	N50° 44.995' E00° 10.792'	Sarsen stone	///guests.couriers.fancied
162	N50° 44.957' E00° 11.020'	The 'Eighth' Sister	///diner.widgets.opposites
163	N50° 44.910' E00° 11.284'	Baily's Hill	///shared.upwardly.denote
164	N50° 44.570' E00° 11.462'	Memorial pillar	///clenching.wiser.overjoyed
165	N50° 44.766' E00° 11.667'	Went Hill	///glossed.fails.remember
166	N50° 44.585' E00° 12.075'	Car park, Birling Gap	///imprints.confronts.familiar
167	N50° 44.302' E00° 12.901'	Belle Tout Lighthouse	///remainder.reinstate.twists
168	N50° 44.112' E00° 13.870'	Path near Shooters Bottom	///winds.contacts.tonsils

Map key

♠	Where to stay	📖	Library/bookstore	●	Other
O	Where to eat and drink	@	Internet	CP	Car park
Δ	Campsite	🏛	Museum/gallery	🚌	Bus station/stop
⊠	Post Office	✝	Church/cathedral	—▯—	Rail line & station
ⓔ	Bank/ATM	①	Phone box		Park
①	Tourist Information	☑	Public toilet	📟 082	GPS waypoint
		▢	Building		

	South Downs Way	✝	Stile	~ ~ ~	Water
	Other Path	⤚	Gate		Stream/river
	4 x 4 track	⬭	Cliffs	🌳	Trees/woodland
	Tarmac road	⤜	Bridge		Beach
	Steps		Fence	🗼	Lighthouse/beacon
	Slope		Wall	4	Golf course
	Steep slope		Hedge	⑭	Map continuation (black = to Eastbourne red = to Winchester)

WPT	COORDINATES	DESCRIPTION	///WHAT3WORDS
169	N50° 44.335' E00° 15.220'	RAF Bomber Command Memorial	///airliners.camera.wiggly
170	N50° 45.113' E00° 16.027'	Eastern end of SDW	///moved.famed.healers

Inland route from Alfriston to Eastbourne via Jevington

WPT	COORDINATES	DESCRIPTION	///WHAT3WORDS
172	N50° 47.518' E00° 12.825'	Crossroads, Jevington	///trains.human.purple
173	N50° 47.222' E00° 14.083'	Turn-off to Willingdon	///wasp.tent.every
174	N50° 47.196' E00° 14.162'	Trig point	///tricks.pines.pays
175	N50° 46.658' E00° 14.575'	Concrete dew pond	///famed.risks.meals
176	N50° 45.901' E00° 14.776'	Road crossing (A259)	///feast.paused.baking
177	N50° 45.729' E00° 15.000'	Finger post	///claim.jets.kick
170	N50° 45.113' E00° 16.027'	Eastern end of SDW	///moved.famed.healers

APPENDIX B: WALKING WITH A DOG

WALKING THE WAY WITH A DOG

Many are the rewards that await those prepared to make the extra effort required to bring their best friend along the trail. However, because the South Downs is a prime sheep-farming area your dog may have to be on a lead for much of the walk.

And you shouldn't underestimate the amount of work involved. Indeed, just about every decision you make will be influenced by the fact that you've got a dog: how you plan to travel to the start of the trail, where you're going to stay, how far you're going to walk each day, where you're going to rest and where you're going to eat in the evening etc.

If you're sure your dog can cope with (and, just as importantly, *enjoy*) walking 10 miles or more a day for several days in a row, you need to start preparing accordingly. Extra thought needs to go into your itinerary. Study the town & village facilities table on pp30-1 (and the advice below), and plan where to stop and where to buy food.

Looking after your dog

To begin with, you need to make sure that your dog is fully **inoculated** against the usual doggy illnesses, and also up to date with regard to **worm pills** (eg Drontal) and **flea preventatives** such as Frontline – they are, after all, following in the pawprints of many a dog before them, some of whom may well have left fleas or other parasites on the trail that now lie in wait for their next meal to arrive. **Pet insurance** is also a very good idea; if you've already got insurance, do check that it will cover a trip such as this. On the subject of your dog's health, perhaps the most important implement you can bring is a **plastic tick remover**, available from vets. These removers, while fiddly, help you to remove the tick safely (ie without leaving its head behind buried under the dog's skin). Being in unfamiliar territory also makes it more likely that you and your dog could become separated. All dogs now have to be **microchipped** but make sure your dog also has a **tag with your contact details on it** (a mobile phone number would be best if you are carrying one with you).

When to keep your dog on a lead

● **On cliff tops** It's a sad fact that, every year, a few dogs lose their lives falling over the edge of the cliffs. It usually occurs when they are chasing rabbits (which know where the cliff-edge is and are able, unlike your poor pooch, to stop in time).

● **When crossing farmland**, particularly in the lambing season (March to May) when your dog can scare the sheep, causing them to lose their young. Farmers are allowed by law to shoot at and kill any dogs that they consider are worrying their sheep. During lambing, most farmers would prefer it if you didn't bring your dog at all. The exception is if your dog is being attacked by cows. Some years ago there were three deaths in the UK caused by walkers being trampled as they tried to rescue their dogs from the attentions of cattle. The advice in this instance is to let go of the lead, head speedily to a position of safety (usually the other side of the field gate or stile) and call your dog to you.

● **On National Trust land**, where it is compulsory to keep your dog on a lead.

● **Around ground-nesting birds** It's important to keep your dog under control when crossing an area where certain species of birds nest on the ground. Most dogs love foraging around in the woods but make sure you have permission to do so; some woods are used as nurseries for game birds and dogs are only allowed through them if they are on a lead.

What to pack
You've probably already got a good idea of what to bring to keep your dog alive and happy, but the following is a checklist:

● **Food/water bowl** Foldable cloth or collapsible silicon bowls are popular with walkers, being light and taking up little room in a rucksack. You can get also get a water-bottle-and-bowl combination, where the bottle folds into a 'trough' from which the dog can drink.

● **Lead and collar** An extendable lead is probably preferable for this sort of trip. Make sure both lead and collar are in good condition – you don't want either to snap on the trail, or you may end up carrying your dog through sheep fields until a replacement can be found.

● **Medication** You'll know if you need to bring any lotions or potions.

● **Bedding** A simple blanket may suffice, or you can opt for something more elaborate if you aren't carrying your own luggage.

● **Hygiene wipes** For cleaning your dog after it's rolled in stuff.

● **A favourite toy** Helps prevent your dog from pining for the entire walk.

● **Food/water** Remember to bring treats as well as regular food to keep up the mutt's morale. That said, if your dog is anything like mine the chances are they'll spend most of the walk dining on rabbit droppings and sheep poo anyway.

● **Corkscrew stake** Available from camping or pet shops, this will help you to keep your dog secure in one place while you set up camp/doze.   ● **Tick remover** See opposite.

● **Poo bags** Essential.   ● **Raingear** It can rain!   ● **Old towels** For drying your dog.

When it comes to packing, I always leave an exterior pocket of my rucksack empty so I can put used poo bags in there (for deposit at the first bin reached). I always like to keep all the dog's kit together and separate from the other luggage (usually inside a plastic bag inside my rucksack). I have also seen several dogs sporting their own 'doggy rucksack', so they can carry their own food, water, poo etc – which certainly reduces the burden on their owner.

Cleaning up after your dog
It is extremely important that dog owners behave in a responsible way when walking the path. Dog excrement should be cleaned up. In towns, villages and fields where animals graze or which will be cut for silage, hay etc, you need to pick up and bag the excrement.

Staying (and eating) with your dog
In this guide we have used the symbol 🐾 to denote where a place welcomes dogs. However, this always needs to be arranged in advance and some places may charge extra. Many B&B-style places have only one or two rooms suitable for people with dogs; hostels (both YHA and independent) do not permit them unless they are an assistance (guide) dog; smaller campsites tend to accept them, but some of the larger holiday parks do not – however, in either case it is likely the dog will have to be on a lead. Before you turn up always double check whether the place you would like to stay accepts dogs and whether there is space for them. When it comes to eating, some cafés accept dogs and most landlords allow dogs in at least a section of their pubs, though few restaurants do. Make sure you always ask first and ensure your dog is on a lead and secured to your table or a radiator so it doesn't run around.   **Henry Stedman**

	START Winchester	Chilcomb	(Cheriton +1½)	Exton	(East Meon + 1)	(Buriton + ½)	(South Harting + ½)	(Cocking + ½)	(Heyshott + ½)	(Graffham + 1)	(Sutton/Bignor + 1)	(Bury + 1)	Houghton Bridge	Amberley	(Storrington + 1½)	(Washington + ½)	(Steyning/Bramber/Upper Beeding + 1)
START Winchester	0																
Chilcomb	2																
(Cheriton +1½)	6½	4½															
Exton	12	10	5½														
(East Meon + 1)	17	15	10½	5													
(Buriton + ½)	24½	22½	18	12½	7½												
(Sth Harting + ½)	28	26	21½	16	11	3½											
(Cocking + ½)	35	33	28½	23	18	10½	7										
(Heyshott + ½)	37	35	30½	25	20	12½	9	2									
(Graffham + 1)	38½	36½	32	26½	21½	14	10½	3½	1½								
(Sutton/Bignor + 1)	42½	40½	36	30½	25½	18	14½	7½	5½	4							
(Bury + 1)	45	43	38½	33	28	20½	17	10	8	6½	2½						
Houghton Bridge	46	44	39½	34	29	21½	18	11	9	7½	3½	1					
Amberley	47½	45½	41	35½	30½	23	19½	12½	10½	9	5	2½	1½				
(Storrington + 1½)	50½	48½	44	38½	33½	26	22½	15½	13½	12	8	5½	4½	3			
(Washington + ½)	53½	51½	47	41½	36½	29	25½	18½	16½	15	11	8½	7½	6	3		
(Steyning/U Bd + 1)	57½	55½	51	45½	40½	33	29½	22½	20½	19	15	12½	11½	10	7	4	
(Fulking + ½)	64	62	57½	52	47	39½	36	29	27	25½	21½	19	18	16½	13½	10½	6½
(Poynings + ½)	66	64	59½	54	49	41½	38	31	29	27½	23½	21	20	18½	15½	12½	8½
Pyecombe	68	66	61½	56	51	43½	40	33	31	29½	25½	23	22	20½	17½	14½	10½
(Clayton + ½)	69	67	62½	57	52	44½	41	34	32	30½	26½	24	23	21½	18½	15½	11½
(Ditchling + 1½)	70½	68½	64	58½	53½	46	42½	35½	33½	32	28	25½	24½	23	20	17	13
(Plumpton + ½)	72½	70½	66	60½	55½	48	44½	37½	35½	34	30	27½	26½	25	22	19	15
(Lewes + 3)	73½	71½	67	61½	56½	49	45½	38½	36½	35	31	28½	27½	26	23	20	16
(Kingston + 1)	78½	76½	72	66½	61½	54	50½	43½	41½	40	36	33½	32½	31	28	25	21
Rodmell/Southease	82½	80½	76	70½	65½	58	54½	47½	45½	44	40	37½	36½	35	32	29	25
(West Firle + 1)	86	84	79½	74	69	61½	58	51	49	47½	43½	41	40	38½	35½	32½	28½
(Alciston/Bwk + 1)	88½	86½	82	76½	71½	64	60½	53½	51½	50	46	43½	42½	41	38	35	31
Alfriston	90½	88½	84	78½	73½	66	62½	55½	53½	52	48	45½	44½	43	40	37	33
[via IR] Jevington*	93	91	86½	81	76	68½	65	58	56	54½	50½	48	47	45½	42½	39½	35½
[via IR] End (E+1½)*	97	95	90½	85	80	72½	69	62	60	58½	54½	52	51	49½	46½	43½	39½
Litlington	91½	89½	85	79½	74½	67	63½	56½	54½	53	49	46½	45½	44	41	38	34
Exceat/Seven Sstrs	93	91	86½	81	76	68½	65	58	56	54½	50½	48	47	45½	42½	39½	35½
Birling Gap	96	94	89½	84	79	71½	68	61	59	57½	53½	51	50	48½	45½	42½	38½
Beachy Head	99	97	92½	87	82	74½	71	64	62	60½	56½	54	53	51½	48½	45½	41½
END (Eastbrn +1½)	100	98	93½	88	83	75½	72	65	63	61½	57½	55	54	52½	49½	46½	42½

* INLAND (ALTERNATIVE) ROUTE FROM ALFRISTON

South Downs Way
DISTANCE CHART

Winchester – Eastbourne

miles (approx) – 1 mile = 1.6km

Note: Where a place name is shown in (brackets) on this chart the distance to the turnoff to this place is shown. Add the (+) number in the brackets to calculate the total distance to that place. Most villages lie below the South Downs.

Place	(Fulking + ½)	(Poynings + ½)	Pyecombe	(Clayton + ½)	(Ditchling + 1½)	(Plumpton + ½)	(Lewes + 3)	(Kingston near Lewes + 1)	Rodmell/Southease	(West Firle + 1)	(Alciston/Berwick + 1)	Alfriston	Jevington [via inland route*]	End (Eastbourne + 1½) [via inland route*]	Litlington	Exceat/Seven Sisters	Birling Gap	Beachy Head	END (Eastbourne + 1½)
(Poynings + ½)	2																		
Pyecombe	4	2																	
(Clayton + ½)	5	3	1																
(Ditchling + 1½)	6½	4½	2½	1½															
(Plumpton + ½)	8½	6½	4½	3½	2														
(Lewes + 3)	9½	7½	5½	4½	3	1													
(Kingston near Lewes + 1)	14½	12½	10½	9½	8	6	5												
Rodmell/Southease	18½	16½	14½	13½	12	10	9	4											
(West Firle + 1)	22	20	18	17	15½	13½	12½	7½	3½										
(Alciston/Berwick + 1)	24½	22½	20½	19½	18	16	15	10	6	2½									
Alfriston	26½	24½	22½	21½	20	18	17	12	8	4½	2								
Jevington [via inland route]*	*29*	*27*	*25*	*24*	*22½*	*20½*	*19½*	*14½*	*10½*	*7*	*4½*	*2½*							
End (Eastbourne + 1½) [via inland route]*	*33*	*31*	*29*	*28*	*26½*	*24½*	*23½*	*18½*	*14½*	*11*	*8½*	*6½*	*4*						
Litlington	27½	25½	23½	22½	21	19	18	13	9	5½	3	1							
Exceat/Seven Sisters	29	27	25	24	22½	20½	19½	14½	10½	7	4½	2½	——		1½				
Birling Gap	32	30	28	27	25½	23½	22½	17½	13½	10	7½	5½	——		4½	3			
Beachy Head	35	33	31	30	28½	26½	25½	20½	16½	13	10½	8½	——		7½	6	3		
END (Eastbourne + 1½)	36	34	32	31	29½	27½	26½	21½	17½	14	11½	9½	——		8½	7	4	1	

INDEX

Page references in red type refer to maps

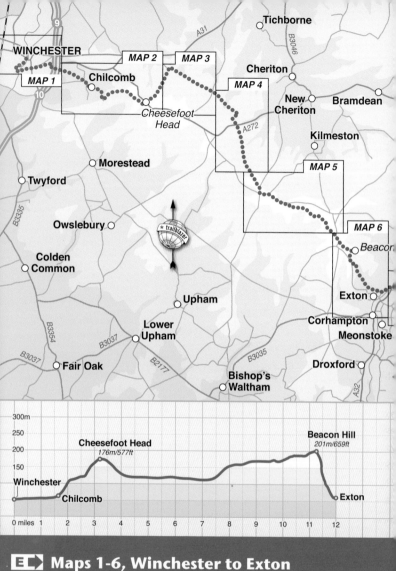

MAP 1

WINCHESTER

MAP 2

Chilcomb

MAP 3

TICHBORNE

Cheriton

MAP 4

New Cheriton

Bramdean

Cheesefoot Head

A272

Kilmeston

MAP 5

Morestead

Twyford

MAP 6

Beacon

Owslebury

trailblazer

Colden Common

Exton

Upham

Corhampton

Lower Upham

Meonstoke

Fair Oak

Droxford

Bishop's Waltham

300m
250
200
150

Cheesefoot Head
176m/577ft

Beacon Hill
201m/659ft

Winchester

Chilcomb

Exton

0 miles 1   2   3   4   5   6   7   8   9   10   11   12

Maps 1-6, Winchester to Exton
12 miles/19.5km – 4¼-5¾hrs

Maps 6-10, Exton to Buriton
12½ miles/20km – 4½-6hrs

Note: Add 20-30% to these times to allow for stops

Winchester
Burito
Exton

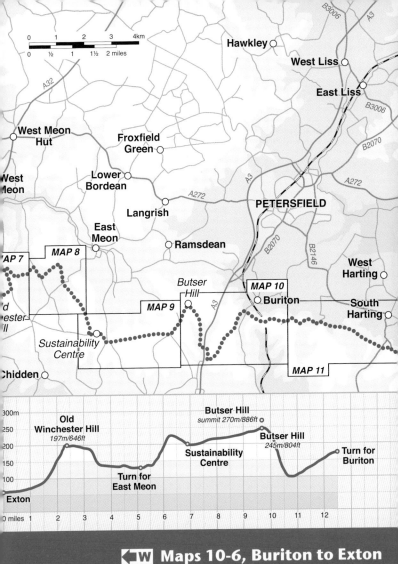

Maps 10-6, Buriton to Exton
12½ miles/20km – 4¼-6hrs

Maps 6-1, Exton to Winchester
12 miles/19.5km – 4¼-6hrs

Eastbourne

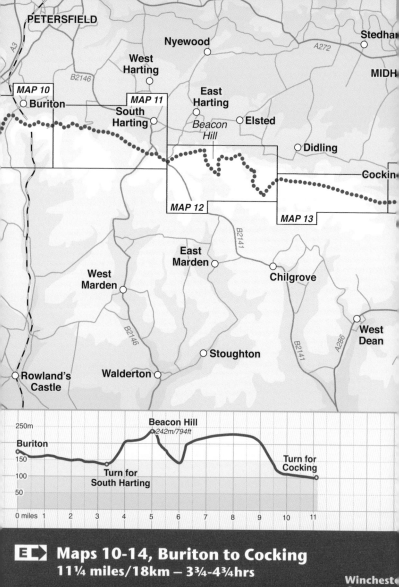

PETERSFIELD

Nyewood

Stedha

A272

A3

B2146

West
Harting

MAP 10

Buriton

MAP 11

South
Harting

East
Harting

*Beacon
Hill*

Elsted

MIDH

Didling

Cockin

MAP 12

MAP 13

B2141

East
Marden

Chilgrove

West
Marden

B2146

Stoughton

B2141

A286

West
Dean

Rowland's
Castle

Walderton

250m

Beacon Hill
242m/794ft

Buriton

150

Turn for
South Harting

Turn for
Cocking

100

50

0 miles 1   2   3   4   5   6   7   8   9   10   11

EC **Maps 10–14, Buriton to Cocking**
11¼ miles/18km – 3¾–4¾hrs

Maps 14–18, Cocking to Amberley
12 miles/19.5km – 3¾–5¼hrs

Note: Add 20-30% to these times to allow for stops

Wincheste

Bur

Cock

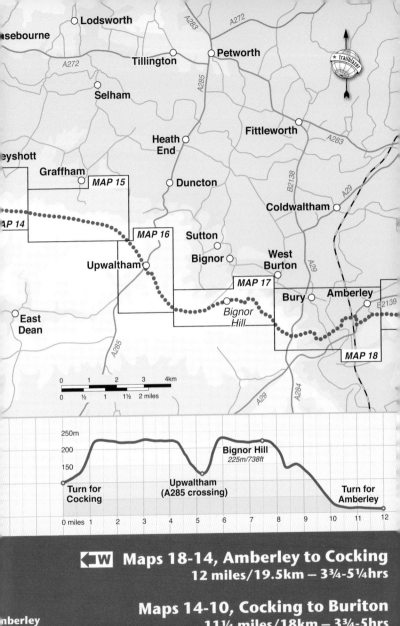

Maps 18-14, Amberley to Cocking
12 miles/19.5km – 3¾-5¼hrs

Maps 14-10, Cocking to Buriton
11¼ miles/18km – 3¾-5hrs

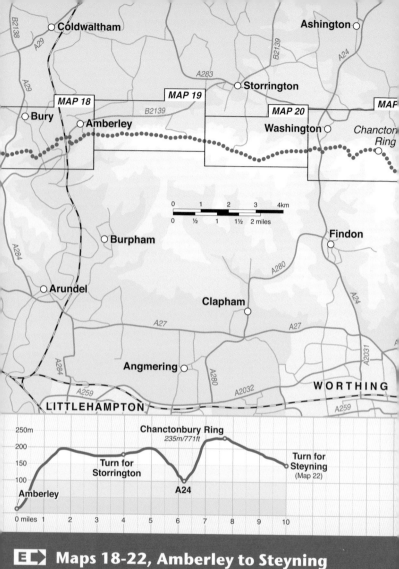

Coldwaltham

Ashington

MAP 18

Storrington

MAP 19

Bury

Amberley

MAP 20

MAP

Washington

Chancton
Ring

0   1   2   3   4km
0   ½   1   1½ 2 miles

Burpham

Findon

Arundel

Clapham

Angmering

WORTHING

LITTLEHAMPTON

Chanctonbury Ring
235m/771ft

Turn for
Storrington

A24

Turn for
Steyning
(Map 22)

Amberley

0 miles 1   2   3   4   5   6   7   8   9   10

Maps 18-22, Amberley to Steyning
10 miles/16km – 3¼-4¾hrs

Maps 22-26, Steyning to Pyecombe
10¼ miles/16.5km – 4-5½hrs
Plus 20-30mins from Steyning to South Downs Way

Note: Add 20-30% to these times to allow for stops

Winchester

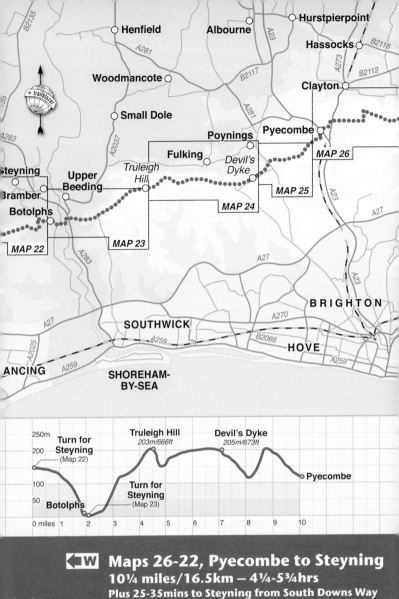

◄W **Maps 26-22, Pyecombe to Steyning**
10¼ miles/16.5km — 4¼-5¾hrs
Plus 25-35mins to Steyning from South Downs Way

Maps 22-18, Steyning to Amberley
10 miles/16km — 3¼-4¾hrs
Add 20-30% to these times to allow for stops

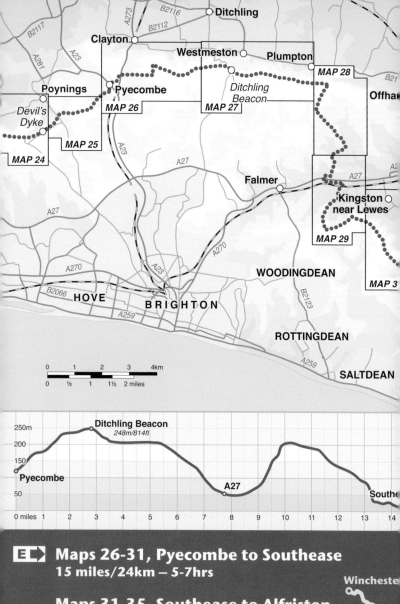

Maps 26-31, Pyecombe to Southease
15 miles/24km – 5-7hrs

Maps 31-35, Southease to Alfriston
7¾ miles/12.5km – 2½-3½hrs

Note: Add 20-30% to these times to allow for stops

Barcombe

Laughton
Common

Chiddingly

Broyle
Side

Laughton

Ringmer

B2124

B2124

Lower
Dicker

Glyndebourne

★ trailblazer

Ripe

Eckington
Corner

Upper
Dicker

Mount
Caburn

Glynde

Chalvington

LES

Arlington

Beddingham

A27

Firle

Selmeston

MAP 33

odmell

Alciston

Berwick

Southease

Firle
Beacon

MAP 31

MAP 32

A27

Wilmington

MAP 35

Milton Street

South
Heighton

MAP 34

Alfriston

CE-
EN

Norton

Litlington

Jevington

NEWHAVEN

250m

Firle Beacon
217m/712ft

200

150

100

Southease

Alfriston

0 miles 1   2   3   4   5   6   7

◄▮W Maps 35-31, Alfriston to Southease
7¾ miles/12.5km – 2½-3½hrs

Maps 31-26, Southease to Pyecombe
15 miles/24km – 5-7hrs

Alfriston

combe

outhease

Eastbourne

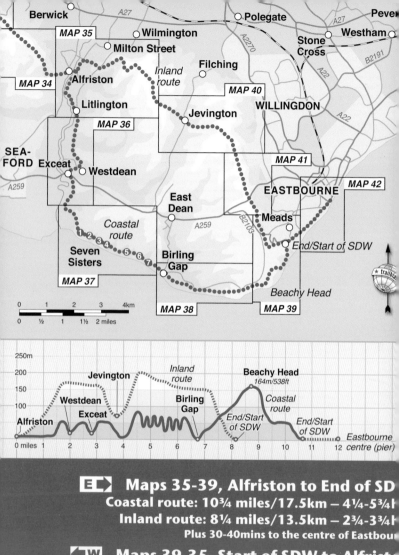

MAP 35
MAP 34
MAP 36
MAP 40
MAP 41
MAP 42
MAP 37
MAP 38
MAP 39

Berwick
Polegate
Pever
Wilmington
Stone Cross
Westham
Milton Street
Alfriston
Inland route
Filching
WILLINGDON
Litlington
Jevington
SEA-FORD
Exceat
Westdean
EASTBOURNE
East Dean
Meads
Coastal route
End/Start of SDW
Seven Sisters
Birling Gap
Beachy Head

0	1	2	3	4km
0	½	1	1½	2 miles

250m
200m
150m
100m

Inland route
Jevington
Westdean
Beachy Head
164m/538ft
Alfriston
Exceat
Birling Gap
Coastal route
End/Start of SDW
End/Start of SDW
Eastbourne
centre (pier)

0 miles 1   2   3   4   5   6   7   8   9   10   11   12

Maps 35-39, Alfriston to End of SD
Coastal route: 10¾ miles/17.5km – 4¼-5¾h
Inland route: 8¼ miles/13.5km – 2¾-3¾h
Plus 30-40mins to the centre of Eastbour

Maps 39-35, Start of SDW to Alfrist
Coastal route: 10¾ miles/17.5km – 4½-6h
Inland route: 8¼ miles/13.5km – 2¾-3¾h
Plus 30-40mins from the centre of Eastbour

Winchester

Alfriston   Eastbourne

[Note: Add 20-3
to these times t
allow for stops

TRAILBLAZER TITLE LIST

For more information about Trailblazer and our
expanding range of guides, for guidebook updates or
for credit card mail order sales visit our website:

trailblazer-guides.com

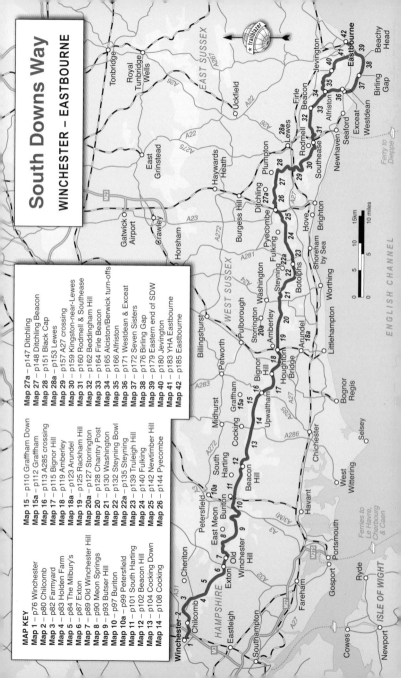

South Downs Way

WINCHESTER – EASTBOURNE